Taylor Swift
In Her Own Words

泰勒·斯威夫特：她说

[美] 海伦娜·亨特 编　孙澳 译

上海社会科学院出版社
SHANGHAI ACADEMY OF SOCIAL SCIENCES PRESS

I feel no need to burn down the house I built by hand. I can make additions to it. I can redecorate. But I built this. And so I'm not going to sit there and say, "Oh, I wish I hadn't had corkscrew-curly hair and worn cowboy boots and sundresses to awards shows when I was 17; I wish I hadn't gone through that fairy-tale phase where I just wanted to wear princess dresses to awards shows every single time." Because I made those choices. I did that. It was part of me growing up. It wasn't some committee going, "You know what Taylor needs to be this year?"

我没必要将亲手搭建的楼阁付之一炬。我可以为其添砖加瓦。我可以将其重新粉饰。毕竟那是我亲手所建。所以我不会呆坐在此，说："哦，我多希望17岁那年，自己没顶着一头小卷发，穿着牛仔靴和无袖背心裙去参加颁奖典礼；我多希望自己没经历过那个童话风格的穿衣阶段，那时每逢颁奖典礼，我都要穿上公主裙。"因为那都是我的选择，是我本人的手笔，是我成长的一部分，而不是什么委员会在断言："你知道泰勒今年得变成什么样吗？"

——*Elle*，2015年5月7日

引　言

十一二岁时，泰勒·斯威夫特（Taylor Swift）在父母的圣诞树农场第一次学弹吉他，从那时起，她就一直坚持塑造形象和讲述故事。她的父母都从事金融行业，母亲安德莉亚·斯威夫特（Andrea Swift）当时在家抚养泰勒和她的弟弟奥斯汀·斯威夫特（Austin Swift），父母俩对音乐行业都知之甚少。尽管如此，泰勒却表现出了超乎寻常的音乐天赋，还十分擅长向听众推销自己的音乐。

泰勒曾说，她一直明白自己要从其他做明星梦的孩子中脱颖而出。她得勤奋努力，她要变得更加优秀。她学弹吉他，在烧烤派对和童子军会议上演出，初中时期就给纳什维尔的音乐高层们寄送自己的录音样带。尽管年纪尚小，她的原创歌曲却充满哲理、琅琅上口、贴近生活，这也是她不同凡响、最终跻身纳什维尔音乐界的关键所在。

泰勒在其早期歌曲中显露出的独特精神气质，一直延续到她后来的专辑《1989》（1989）和《名誉》（reputation）[1]中。例如，她

---

[1] 泰勒的第五张专辑《1989》发行于2014年10月27日。泰勒的第六张专辑《名誉》发行于2017年11月10日。本书中使用的专辑/迷你专辑、歌曲/单曲、电视节目/影视作品、公司/机构、奖项、媒体报刊等译名，以相关官方在中国大陆地区使用的中文（引进版）译名为重要参考，歌曲名选用更贴合歌曲表达之意的译名。泰勒的专辑、歌曲、巡演、纪录片等英文原名的字母大小写，均与发行版本字母大小写保持一致。另，本书如无特别说明，脚注均为译者注。

最早写成的歌曲之一《局外人》("The Outside")讲述了自己在初中学校里遭遇霸凌和孤立的经历。在《局外人》和其他歌曲中,她将自己的痛苦经历淬炼成一种个人形象。曾是局外人的泰勒化失意痛苦为成功,将大家都经历过的排斥创作为饱受大众喜爱的音乐。

在纳什维尔(14岁时,泰勒说服父母,举家迁居至此),大多数唱片公司都认为,泰勒在课堂上创作的那些关于校园霸凌、高中恋情和孤立排斥的歌曲不会引起乡村音乐听众的兴趣。但泰勒比这些唱片公司更了解自己的形象定位和魅力所在。比如,歌曲《我们的歌》("Our Song")在她的高中同学间广受欢迎,因为泰勒笔下的深夜密谈和恼人父母引起了大家的共鸣。即使当时创作的歌曲还没有固定的受众,泰勒对自己已经有明确的形象定位和塑造体系。她只是需要业内人士的发掘,将其形象和创作传递给听众。

斯科特·波切塔(Scott Borchetta)就是这个伯乐。波切塔当时在环球音乐集团[1]就职,正打算自立门户,成立自己的唱片公司。他在纳什维尔的蓝鸟咖啡馆发掘了泰勒,邀请她与自己尚未成立的大机器唱片公司[2]签约。泰勒同意了波切塔的提议,与大机器合作发行了自己的前6张专辑,取得了前所未有的成功。

泰勒很快发现了久候自己的音乐受众。她的首张单曲《蒂姆·麦格劳》("Tim McGraw")和同名专辑《泰勒·斯威夫特》(*Taylor Swift*)[3]成功登上了各大乡村音乐排行榜,引起了诸多颁奖

1　环球音乐集团(Universal Music Group):全球最大的音乐公司之一。
2　大机器唱片公司(Big Machine Records):成立于2005年9月1日。
3　泰勒的首张专辑《泰勒·斯威夫特》发行于2006年10月24日。

典礼的关注,其歌迷群体也在不断壮大。她不遗余力地推广自己的音乐作品,决定居家自学以便兼顾巡演和歌曲录制日程,由此成功进军乡村音乐界。接受电台DJ和电视节目主持人采访时,她的举止与平常少女无异——对自己取得的成就充满敬意,听到笑话就会开怀大笑,热衷于八卦男友和初中时的霸凌者。泰勒向人们证明,青春少女们的经历自然而有趣,一样值得被歌唱,她将自己的生活日常耕耘为非同凡响的成功。

《放手去爱》(Fearless)和《爱的告白》(Speak Now)时期[1],泰勒取得了毋庸置疑的成功。她发行的第二张专辑《放手去爱》登上了公告牌200强专辑榜榜首,拿下了格莱美的年度专辑奖项,并为她开启了全球瞩目的首次巡回演唱会。这也标志着泰勒的形象发生了改变,从小镇乡村女孩转变为歌曲《你应该和我在一起》("You Belong With Me")里被冷落的书呆子和《爱情故事》("Love Story")里的童话公主——也正是这种差异,让许多高中女生产生了共鸣——她们在学校生活和自己天地中的形象迥然不同。

专辑《爱的告白》与首张专辑《泰勒·斯威夫特》有着相同的主题——霸凌和失恋,但在《爱的告白》中,这两大主题已然超越了高中校园故事。斩获两座格莱美奖杯的歌曲《卑鄙》("Mean")是泰勒对一位音乐评论家的回应,这位评论家曾猛烈抨击她和史

---

[1] 泰勒的第二张专辑《放手去爱》发行于2008年11月11日,第三张专辑《爱的告白》发行于2010年10月25日。此处指自《放手去爱》发行至2012年10月22日第四张专辑《红》发行前的时期。

蒂薇·妮克丝在格莱美颁奖现场带来的《瑞安农》表演[1]。而在歌曲《无辜者》("Innocent")中,泰勒表达了对坎耶·韦斯特[2]的原谅,算是对他的窘境施以援手——韦斯特因在MTV音乐录影带大奖[3]的颁奖现场打断了她的领奖致辞而臭名昭著[4]。

在这张专辑中,她的恋爱对象也不再是橄榄球队队长或隔壁的邻居男孩,据报道(泰勒鲜少在媒体上谈论自己的感情生活),这张专辑涉及的恋爱对象则是:约翰·梅尔(John Mayer)、乔·乔纳斯(Joe Jonas)、泰勒·洛特纳(Taylor Lautner)——都是星光熠熠的名人。她的音乐也更加宏大。《摇摇欲坠》("Haunted")等歌曲采用了雄心勃勃的管弦乐编曲,歌曲《分手信》("Dear John")和《着迷》("Enchanted")不仅在时长上超过了一般乡村歌曲的3分钟长度,形式上还更为灵巧轻盈,在简单的旋律基础上过渡到更为宽广的流行和声。

媒体对这张专辑进行了持续宣传,《爱的告白》巡回演唱会(Speak Now World Tour)结束之际,泰勒显然已经准备告别天真童话的音乐风格,转而涉足更加成熟的音乐领域。2011年,《纽约客》(The New Yorker)杂志对正在进行《爱的告白》巡演的泰勒进行了报道,称:"她近来决定人生要'知足常乐……没人能一直维持喜

---

1 2010年,第52届格莱美颁奖典礼上,泰勒与史蒂薇·妮克丝(Stevie Nicks)同台表演歌曲《瑞安农》("Rhiannon")和《你应该和我在一起》。
2 坎耶·韦斯特(Kanye West):美国说唱男歌手,2018年宣布改名为耶(Ye)。
3 MTV音乐录影带大奖(MTV Video Music Awards,VMAs):也称MTV音乐电视大奖,是为表彰优秀音乐录影带(MV)设置的奖项。
4 事件的详细经过请参见书末"大事记"2009年MTV音乐录影带大奖部分。

出望外的状态'。泰勒目前已为新专辑写了大约10首歌。被问及这些歌曲有什么特点时，她说：'这些歌都比较伤感？坦白来讲。'"

泰勒的下一张专辑《红》（Red）[1]，是她从原来的乡村音乐领域迈向流行音乐和一系列更加成熟主题的重要一步。《红》是泰勒迈入20岁后写的第一张专辑，其中大部分歌曲以失恋为主线——据称与她和演员杰克·吉伦哈尔（Jake Gyllenhaal）的恋情有关——展现了她成为青少年明星后的成长。泰勒与老搭档利兹·罗斯（Liz Rose）合作完成的歌曲《回忆太清晰》（"All Too Well"）饱受粉丝喜爱，该曲将故事细节娓娓道来，传递出分手后强烈的怀念之情。专辑中，包括《我们再也回不去了》（"We Are Never Ever Getting Back Together"）、《我知道你是大麻烦》（"I Knew You Were Trouble"）和《22》（"22"）在内的流行歌曲，由泰勒与瑞典传奇制作人马克斯·马丁（Max Martin）及希尔贝克（Shellback）制作完成，这些歌曲不仅证明了她在音乐方面的成长，也表明她愿意与新制作人合作，尝试新音乐风格。

虽然专辑《红》对泰勒的心碎进行了刻意包装，但这张专辑传递出的情感依然强烈而直白。专辑宣传期间，泰勒在采访中常常显得不似从前那般直言不讳。《幸运儿》（"The Lucky One"）等歌曲揭露声名显赫并非表面那般光鲜，与其个人生活有关的谣言和诸多演出要求施加在她身上的压力也显而易见。泰勒与其粉丝共同成长，虽然她20多岁时的烦恼似乎多于大多数年轻人，但专

---

[1] 泰勒的第四张专辑《红》发行于2012年10月22日。

辑《红》中极度私人化的不确定性和心碎依然能引起听众的强烈共鸣。泰勒在成长过程中并未丢掉将个人经历转化为公众形象的嗅觉，这种公众形象既不可触及（毕竟她是一位流行明星），又极其脆弱。

如果说专辑《红》在一定程度上代表了名气、事业及个人生活带给泰勒的重担，专辑《1989》则卸下了这些负担。《1989》是她公开发行的第一张流行专辑，远离了自己的乡村音乐根基，这在某种程度上是一场豪赌。在这张专辑中，泰勒在歌曲《释怀》("Clean")里放下了一段感情，在《统统甩掉》("Shake It Off")里无视流言蜚语，在《空白格》("Blank Space")里反讽了媒体报道对于她不断约会的谣言，在《欢迎来纽约》("Welcome To New York")里做出不再由专辑周期、名气及恋情决定个人生活的重大决定。尽管此前大机器唱片公司曾对发行纯流行乐专辑抱有疑虑，但专辑《1989》最终取得了空前成功，首周销量达到128.7万张，成为2014年美国最畅销的专辑，泰勒也凭借这张专辑再度获颁格莱美年度专辑奖项。泰勒坚守自我，不受身边反对声音的干扰，向人们证明唱片公司、媒体乃至整个音乐行业都无法掌控她的事业和形象，她本人才是自己的主宰。

泰勒还做出了不在流媒体音乐平台声破天（Spotify）上架专辑《1989》的重大决定，随后又将自己的全部过往专辑从流媒体服务上下架。她还写了一封批评苹果音乐的公开信，指责该平台在用户3个月的免费试用期内，拒绝向艺人支付流媒体音乐的版税。有人认为，泰勒将专辑下架声破天平台意在提高自己的音乐销量，或是该服务平台并未就播放其音乐支付足够款项。然而泰勒回应道，自己的决定旨在引起大家对这一不公正体系的关注，受益者不单单包括像她一样的流行歌星，还有那些独立音乐新人，以及刚刚开始学习音乐、未来想自己组建乐队的孩子。所有音乐人理应从自己的音乐中得到报酬，歌迷和公司都应认识到音乐的价值，认识到音乐值得他们买账。音乐行业在某种程度上对此做出了回应——苹果音乐同意在用户3个月免费试用期内向艺人支付报酬；2018年，环球音乐集团与泰勒签约时，同意即使艺人尚未赚回预付给他们的所有款项，也能得到环球音乐出售声破天股份所得的资金[1]。泰勒以其上百万的专辑销量证明，虽然流媒体平台上可以在线播放音乐，人们依然愿意为音乐付费（至少为她的音乐消费）。

然而，作为流行歌星的泰勒，就算为音乐行业存在的问题发声，就算在自己的事业上取得了重大突破，也免不了背负种种包袱，比如对其私生活的无厘探究，以及专辑《1989》发行几年后她本人遭受的争议，后者则为其事业发展指明了新方向。2009年，泰勒在MTV音乐录影带大奖颁奖典礼上遭到了坎耶·韦斯特的公然羞辱，两人后来重归于好（但有时貌合神离）。后来，韦斯特在录制自己的歌曲《颇负盛名》("Famous")时，询问泰勒是否可以在歌词"我感觉自己和泰勒可能还会做爱"中提到她。然而歌曲发布后，泰勒的团队则表示泰勒本人并未同意韦斯特在这首歌中用"贱

---

[1] 2018年底，环球音乐集团持有声破天3.5%的股份（估值约8.5亿美元），根据合约，若环球音乐未来将这些股份出售，所获资金将分配给旗下艺人。

人"（bitch）指代自己[1]。双方各执一词，坎耶当时的妻子金·卡戴珊发布了一则泰勒支持这首歌的电话录音[2]，泰勒则要求终止这场争议事件。

凡此种种，加上泰勒与前男友加尔文·哈里斯（Calvin Harris）及女歌手凯蒂·佩里（Katy Perry）间的一些恩怨纠葛（媒体宣称她与后者不和），泰勒在一些人眼中的形象变为阴险狡诈、背后捅刀、借自己的名气破坏他人事业的女歌手，同名专辑《泰勒·斯威夫特》时期的那个纯真烂漫、满头卷发的少女已恍如隔世，专辑《红》时期诚挚坚定、黯然心碎的歌手也已远去。然而，面对流言蜚语，泰勒的回应方式一如既往——她已准备好用全新的形象一击碎这些谣言。

2017年末，泰勒清空了自己所有社交媒体账号上的内容。数日后，她发布了一系列视频，视频内容为一条盘绕的蛇（在卡戴珊/韦斯特闹剧中，卡戴珊及其拥趸以蛇代指泰勒）。不久后，泰勒宣布即将发行新专辑《名誉》，并发行了单曲《瞧你们让我做了什么》（"Look What You Made Me Do"）。这首歌的歌词和音乐录影带提到了泰勒此前纠缠其中的种种恩怨纠纷，而从这些恩怨情仇中走出来的她则变得更为坚韧强硬。在这首歌的间奏中，

---

1 争议歌词："I feel like me and Taylor might still have sex / Why? I made that bitch famous."（我觉得自己和泰勒可能还会做爱／为什么？我让那个贱人出名了）。

2 金·卡戴珊（Kim Kardashian）：美国娱乐界名媛、服装设计师，坎耶·韦斯特前妻，两人2014年完婚，2022年离婚。该录音片段于2020年被证实为刻意歪曲事实的蓄意剪辑版本。

她宣布"过去的泰勒已无法接通——为什么？因为她已经死了！"（"the old Taylor can't come to the phone right now—Why? Oh, 'cause she's dead！"）与歌曲《空白格》有异曲同工之妙的是，泰勒正试图透过这首歌掌控自己的名誉，通过掌握主动权，让试图取笑或攻击自己的人无路可走。她在自己的整个职业生涯中都称自己脸皮薄——对于一个脸皮薄的人来说，要回击霸凌者，还有比化身为难以对付的蛇更好的办法吗？

但泰勒的音乐并不仅仅用来塑造其自身形象。在专辑《名誉》中，歌迷一如既往能够探索这位巨星的真实感受——愤怒、背叛之外，还有受伤、希望和爱。用泰勒的话说，《名誉》狂轰滥炸般的宣传是诱饵，也是调包，目的是在她揭露这张专辑的情感核心前分散公众的注意力——《易碎》（"Delicate"）和《新年日》（"New Year's Day"）等歌曲透露出泰勒在名誉受损的阴霾中爱上了某人。虽然这也算得上一种公关手段，但专辑《名誉》刻画的泰勒，依然能引起听者的共鸣。谁没为他人的看法烦忧过？泰勒经久不衰的成功，源自她将自己的音乐建立在人类共通的恐惧和喜悦之上——遭到霸凌、受伤心碎以及坠入爱河。

2019年夏，泰勒又一次在社交媒体上预告即将发行新专辑，发布数张色彩明亮、风格淡雅的照片后，节奏欢快的流行歌曲《我！》（"ME！"）发行。她随后发行的专辑《恋人》（Lover）[1]拉开了新时期的帷幕，将听众带回那个天真烂漫、情感真挚的青少年时期——同

---

[1] 泰勒的第七张专辑《恋人》发行于2019年8月23日。

时向听者证明这样的泰勒从未远去。当时,泰勒没有为这张专辑举办全球性的巡回演唱会,只计划举办几场小型音乐节性质的演出宣传专辑。

新冠疫情期间,泰勒惊喜发行专辑《民间故事》(*folklore*)[1],更令人惊喜的是,她在这张专辑中再一次实现了音乐风格上的转变,《民间故事》听起来更像轻盈柔和、细节满满的独立民谣。这是泰勒首张较少涉及其个人生活,反而更多描述想象中的虚构人物的专辑。然而,惊喜尚未落幕。数月后,泰勒发行《民间故事》的姊妹专辑《永恒故事》(*evermore*)[2],这张专辑延续了前一张专辑独立民谣的音乐风格和落笔于虚构的故事情节,她当时沉迷于此类创作。

翌年,泰勒着手发行由大机器唱片公司发行的前6张专辑的重录版本。她与大机器公司的合约到期时,后者不仅拒绝将前6张专辑的母带卖给她,还将母带卖给了音乐经纪人斯库特·布劳恩(Scooter Braun),而在泰勒看来,布劳恩为人处事欺人太甚[3]。歌迷们欣然接受了这些重录专辑[4],并将自己流媒体歌单中的旧版专辑替换成了重录版本,泰勒似乎也得到了音乐评论家们的广泛支持,公告牌称其为"2021年最伟大的流行巨星"。

---

1 泰勒的第八张专辑《民间故事》发行于2020年7月24日。
2 泰勒的第九张专辑《永恒故事》发行于2020年12月11日。
3 布劳恩曾是坎耶·韦斯特的经纪人,并在韦斯特/卡戴珊事件中有所牵连。
4 截至2024年12月,泰勒已发行《放手去爱(重制版)》[*Fearless (Taylor's Version)*]、《爱的告白(重制版)》[*Speak Now (Taylor's Version)*]、《红(重制版)》[*Red (Taylor's Version)*]和《1989(重制版)》[*1989 (Taylor's Version)*]4张重录专辑。

引 言

2022年，泰勒重回流行音乐领域，发行电子流行专辑《午夜》（Midnights）[1]，这张专辑的灵感来源于她在无数失眠夜晚里感到的焦虑与不安。《午夜》打破了多项纪录，比如，它是声破天音乐平台上单日播放量最高的专辑，还是有史以来首张一周内全部占据公告牌热门单曲100强榜前10位的专辑。

5年没有举行巡演的泰勒，终于再度踏上了舞台，这就是时代巡回演唱会（The Eras Tour）[2]，一场横跨五大洲、囊括她所有专辑和音乐时期的体育场巡演。时代巡演的美国预售首日，1400万歌迷在线抢票，票务网站票务大师（Ticketmaster）一度因此瘫痪。与泰勒事业的诸多方面一样，这场巡演在全球范围内售罄，打破了多项纪录，成为一种文化现象。

在2020年上映的纪录片《美利坚女士》（Miss Americana）中，泰勒表达了自己的担忧，她担忧音乐行业的女性从业者一旦步入30岁，就可能会被抛弃，因为公众期待她们永葆年轻亮丽，不会容忍30多岁的女性音乐家。虽然有此忧虑，她却越战越勇。自本书第一版上市起[3]，泰勒已经发行了5张新专辑和4张重录专辑，并开启了一场创纪录的全球巡回演唱会。

泰勒自有一套革新自我形象的方式，她在独立民谣专辑《民间

---

1 泰勒的第十张专辑《午夜》发行于2022年10月21日。
2 时代巡回演唱会：2023年3月17日在美国格伦代尔首演，于2024年12月8日结束。巡演电影《泰勒·斯威夫特：时代巡回演唱会》（Taylor Swift: The Eras Tour）于2023年10月13日在北美上映，12月31日在中国大陆上映。
3 英文原版图书 Taylor Swift: In Her Own Words 第一版于2019年9月出版，第二版 Taylor Swift: In Her Own Words (In Their Own Words) 于2025年3月出版。

故事》中展现出了创作虚构故事的天赋,在最新发行的专辑《苦难诗社》(THE TORTURED POETS DEPARTMENT,简称TTPD)[1]中将自我在名利之间的挣扎转化为艺术。她并未沦为音乐行业追逐新事物的猎物,恰恰相反,她一再提升业内能够企及的成功高度。

虽然本引言对泰勒的经历进行了评论性介绍,本书却并不是针对泰勒·斯威夫特的分析或评论之作。书中收录了泰勒的诸多话语,希望读者在阅读中听她本人讲述自我。这些话语再现了泰勒·斯威夫特如何做出改变、跌倒失利、重整旗鼓,又是如何为自己发声,开拓创新并成为传奇。这位年轻女性不仅是一位歌手,更是一位文化偶像,她为艺术家发声,虽然曾经不得不迅速成长起来,但她迎难而上、竿头日进。

---

[1] 泰勒的第十一张专辑《苦难诗社》发行于2024年4月19日。

目 录

个人生活

《不要长大》：早期生活与纳什维尔之路　　3
《我！》：成为泰勒·斯威夫特　　20
《爱情故事》：恋情、心碎与名誉　　41

帝国缔造者

《空白格》：音乐之内　　65
《不朽》：泰勒最伟大的传奇故事　　118
　　　　——与粉丝共谱
《一切皆变》：日新月异的音乐行业　　133
《随你怎么说》：名人与争议　　146

人生智慧

《爱的告白》：勇敢发声　　173
《统统甩掉》：其他人生教训　　194

大事记　　227
粉丝告白　　261
译名对照表　　275
致谢　　279

个人生活

《不要长大》：
早期生活与纳什维尔之路

I grew up on a Christmas tree farm, and I just remember having all this space to run around and be a crazy kid with tangled hair. And I think that really had a lot to do with me being able to have an imagination and become obsessed with, like, little stories I created in my head. Which then, later in life, led to songwriting.

我在一个圣诞树农场长大，我记得那里有足够大的空间任我到处跑来跑去，我的头发乱糟糟地缠在一起，像个野孩子一样。这样的成长经历不仅激发了我的想象力，让我痴迷于在自己脑海里创作一个个小故事，而且在后来的生活中，又带我走上了写歌的道路。

——第52届格莱美颁奖典礼排练现场，2010年1月31日

My mom thought it was cool that if you got a business card that said "Taylor" you wouldn't know if it was a guy or a girl. She wanted me to be a business person in a business world.

我妈妈觉得，要是你名片上印的名字是"Taylor"，别人就不会从名字

上看出你是男性还是女性,她觉得这很酷。她当时希望我从商。

——《滚石》(*Rolling Stone*)杂志,2009年3月5日

I used to come home from Disney movies, you know, where they'd have all these songs in the Disney movies like *Lion King* and stuff. And I'd be singing the words to the songs that I had heard once in the movie, but I had changed the lyrics to my own.

我小时候看完迪士尼电影回家,《狮子王》之类的电影里有很多配乐歌曲,我只需要听一遍就能唱出来,但我会把里面的歌词改成我自己的版本。

——美国电视节目 *CBS This Morning*[1],2014年10月29日

I actually learned on a twelve-string, purely because some guy told me that I'd never be able to play it, that my fingers too small. **Anytime someone tells me that I can't do something, I want to do it more.**

其实我当初学的是十二弦吉他,因为那时有人说我手指太细小,没法弹奏这种乐器。**一旦有人说我做不成什么事,我就会加倍努力去做。**

——美国杂志 *Teen Vogue*,2009年1月26日

I started writing songs when the guy who came over to fix my computer

---

1 部分较为小众的国外节目、杂志保留其外文原名,以方便读者进一步查阅。——编者注

had a guitar with him because he had just come from a show. And he asked me if I wanted to learn a few guitar chords, and I said, "Yeah!" So he taught me three guitar chords and left his guitar with me that week and I wrote my first song.

我开始写歌的契机要追溯到一个来帮我修电脑的人,他当时刚演出完,随身带着一把吉他。他问我想不想学几个吉他和弦,我回答:"好啊!"他就教了我3个吉他和弦,还把吉他借给我一周,于是我写了自己的第一首歌。

——英国音乐访谈节目 *The Hot Desk*,2009年5月

When I picked up the guitar, I could not stop. I would literally play until my fingers bled—my mom had to tape them up, and you can imagine how popular that made me: "Look at her fingers, so weird."

我一抱起吉他就无法放下,甚至能一直弹到手指流血——我妈妈就得用胶布把我的手指缠起来,你能想象这让我在同学间多么"出名":"看她的手指,真奇怪。"

——《滚石》杂志,2009年3月5日

I started writing songs because, when I'd have a difficult day at school or I'd be going through a hard time, I'd just tell myself, like, "It's OK, you can write a song about this later." And so I think I trained my brain to be like, "Pain? Write a song about it. Like, intense feeling? Write a song about it."

我开始写歌是因为在学校度过了艰难的一天,或者经历了一段难挨

的时光,这时我就会告诉自己,"没事的,你可以在事情过后把这些经历写成歌"。于是我好像把自己的大脑训练成,"感到痛苦?把它写成歌吧。情绪激烈?把它写成歌吧。"

——澳大利亚电视节目 *Today*,2012年11月26日

When you're in school, anything that makes you different makes you weird, and anything [that] makes you weird makes you just off-limits… And I think that you run into that same story line a lot with musicians and people who end up in the music industry or Hollywood or whatever, because they loved something from a very early age that not a lot of other kids loved.

在学校时,要是你有与众不同的地方,别人就会觉得你稀奇古怪;要是别人觉得你稀奇古怪,你就会被大家孤立……很多音乐家,很多在音乐行业或好莱坞从业的人都有类似的经历,因为他们从小热爱的东西,并不为大部分孩子所热衷。

——美国广播电台Beats 1[1],2015年12月13日

I wrote ["The Outside"] about the trouble I was having at school when I was younger. You know, I'd go to school some days and not know if I was gonna have a conversation with anybody. I mean, I was really sort of an outcast and spent a lot of time on the outside looking in. And I think, you know, this song is really sort of the basis on why I started to write songs, because I was at a point in my life where I just kind of said, "You know what? People haven't always been there for me, but music always has."

1　美国广播电台Beats 1:2020年更名为苹果音乐1台(Apple Music 1)。

歌曲《局外人》[1]写的是我从前在学校里遇到的困境。总有那么几天，我去上学时都不知道是否会有人和我说话。我是被大家排斥的那个人，总是游离在人群之外，总是向人群中张望。可以说这首歌是我写歌的起点，因为处于那个人生节点的我意识到："你知道吗？人们不会一直陪着我，但音乐一直都在。"

——美国电视节目 *Studio 330*（不插电表演现场），2006年12月5日

The first song that I really finished... it's called "Lucky You". And it was this song that I wrote about a girl who's different from everybody else, and she's unique, and she, like, sings her own song, and she goes her own way... It was very 12. It was very uplifting and inspirational and sugarcoated. And I look back on it and I sounded like a little chipmunk singing back then.

我真正完成的第一首歌……歌名是《幸运的你》。我在这首歌里写了一个与众不同的女孩，她独一无二，唱自己的歌，走自己的路……这首歌很有12岁的感觉，极度意气风发、鼓舞人心，裹着甜蜜的外壳。现在回想起来，我唱这歌的时候听起来就像只小花栗鼠。

——英国音乐访谈节目 *The Hot Desk*，2009年5月

I remember the girls who would come to talent shows and say to anyone

---

[1] 本书话语部分为中英文对照格式，故中文歌曲名首次出现处不再另外加括号注明对应英文歌曲名。——编者注

they met, "I'm so-and-so—I'm going to be famous someday." I was never that girl. I would show up with my guitar and say, "This is a song I wrote about a boy in my class." And that's what I still do today.

我记得有些参加才艺表演节目的女孩会对遇到的每个人说:"我如何如何优秀,总有一天我会出名。"我不是这种女孩。我会带着我的吉他上场,说:"下面这首歌写的是我班里的一个男孩。"如今,我仍在这样做。

——英国时尚周刊 Glamour,2009年7月1日

My love for country was cemented by three great female acts: Shania Twain brings an independence and a crossover appeal. Faith Hill has this beauty and grace and old-school glamour. And the Dixie Chicks have this "we don't care what you think" quirkiness.

几位伟大的女性音乐表演者/组合奠定了我对乡村音乐的热爱:仙妮亚·唐恩[1]个性独立,勇于跨界而魅力十足;菲丝·希尔[2]美丽优雅,充满复古魅力;南方小鸡[3]标新立异,高喊着"我们不在乎你怎么看"。

——《滚石》杂志,2008年11月27日

---

1 仙妮亚·唐恩(Shania Twain):加拿大乡村音乐女歌手,曾获格莱美最佳乡村专辑、最佳乡村歌曲等奖项,并在好莱坞星光大道留名。
2 菲丝·希尔(Faith Hill):美国乡村音乐女歌手、演员,曾获最佳乡村女歌手、最佳乡村专辑、最佳乡村合作歌曲等奖项,并在好莱坞星光大道留名。
3 南方小鸡(The Chicks,原名Dixie Chicks):美国得克萨斯州女子乐队,多次获得格莱美最佳乡村专辑奖项。

I think that the way music can transport you back to a long forgotten memory is the closest sensation we have to traveling in time. To this day, when I hear "Cowboy Take Me Away" by the Dixie Chicks, I instantly recall the feeling of being twelve years old, sitting in a little wood paneled room in my family home in Pennsylvania.
I'm clutching a guitar and learning to play the chords and sing the words at the same time, rehearsing for a gig at a coffee house.

音乐能带你回到那些久远的、逝去的记忆中，这是最像时间旅行的一种感觉。时至今日，每当听到南方小鸡的歌曲《牛仔，带我走吧》，我就像立马回到了12岁，回到宾夕法尼亚州的家中，坐在木板小房间里。
我抱着吉他，一边学和弦、一边唱歌词，为咖啡馆的演出排练。

——*Elle*（英国版），2019年2月28日

When I was 10 I saw this TV program about Faith Hill, and it said, you know, "When Faith Hill was 19 or so she moved to Nashville, and that's how she got into country music." And so I had this epiphany when I was 10. I was like, I need to be in Nashville. That's a magical dream world where dreams come true... That's when I started on my daily begging rant with my parents of, "I need to go to Nashville, please, please, please take me to Nashville. I need to go!"

10岁时，我看了一个关于菲丝·希尔的电视节目，节目里提到："菲丝·希尔在大约19岁时搬到了纳什维尔，此后便涉足乡村音乐圈。"10岁的我恍然大悟，我也要到纳什维尔去。那是个神奇的梦

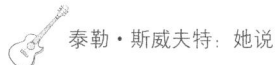

幻世界,在那里我能梦想成真……从那时开始,我就日日央求父母:"我得去纳什维尔,求你们了,求你们了,求你们带我去纳什维尔吧。我真的得去纳什维尔!"

——英国访谈节目《保罗·奥格雷迪秀》
(*The Paul O'Grady Show*),2009年5月8日

It sounds really crazy to move across the country for your 14-year-old, but I was really persistent. And from the time I was about nine years old I was doing theater productions every time I got a chance. I was performing in cafes and writing songs and recording demos. Looking back, I feel a little weird about it because it doesn't seem normal for a kid. But it felt normal to me.

为一个14岁的孩子跨越小半个美国搬家,这听起来很疯狂,但我非常坚定。我从9岁起,只要有机会就去参与剧场演出。我在咖啡馆表演,写歌,录样带。现在回想起来确实有些不可思议,因为这些似乎都不是寻常孩子会做的事。但于我而言,这些事却稀松平常。

——南非电视节目 *Top Billing*,2014年11月7日

They are the opposite of stage parents. They had no idea what to do with me when they discovered that their kid was obsessed with music, because neither of them sang or play instruments. It was very out of left field for them, so they had to learn about this industry just because I was obsessed with it.

他们不是那种专横强制的父母。发现自己的孩子痴迷音乐时，我父母有些无所适从，因为他们既不会唱歌，也不会演奏乐器。音乐对他们来说是天方夜谭，但就因为我痴迷于此，了解这个行业对他们而言成了必需之事。

——加拿大电视节目 *Tout le monde en parle*，2014年9月28日

My mom and I have always been really close, and she's always been the friend that was always there. You know, there were times when, in middle school and junior high, I didn't have a lot of friends. But my mom was always my friend. Always. And you can never forget those people who were always there for you from the beginning.

我和妈妈的关系一直很亲密，她一直是我的朋友，一直陪着我。初中和高中时，我没有多少朋友。但我妈妈一直是我的朋友，一直都是。你永远不会忘记那些从一开始就陪在你身边的人。

——美国电视节目 *CMA Celebrity Close Up*，2008年7月19日

My mom thinks of things in terms of reality and my dad always thinks in terms of daydreams—and, "How far can we go with this?" I never really went there in my mind that all of this was possible. It's just that my dad always did.

在为人处事方面，我妈妈注重现实，我爸爸则极度理想——"我们能走多远？"我从未设想过自己能取得今天的成就。但我爸爸却对此深信不疑。

——《滚石》杂志，2012年10月25日

When I was 10 years old, I'd lie awake at night and think about the roaring crowd and walking out onstage and that light hitting me for the first time. But I was always very calculated about it. I would think about exactly how I was going to get there, not just how it would feel to be there.

10岁时,夜里躺在床上,我会想象自己在人群欢呼中首次登台亮相,灯光照在我身上。但我对自己的梦想向来计之深远。我会思考如何脚踏实地地实现梦想,而非仅仅沉溺于实现它的想象。
——美国杂志《乡村音乐周刊》(*Country Weekly*),2007年12月3日

It takes a lot of different stepping stones, and meeting different people who introduce you to this person, and then working really hard. Playing venues that aren't even venues. Playing Boy Scout meetings, and garden club meetings, and coffee shops, and anywhere you can, just because you love it.

(实现梦想)需要许多敲门砖,需要见很多人,由他们将你引荐给别人;需要埋头苦干;需要在根本算不上演出场所的地方演出;需要在童子军会议、花园俱乐部会议、咖啡馆等一切可以演出的地方演出。原因无他,只因热爱。
——美国系列电视节目 *My Date With…*,2009年11月13日

When I was 11 I came to Nashville and just kind of knocked on doors of record labels. Like, my mom was waiting in the car. And I had this little demo karaoke CD and would walk into every major record label and was like, "Hey, I'm Taylor, I'm 11, I want a record deal. Call me."

《不要长大》：早期生活与纳什维尔之路

11岁时，我在纳什维尔挨门逐户地拜访各家唱片公司。那时我妈妈在车里等我。我带着自己的卡拉OK样带光盘，走进各大唱片公司，说："嗨，我是泰勒，今年11岁，我想和唱片公司签约。请联系我哦。"
——美国新闻广播节目 *CNN Spotlight*，2014年12月7日

I got a job as a songwriter for Sony/ATV [Music] Publishing when I was 14… I was in eighth grade, and my mom would pick me up from school and drive me downtown, and I would go write songs with these great songwriters in Nashville. And then I'd go home and do my homework.

14岁时，我在索尼/联合电视音乐出版公司[1]旗下任词曲作者……那时我上八年级，放学后我妈妈开车送我到市中心，在那里我和纳什维尔最杰出的词曲作者们一起写歌。然后我再回家做作业。
——美国脱口秀节目《艾伦秀》(*The Ellen DeGeneres Show*)，2008年11月11日

I knew every writer I wrote with was pretty much going to think, "I'm going to write a song for a 14-year-old today." So I would come into each meeting with 5 to 10 ideas that were solid. I wanted them to look at me as a person they were writing with, not a little kid.

我知道和我一起写歌的词曲作者大概都会想："今天我要给一个14

---

[1] 索尼/联合电视音乐出版公司：2021年更名为索尼音乐出版公司（Sony Music Publishing）。

岁的女孩写歌。"所以每次我去参加会议前都会想5到10个切实可行的点子。我希望他们视我为合作者,而不是一个小孩。
——《纽约时报》(*New York Times*),2008年11月7日

When I was 13, I got a meeting with RCA Records, and they said they wanted to sign me to a development deal. That means they want to watch you, but they're not promising to make an album with you—kind of like a guy who wants to date you but not be your boyfriend. After a year you turn in your songs, and they decide whether they want to shelf you—keep watching you—drop you or sign you to a record deal. They decided to shelf me, and I had a choice to make. I could have stayed in development with them, but I figured that if they didn't believe in me then, they weren't ever going to believe in me. So I made a tough decision and struck out on my own.

13岁时,我与美国广播唱片公司[1]会面,他们希望与我签订发展合约[2]。这意味着他们想先观察你,但并不承诺和你制作专辑——有点儿像那种只想和你约会但不想当你男友的家伙。一年后你拿出创作的歌曲,由他们决定是搁置你,也就是继续观察你,还是放弃与你合作,又或是与你签订唱片合约。他们决定暂时搁置我,我面临是去还是留的选择。我当时仍然可以与他们保持发展合约关系,但我觉得如果他们那时候还不信任我,就永远不会信任我。我做了个艰

---

1 美国广播唱片公司(Radio Corporation of America Records):贝图斯曼唱片集团(Bertelsmann Music Group, BMG)旗下的一家名牌唱片公司。
2 发展合约(development deal):唱片公司与具有发展潜力的艺人签订此类合约,作为对艺人未来发展的投资。

难的决定，我要自食其力。

——英国时尚周刊 *Glamour*，2009年7月1日

When I was making the rounds first trying to get a record deal, the thing that I heard the most is, "Country music does not have a young demographic. The country music demographic is 35-year-old females, and those are the only people that listen to country radio..."
That's what I heard everywhere I went, and I just kept thinking that can't be true. That can't be accurate because I listen to country music and I know there have to be other girls everywhere who listen to country music and want some music that is maybe directed more towards them, toward people our age.

我早年四处奔走，试图获得一份唱片合约时，听到的最多的一句话就是，"乡村音乐的受众不是年轻群体，而是35岁的女性群体，只有她们才会收听乡村音乐电台……"
所到之处人人都这样说，但我就是不愿被他们说服。因为这和实际情况有出入，我本人就是乡村音乐的听众，我知道肯定还有很多地方的女孩也听乡村音乐，并且大家都希望听到为我们这个年龄群体所创作的乡村音乐。

——美国电视节目 *CMT Insider*，2008年11月26日

All the songs I heard on the radio were about marriage and kids and settling down. I just couldn't relate to that. I kept writing songs about the guy who I dated for a couple of weeks and who cheated on me, about all the things I was going through... I felt there was no reason why country music shouldn't relate to someone my age if someone my age was writing it.

我在电台里听到的歌曲,内容无外乎都是结婚生子和安居某地。我根本无法与这些歌曲产生共鸣。我不停创作,写一起约会了几周但最后背叛我的家伙,写我经历的一切……我觉得只要有我这个年纪的人在写乡村歌曲,乡村音乐就没理由脱离我所在的年龄群体。
——英国《每日电讯报》(*Telegraph*),2009年4月26日

One of my favorite songs that I've ever put out is called "Fifteen". And it's about my freshman year of high school, and it kind of chronicles my best friend, Abigail, and me and the way that we went through our freshman year of high school and the lessons we learned. And that's kind of how I like to tell a story, is from the point of view of really knowing what you're talking about and knowing where you're coming from because you were there.

在我已发行的歌曲中,《15岁》是我最喜爱的歌曲之一。这首歌写的是我在高中一年级的经历,我在歌里记述了和最好的朋友阿比盖尔一起度过的高一生活,以及我们共同成长的经验教训。我喜欢用这种方式讲故事,知道自己在讲什么,知道自己来自何处,因为那是我的亲身经历。
——YouTube频道YouTube Presents,2011年9月1日

When you are trying to shop for a label deal, never use the phrase "I sound just like [another famous artist]." Don't say that to the labels.

They'll say "Well, we already have those big-name artists [so we don't need to sign you]." For young artists, try to sound original, so you don't sound like anyone else.

向唱片公司寻求合约时，千万别说"我唱歌就像'某位著名艺术家'"。别对唱片公司用这套说辞。因为他们会说："我们已经有那些大牌艺人了（潜台词：所以就没必要和你签约了）。"对年轻艺人来说，你的歌要尽量保有原创特色，这样才能使自己独一无二。

——网络杂志 *Songwriter Universe*，2007年2月16日

I took tiny, little things, like, inspiration, from Faith Hill. She's nice to everybody, so that rubbed off on me. You know, Shania Twain is confident and knows who she is, and that's something that I took as inspiration. So, I guess it's all about being different from as many people as you can possibly be different from. Find something that really is you.

我从菲丝·希尔那里获得了许多小启发。她待人友善，这影响了我。仙妮亚·唐恩充满自信，自我认知明确，她也启发了我。我想这说明你要尽可能变得与众不同。要找到自己的独特之处。

——美国系列电视节目 *My Date With...*，2009年11月13日

I had this showcase at The Bluebird Cafe, ironically the place where Faith Hill got discovered. And I played my guitar and sang a bunch of songs that I'd written. There was one guy in the audience named Scott Borchetta. So he came up to me after the show and he said, "I want you on my record label, and I want you to write all your own music," and I was so excited.

And I get a call from him later that week and he goes, "Hey, so, good news is I want you on my record label. Bad news is that I don't actually have a record label yet."

我曾在蓝鸟咖啡馆演出,那里恰巧也是菲丝·希尔被发掘的地方。我在台上弹奏吉他,唱了很多自己写的歌。斯科特·波切塔在台下观众里。演出结束后他找到我,说:"我想签你到我们唱片公司来,你可以完全自主地创作音乐,"我当时很激动。那周晚些时候,他给我打了个电话,说:"嗨,好消息是我的唱片公司想和你签约,坏消息是我的唱片公司还没成立。"

——美国系列电视短片节目《泰勒·斯威夫特:无畏之旅》(*Taylor Swift: Journey to Fearless*),2010年10月22日

They only had 10 employees at the record label [Big Machine] to start out with, so when they were releasing my first single, my mom and I came in to help stuff the CD singles into envelopes to send to radio. We sat out on the floor and did it because there wasn't furniture at the label yet.

大机器唱片公司起步时只有10名雇员,所以我的首张单曲发行时,我和妈妈都去给大家帮忙,帮着把要送去电台的单曲光盘塞进信封里。当时大机器唱片公司里还没有家具,所以我们就坐在地板上干活。

——美国杂志《娱乐周刊》(*Entertainment Weekly*),2008年2月5日

I've never wanted to use my age as a gimmick, as something that would get me ahead of other people. I've wanted the music to do that. So we've never hidden the fact that I'm 17, but we've never wanted it to be the headline. Because I want the music to win. I think the actual truth of the matter is that being 17 has been sort of an obstacle, just in proving yourself to radio and proving yourself to middle-aged people listening to the radio.

我从来都不用年龄作噱头,从来不靠年龄小超越他人。我希望用音乐超越他人。所以我们从未隐瞒过我只有17岁的事实,但也并不希望我因为年龄小而上头条。因为我想靠自己的音乐获胜。对我来说,17岁的年纪未尝不是一种阻碍,你得向电台证明自己,还得向收听电台的中年听众们证明自己。

——美国杂志《娱乐周刊》,2007年7月25日

Even when I go back to high school now, when I go back to functions like a football game or a band concert or something like that, it doesn't matter how many people come up and ask me for my autograph, if I see like one of those popular people, I still feel like my hair is frizzy and people are looking at me.

即使我现在回到高中,再去参加橄榄球比赛或乐队演唱会之类的社交活动,有多少人凑上前来找我签名都无关紧要,就算我看上去像个名人,我还是感觉自己处在顶着一头小卷发,正被人们盯着看的往常状态里。

——美国杂志《17岁》(*Seventeen*),2009年1月20日

《我!》:

成为泰勒·斯威夫特

I'm kind of used to being shot out of a cannon, you know? That's kind of like what my life has become, and it's an exhilarating feeling, for sure. And, yeah, you're exhausted, but it's an exhausted feeling with, like, a sense of accomplishment too.

我已经习惯那种应接不暇的忙碌状态了,你知道吗?那就是我现在的生活状态,那种状态令人亢奋。当然,你也会筋疲力尽,但这种筋疲力尽也会带来成就感。

——堪萨斯州音乐电台 Mix 93.3,2012年10月29日

People talk to me a lot about, "Why don't you ever rebel?" And I feel like I do rebel. To me, rebelling is—is that rush you get when you sing a song about someone and you know they're in the crowd.

人们经常问我:"你怎么从不叛逆?"其实我也会叛逆。对我来说,在台上唱着一首写给某人的歌,并且知道那人就在台下时的澎湃心潮,就是我的叛逆。

——美国电视节目 *Dateline*,2009年5月31日

I never won anything in school or in sports, and then all of a sudden, I started winning things. People always say, "Live in the moment"—if you really live in the moment at a big awards show and you win, you freak out!

我从未在学业或运动方面赢过什么,然后一夕之间,我开始收获一些成果。人们常说"活在当下"——如果你在一场大型颁奖典礼上赢得了奖项,活在当下的感觉就是欣喜若狂!

——《滚石》杂志,2012年10月25日

I know where I'll be on tour a year from now... so I try to kind of implement as much spontaneity in my life as I possibly can, especially because, you know, **this actually is really fun.**

我知道自己一年后会在哪里举办巡演……所以我试着在生活中尽可能随心而为,**而这真的很有趣**。

——英国广播电台BBC Radio 1,2014年10月9日

I was raised by two parents who raised me to never be presumptuous about success or winning, and they always would say you have to work for every single thing that you get. And, you know, so every single time I've won an award or something like that, it's been like I win it like it's the last time I'll ever win anything.

我父母从小就教育我,永远不要觉得成功或胜利是你的囊中之物,他们常说,一点一滴的收获都来自一分一毫的耕耘。所以每次我获

奖或赢得什么荣誉，都感觉那是我最后一次赢得什么东西。
——英国访谈节目《艾伦·蒂托马奇秀》
(The Alan Titchmarsh Show)，2010年10月28日

Words are everything to me. Words can build me up and make me feel so good. And on the flip side, words can absolutely demolish me. I am nowhere close to being bulletproof when it comes to criticism.

文字是我的一切。文字让我振作起来，让我感觉如此美好。反之，文字也能让我一蹶不振。面对批评，我还做不到刀枪不入。
——美国杂志《娱乐周刊》，2010年12月3日

My confidence is easy to shake. I am very well aware of all of my flaws... I have a lot of voices in my head constantly telling me I can't do it... And getting up there on stage thousands of times, you're going to have off nights. And when you have an off night in front of that many people, and it's pointed out in such a public way, yeah, that gets to you. I feel like, as a songwriter, I can't develop thick skin. I cannot put up protective walls, because it's my job to feel things.

我的信心很容易动摇。我很清楚自己的那些缺点……每时每刻，我的脑海里都有很多声音叫嚣着我做不到……在舞台上表演上千次，总会有搞砸的时候。当你在那么多人面前表现不佳，当你的失误在公众面前被大肆宣扬，你也会心烦意乱。作为词曲作者，我无法视若无睹。我没法对此竖起保护墙，因为我的工作就是去感受事物。
——美国新闻电台节目 All Things Considered，2012年11月2日

My mom tells me that when I was a little kid she never had to punish me for something I did wrong because I'd punish myself worse than she ever could. That's how I am when I make a mistake.

我妈妈告诉我，我小时候她从不会因为我做错了什么事而惩罚我，因为我会用比她更狠的方式惩罚自己。我犯错时便是如此。
　　　　　　——美国杂志《娱乐周刊》，2010年12月3日

I'm intimidated by the fear of being average.

我害怕沦为平庸无奇之辈。
　　　　　　——美联社（Associated Press），2006年11月21日

I doubt myself like 400,000 times per 10-minute interval… I have a ridiculously, terrifyingly long list of fears—like, literally everything. Everything. Diseases. Spiders. Like, the support of roofs. Or I get scared of the idea of people, like, getting tired of me in general, which is a broader concept.

每隔10分钟，我就会怀疑自己成千上万次……我无可救药地害怕很多东西——一切都让我感到恐惧。一切事物，疾病、蜘蛛乃至屋顶的支撑结构都让我恐惧。人们的看法也让我恐惧，总体来说我害怕被人们厌倦，这是一种更宽泛意义上的恐惧。
　　　　　　——美国VH1频道音乐节目 *Storytellers*，2012年11月11日

My mom is the last straw. She is the last-ditch effort for me to feel better because she's really good at being rational and realistic. She's going to always bring me back to a place where I'm not so imbalanced.

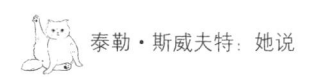

妈妈是我的救命稻草。她非常理性，又足够注重现实，因此是我最后的解药，她能让我的状态好起来。妈妈总能把我从失衡的状态中解救出来。

——美国杂志《名利场》（Vanity Fair），2015年8月11日

My dad is, like, a legendary photobomber. It's his favorite thing to do. He loves to just jump into the back of pictures at any given moment. And it's fun having parents who are really enthusiastic about what I do for a living.

我爸爸简直是个抢镜大师。他酷爱抢镜，喜欢随时随地跳进镜头里。我父母对我的事业充满热情，这很有趣。

——英国电台KISS FM，2014年10月9日

I honestly think my lack of female friendships in high school and middle school is why my female friendships are so important now. Because I always wanted them. It was just hard for me to have friends.

老实说，现在我这么重视与女性朋友间的友谊，可能与我在初中和高中时缺少女性朋友有关。那时我一直渴望有几个女性朋友。交朋友对那时的我来说实非易事。

——GQ，2015年10月15日

I'm really not interested in, like, an entourage of people who tell me what

I want to hear all the time. That doesn't thrill me or excite me at all. I have friends who are all passionate about what they do. They all have their own lives, their own jobs, their own things that they're obsessed with like I'm obsessed with music.

我对那些只讲我想听的内容的人不感兴趣。那不会让我激动和兴奋。我有些朋友对自己从事之事充满了热情。他们有各自的生活和工作，像我痴迷音乐一样有自己的痴迷之物。

——英国广播电台 BBC Radio 1，2014年10月9日

I'll walk into the room and I'll be like, "What do you think about this outfit for the show next week?" And [Ed Sheeran] will be like, "You look like a blackjack dealer." If he's gonna tell me my outfit looks bad, he's gonna tell me if my song isn't good enough. And those are the people that I really want to be the ones who I bounce ideas off of.

当我走进房间，问：“你觉得我下周穿这件表演怎么样？”艾德·希兰[1]会说：“你看起来像21点纸牌游戏里的荷官。”他能直接点评我的表演服装，也会对我的歌曲质量直言不讳。我很想与希兰这类人分享观点，征求他们的反馈。

——2013年MuchMusic音乐录影带颁奖典礼后台，
2013年6月16日

---

1 艾德·希兰（Ed Sheeran）：英国流行男歌手，曾获全英音乐奖年度专辑奖、格莱美最佳流行专辑奖等，与泰勒合作发行《一切皆变》（"Everything Has Changed"）、《游戏终结》（"End Game"）等多首歌曲。

We even have girls in our group who have dated the same people. It's almost like the sisterhood has such a higher place on the list of priorities for us... When you've got this group of girls who need each other as much as we need each other, in this climate, when it's so hard for women to be understood and portrayed the right way in the media... now more than ever we need to be good and kind to each other and not judge each other—and just because you have the same taste in men, we don't hold that against each other.

我的姐妹圈里有几个女孩甚至和同一个人约会过。但对我们来说，姐妹情谊才是彼此更看重的东西……当前环境中，女性很难得到媒体的正确理解和刻画，姐妹圈里的女孩们需要彼此，全体女性也需要彼此……现如今，我们比以往任何时候都要友好相处，而非去评判彼此——我们不会仅仅因为喜欢同样类型的男人就剑拔弩张。

——美国杂志《名利场》，2015年8月11日

It's always a priority for me to make a great record... But if I were handed a script that blew my mind, that would be the next priority. I would really jump into that because I think that, you know, acting has always been something I've been fascinated by, and I've always loved doing it. It's an amazing, cathartic experience to become another person.

制作一张好专辑始终都是我的首要任务……但要是有让我大开眼界的剧本邀约，演戏就成了我下一阶段的当务之急。我很乐意参与其中，因为我一直都对演戏很感兴趣，并且也以此为乐。演戏的感觉

很棒,成为另一个人是种酣畅淋漓的体验。
——美国视频频道Monsieur Hollywood,2012年7月26日

Every night before the show, the band and the dancers and the singers and I, we all get together in a huddle. It's a way for us to all get together and have somebody from the group make a speech.
It's really amazing to get to hear from everyone who we perform with, because you hear their life stories, you hear, sometimes, funny stories, you hear what's motivating them lately, and it just makes you realize that you're performing with people who've been dreaming about this their whole life. The same way I started writing songs when I was 12, those dancers, you know, woke up one day when they were four and decided dancing was all they ever wanted to do, and now they're doing it.

每晚演出开始前,我和乐队成员、舞蹈演员以及伴唱歌手们都会围成一圈,大家聚在一起,听团队里的某个成员讲话。
能有机会听巡演团队里的每个人讲话实在很棒。因为我能听到他们的人生故事、生活趣事或是最近的动力来源,这让我意识到,这些和我一起演出的人,一直梦寐以求的就是登台表演。就像我12岁时开始写歌,可能那些舞者4岁时,某天醒来决定将跳舞作为毕生所求,而现在他们正在实现自己的梦想。
——巡演纪录片《泰勒·斯威夫特:1989世界巡回演唱会》
(*Taylor Swift: 1989 World Tour Live*),2015年12月20日

I'm around people so much. Massive amounts of people. I do a meet-and-greet every night on the tour, and it's 150 people. Before that, it's a radio meet-and-greet with 40 people. After the show, it's 30 or 40 more people. So then when I go home and turn on the TV, and I've got Monica and Chandler and Ross and Rachel and Phoebe and Joey on a *Friends* marathon, I don't feel lonely. I've just been onstage for two hours, talking to 60,000 people about my feelings. That's so much social stimulation. When I get home, there is not one part of me that wishes I was around other people.

我身边围绕着太多人。简直是人山人海。每晚都有150个人参加我的巡演见面会。那之前还有一个40人参加的电台见面会。演出结束后我还得参加一个30至40人的见面会。等我回到家，打开电视看滚动播放的《老友记》，还有莫妮卡、钱德勒、罗斯、瑞秋、菲比和乔伊[1]陪着我，我不会觉得孤单。那时候我刚刚完成了两小时的表演，和6万观众分享了我的感受。这是多大的社交刺激啊。所以回到家时，我一点儿也不想有其他人在身旁了。

——GQ，2015年10月15日

I've always felt, you know, 40, in my career sensibilities and things like that. I've had to grow up fast. But then I think on the opposite end that's kind of stunted my maturity as far as, like, my interests and my hobbies. My ideal Fourth of July celebration was creating a giant slip and slide on my lawn.

从职业敏感度之类的方面来说，我一直觉得自己已经40岁了。我

---

[1] 均为美国系列电视剧《老友记》（*Friends*）中的角色。

必须（在这方面）快速成长起来。但反过来看，我的兴趣爱好又极大地阻碍了自己的成长。我理想中的7月4日国庆节庆祝活动，是在自家草坪上搭一个巨大的滑梯。

——美国杂志《幸运》(Lucky)封面拍摄幕后，2014年12月

I get as excited about being onstage as I get about cozy things... This is the time of year where I'm so out of control excited about the fact that it's fall. Guess what's next? Winter. So it's two seasons in a row that I love, and I can bake stuff all the time, and then I can give it to people. I can try out new recipes. I can wear sweaters. I can wear knee socks. I can even buy sweaters for my cats to wear.

登台表演让我兴奋，温馨的事物也让我兴奋……每年这个时候，我都无法抑制住自己的兴奋之情，因为现在是秋天了。接下来是什么？是冬天。我很喜欢秋冬这两个接续的季节，我可以经常烤点儿什么，然后分享给大家。我还可以试试新菜谱，可以穿毛衣，可以穿及膝袜，甚至还可以给我的几只猫买毛衣穿。

——"泰勒·斯威夫特1989"，2014年10月27日

[Baking] kind of calms me down, because if I'm thinking about measuring out all these ingredients and just kind of following sort of a recipe, I'm not thinking about things that stress me out.

烘焙能让我放松平静下来，称量所有食材和按照食谱操作占据了我的脑海，我就没空为那些让我倍感压力的事情分心了。

——英国电台KISS FM，2014年10月9日

All I think about are metaphors and cats.

隐喻和猫咪占据了我全部的思绪。

——雅虎直播，2014年8月18日

My cats are named after my favorite female lead TV show characters. My first cat is named Meredith after Meredith Grey. My second cat is named Olivia after Detective Olivia Benson. Let's set the record straight: I'm not getting a third cat because, you know, two cats is a party, three cats is a cat lady. But if I *were* to—you know, you *have* to get another cat, you *have* to name it something—I might name it Monica Geller.

我的猫咪们都以我最爱的电视剧女主角命名。第一只猫梅雷迪斯的名字取自梅雷迪斯·格蕾[1]。第二只猫奥利维亚的名字来自奥利维亚·本森探长[2]。我们把话说清楚：我不打算养第三只猫，因为养两只猫家里其乐融融，养三只猫我就成了可悲的单身猫奴。但要是我养——要是真得养第三只猫，你就得给它取名——我可能会叫它莫妮卡·盖勒[3]。

——美国杂志《幸运》封面拍摄幕后，2014年12月

Meredith, she was the first cat that I got. I post pictures of her on

---

1 梅雷迪斯·格蕾（Meredith Grey）：美剧《实习医生格蕾》（*Grey's Anatomy*）的主角。
2 奥利维亚·本森探长（Detective Olivia Benson）：美剧《法律与秩序：特殊受害者》（*Law & Order: Special Victims Unit*）中角色。
3 莫妮卡·盖勒（Monica Geller）：美剧《老友记》中角色。

Instagram and stuff. And she was a really beautiful kitten, so she became named, like, the year-end top celebrity pet. I think on some level she knew because she changed after that. Less likely to frolic, more likely to brood and just stare at me like I don't matter.

梅雷迪斯是我养的第一只猫。我把它的照片发到了照片墙之类的平台上。它真的是只很漂亮的小猫咪,后来还被提名为年度最佳名人宠物。我想冥冥之中它好像知道了这事,因为从那之后它就像变了只猫。不再经常嬉戏,反而爱作沉思状,它就那么盯着我,好像我无关紧要一样。

——美国脱口秀节目《凯莉与麦克现场秀》
（*Live with Kelly and Michael*），2014年11月26日

I do have a new kitten. Her name's Olivia. Her full name is Detective Olivia Benson, obviously. What better to name a tiny little kitten than the name of a fierce female detective? I just really wanted a name that stood for, like, crime fighting and, like, cleaning up the streets of New York, which is clearly what this cat's going to do.

我确实养了一只新小猫,它叫奥利维亚。是的,全名是奥利维亚·本森探长。我觉得用这位雷厉风行的女探长的名字为小猫咪命名再合适不过了。我就是想给它取一个寓意为纽约市打击犯罪、清理门户的名字,显然这也是这只小猫的职责所在。

——时尚杂志 *InStyle* 封面拍摄幕后,
2014年10月27日

This kitten [Benjamin Button] was brought in [for the "ME!" music video]… because he didn't have a home, and they did a program where they try to get kittens adopted by putting them in, like, commercials and stuff. And oh my God, it worked. I fell in love. The woman who was handling him… hands me this tiny cat, and he just starts purring, and he looks at me like, "You're my mom, and we're gonna live together."

这只小猫（本杰明·巴顿）被带进来（拍摄歌曲《我！》的音乐录影带）……因为它无家可归。他们有人发起了一个项目，让这些小猫出演广告，以便为它们寻找领养人家。天啊，这办法真奏效。我爱上这只猫了。负责照顾这只小猫咪的女士……一把它递给我，它就开始咕噜咕噜叫唤，它看着我的眼神好像在说："你就是我的妈妈，我们以后一起生活。"

——照片墙直播，2019 年 4 月 26 日

[Cats are] very dignified. They're independent. They're very capable of dealing with their own life, and if you fit into that on that day, they'll make some time for you, maybe. **I just really respect it.**

猫非常从容稳重。它们个性独立，有能力过好自己的生活。要是哪天时机合适，它们也许愿意为你腾出些时间。**我对猫咪充满敬意。**

——《时代周刊》（*Time*）网站视频，2019 年 4 月 24 日

Anywhere in America, I can bring them. Anywhere outside of America is not legal. But in America, if I'm in the country, I have the cats.

在美国境内，我能随时把猫咪带在身边。在美国以外这就不合法了。但只要在美国，只要我在国内，我一定会带着我的猫。

——iHeartRadio音乐节后台，2014年5月10日

I'm very organized in weird ways, and I kind of like to be able to look at old pictures and see what my hair looks like and what I'm wearing and be like, "Oh, that was the second album!"

我在一些奇怪的方面很有条理，比如我只要看看旧照片里的发型和服饰，就能反应过来："哦，那是第二张专辑时期！"

——雅虎直播，2014年8月18日

I'll have these style epiphanies. When I was 15, I realized that I loved the idea of a dress—like a sundress—and cowboy boots. And that's all I wore for, like, two years. And then I just started loving the bohemian, like, fairy-type look... so I dressed like how a fairy would dress for two years. And now I see pictures from the 50s and 60s where women had, like, red lips and a pearl earring and, like, those very classic looks. And I kind of dress now a little more vintage-y. So it's always got a direction to it.

我会有时尚风格方面的领悟。15岁时，我意识到自己喜欢裙子——像那种无袖背心裙——还喜欢牛仔靴。那两年我都是这么穿的。然后我开始着迷于波希米亚风格，着迷于那种仙女风的服饰……所以那两年我打扮得像个仙子。现如今，我看到照片里20世纪五六十年代的女性经典造型，她们涂红唇、戴珍珠耳环，所以我现在的穿

衣风格更复古风一些。我的风格总是有方向可循。

——与科迪斯（Keds）品牌的联名合作视频，2013年5月15日

I'm never gonna have the moment where I'm like, "I'm a woman now, guys. I'm only gonna write dark songs and I'm gonna dance in my bra all the time." Like, I just—that's not really me. I hope things will gradually evolve into growing up kind of as people naturally grow up.

我永远不会经历那种时刻，比如"大家，我现在是个成年女性了，我要只写暗黑的歌，还要一直穿着内衣跳舞"。诸如此类——那不是我。就像人们自然长大一样，我希望有个循序渐进的成长过程。

——美国杂志《今日》(Today)，2012年2月14日

I don't necessarily remember the first time that I wore red lipstick, but I know that in the last couple of years it's become my comfort zone, just because I think that it's an easy way to make an outfit or a look pop. Sometimes I'll just completely put nothing on my face except for a red lip, and it somehow looks like you have makeup on.

我不太记得自己第一次涂红唇是什么时候了，但我知道红唇是我过去几年间的"舒适区"，因为它很容易就能让一套服装或造型给人眼前一亮的感觉。有时候我就算素面朝天也会涂上红色唇膏，看起来就像化了妆一样。

——时尚杂志 *InStyle* 封面拍摄幕后，2013年10月23日

I don't like showing my belly button. When you start showing your belly button then you're really committing to the midriff thing. I only partially commit to the midriff thing—you're only seeing lower rib cage. I don't want people to know if I have one or not. I want that to be a mystery.

我不喜欢露肚脐。一旦开始露肚脐，你就会对露脐装情有独钟了。我只喜欢露出部分腹部——人们只能看到我的上腹部[1]。我不想让人们知道我有没有肚脐。我希望这成为一个谜。

——美国杂志《幸运》，2014年12月

Thirteen is the day I was born in December, and ever since then, it's kind of shown up around good times. Like, when good things are about to happen I'll see a 13 everywhere I go, and, you know, [at] awards shows I'll see a lot of 13s and then I'll end up winning. It's a really good sign.

12月13日是我出生的日子，从那之后，13这个数字每次出现都会有好事发生。要是好事将近，我随处都能看到这个数字，比如在颁奖现场我看到13很多次，最后就会得奖。13预示着好运。

——巴西电视节目 *Acesso MTV*，2012年9月17日

I have written lyrics on my arm for the last tour, and it was really a fun thing to do because, you know, it could be a song I'd never heard before. It could be a song that somebody just said, "Oh, here, I really like this one

---

[1] 露腹装是泰勒在专辑《1989》时期的标志性着装，指上衣较短、下装为高腰遮住肚脐的服装款式。

line in this one song," you know, like, in the dressing room before I'd go on. And I'd just write it on my arm.

上一场巡演中，我会在自己的胳膊上写歌词，我乐在其中，有时候写的歌词可能出自某一首我从未听过的歌曲。可能出自登台前某人在我更衣室里说的话，"哦，我很喜欢这首歌里的这句词"。我就会把它写在自己的胳膊上。

——美国音乐网站 Taste of Country 视频，2012 年 10 月 22 日

If I had to have a theme song, like if I were going out into a boxing ring to fight or something, it would be "Backseat Freestyle" by Kendrick Lamar. And that may seem like a little bit of a unique choice for me, but if you really knew me you would know that it's not, and you would know that I know every single word to that song and I really wish that I was best friends with Kendrick Lamar.

如果非要给我配首主题曲，比如我要去搏击场参加搏斗之类，那么我的主题曲应该是肯德里克·拉马尔[1]的《后座自由式》。选这首歌看起来可能有点不同寻常，但要是你真的了解我，你会觉得没什么不合适，因为你知道我熟悉那首歌的每一个词，并且我非常希望和肯德里克·拉马尔成为好朋友。

——美国杂志《好莱坞报道》(*Hollywood Reporter*) 视频，2014 年 12 月 17 日

---

1 肯德里克·拉马尔（Kendrick Lamar）：美国说唱男歌手、词曲作者，斩获多座格莱美奖项，也是第一位获得普利策音乐奖的非古典和爵士音乐人。

We're taught to find examples for the way we want our lives to wind up. But I can't find anyone, really, who's had the same career trajectory as mine. So when I'm in an optimistic place I hope that my life won't match anyone else's life trajectory, either, going forward.

旁人教导我们要找到自己理想生活的榜样。但我找不到那种榜样，因为我的事业轨迹与他人的事业轨迹截然不同。所以要是乐观点看，我希望自己走出一条与旁人截然不同的路。

——《时代周刊》，2014年11月13日

We're people-pleasers, that's why we became entertainers, so if people don't want you to be on stage anymore in sparkly dresses singing songs to teenagers when I'm 40, then I'm just not going to do it. It's just a goal of mine to not try and be something I'm not.

我们总是讨好他人，所以我们成了艺人，如果40岁的时候，人们不愿再看我在台上穿着亮闪闪的裙子给青少年唱歌，我就不会做这事了。我的目标之一，就是不要尝试违背我本性的事，不要成为违背我本性的人。

——*Vogue*（澳大利亚版），2015年11月14日

I get so ahead of myself. I'm like, "What am I going to be doing at 30?" But there's no way to know that! So it's this endless mind-boggling equation that you'll never figure out. **I overanalyze myself into being a big bag of worries.**

我太过未雨绸缪。时常疑惑："30岁时我在做什么？"但你根本无法未卜先知！这种念头盘踞在脑海，挥之不去，却也无法穷根究底。**我自我剖析过多，因而满心忧虑。**

——Vogue，2012年1月16日

My life would kind of go, like, you record an album, you put out the album, you go on tour... And it kind of went like that over and over again until I finished with the *1989* World Tour. And I just felt like I needed to kind of stop for a second and think about who I would be as a person if I broke that kind of cycle of constantly making something and putting it out— like, if I stopped to reflect. What kind of life would I have if there wasn't a spotlight on that life?
And I was a little afraid to do that because I was like, "Oh my God. What if they don't wanna hang out with me anymore? They'll forget about me, they're gonna move on, go see someone else who wears sparkly dresses, I don't know." And I was so honored and pleasantly surprised that you guys were so supportive of me taking a break. You're so empathetic. You guys were like, "Go, be happy! We just want you to be happy!"

过去我的生活就是录制专辑、发布专辑、开始巡演……这套流程循环往复，直到我结束了《1989》巡回演唱会。那时候我觉得自己得停下来思考一下，要是我打破了那套持续制作什么和发布什么的生活循环，要是我暂停反思复盘，我会成为什么样的人？我在聚光灯外的生活，又会是什么模样？
这想来让人有些害怕，因为我会觉得："天啊。要是他们再也不想和我一起玩了怎么办？他们会忘了我，继续生活，去看其他穿着亮闪闪裙子的人演出，我不知道。"但你们非常支持我休息一段时间，对此我真的倍感荣幸，也非常开心。你们那么善解人意。就好像在说："去休息吧，开心点儿！我们只希望你开心！"

——《名誉》巡回演唱会（The reputation Stadium Tour），
马萨诸塞州福克斯伯勒，2018年7月26日

I was so fulfilled by approval... I became the person who everyone wanted me to be.

他人的认同给了我极大的满足感……我变成了众人希望我成为的那个人。

——纪录片《美利坚女士》，2020年1月23日

There's this thing people say about celebrities, that they're frozen at the age they got famous, and that's kind of what happened to me. I had a lot of growing up to do, just trying to catch up to 29.

有人说，一旦成名，人的成长便停滞不前了，这种说法有点符合我的处境。我还需要变得更加成熟，才能配得上我29岁的实际年龄。

——纪录片《美利坚女士》，2020年1月23日

Taylor Swift: [I'm] definitely not ready for all this grown-up stuff.
Joel Little: I don't think anybody's ever ready for that stuff. You just figure it out when it happens.
Taylor Swift: I kind of don't really have the luxury of figuring stuff out because my life is planned, like, two years ahead of time.

泰勒:"(我)完全还没准备好应对这些大人的事。"
乔尔·利特[1]:"我觉得没人能等准备好了再应对那些事。事情发生的时候,顺其自然就好了。"
泰勒:"顺其自然对我来说是一种奢望,因为我(当下)的生活几乎在两年前就被规划好了。"

——谈及没有准备好成为母亲等,纪录片《美利坚女士》,
2020年1月23日

Over the years, I've learned I don't have the time or bandwidth to get pressed about things that don't matter. Yes, if I go out to dinner, there's going to be a whole chaotic situation outside the restaurant. But I still want to go to dinner with my friends. Life is short. Have adventures. Me locking myself away in my house for a lot of years—I'll never get that time back. I'm more trusting now than I was six years ago.

这几年来,我发现自己没有时间和精力为那些无关紧要的事情烦恼。没错,如果我外出吃晚餐,餐厅外将陷入一片混乱。但我还是想和朋友们共度晚餐。人生苦短,及时纵情。过去我把自己关在家里好几年[2]——我再也不会重蹈覆辙。我现在比6年前更容易相信别人了。

——《时代周刊》,2023年12月6日

---

1 乔尔·利特(Joel Little):音乐制作人,参与制作泰勒专辑《恋人》中《我!》、《你需要冷静》("You Need To Calm Down")等歌曲。
2 此处指2016年在歌词争端、卡戴珊录音事件等影响下,很长一段时间内泰勒都消失于公众视野之中。

《爱情故事》：
恋情、心碎与名誉

I'm fascinated by love rather than the principle of "Oh, does this guy like me?" I love love. I love studying it and watching it. I love thinking about how we treat each other, and the crazy way that one person can feel one thing and another can feel totally different.

令我着迷的是爱情，而非"哦，他喜欢我吗？"的答案。我热衷于爱情本身。我喜欢研究爱情，喜欢观其生发，喜欢思考爱人间如何相处，喜欢那种两人的感受截然不同的疯狂。

——《滚石》杂志，2009年3月5日

I wrote ["Teardrops On My Guitar"] about a guy that I had a crush on, and he didn't know. Inevitably, he knows now. And, you know, I have this habit of writing songs about guys and naming them. I can't seem to stop doing that.

歌曲《泪洒吉他》写的是我曾经迷恋过的一个男孩，但他当时并不知道我暗恋他。当然，现在他知道了。我写歌时习惯直接挑明所写男孩的名字，这个习惯好像难以戒掉。

——英国访谈节目《保罗·奥格雷迪秀》，2009年5月8日

I like to encode capital letters in the printed lyrics, so they spell out phrases. I encoded the "Should've Said No" guy's name over and over. It was only his first name, but everyone figured it out. I'd get texts from him. He was scared out of his mind I'd crucify him on a talk show. All I could think was, "Well, you should've said no. That's what the song is about."

我喜欢在歌词本中用大写字母编码隐藏信息,大家能据此拼出一些词语。我在《本应拒绝》的歌词里一遍一遍加密重复那个男生的名字。虽然没道出他的姓,但大家都知道他是谁。他可能会给我发短信,怕我在脱口秀里将他描述得罪大恶极。我满脑子想的都是:"你本应拒绝的。这就是这首歌想传递的信息。"

——美国杂志《健康女性》(Women's Health),
2008年11月3日

When people need music the most is when they're either falling in love or falling out of it.

人们在坠入爱河或分道扬镳时最需要音乐。
——2012年加拿大乡村音乐协会奖(Canadian Country Music Association Awards)颁奖典礼后台,2012年9月9日

"White Horse" is about that first letdown, when you realize that somebody isn't who you thought they were and that they're not gonna end up being your future, they're gonna end up being your past.

歌曲《白马》写的是第一次觉得心灰意冷的时刻,那一刻你意识到

某人与你想象的有所出入，你意识到他们不会参与你的未来，他们终将成为你的过往。

——与粉丝们的直播聊天，2008年11月13日

I think I fall into the category of the hopeless romantics, and I think that you do too, because you're here. The tricky thing about us, the tricky thing about the hopeless romantics, is that when we fall in love with someone, when we say hello, and it's magical, we never imagine that that hello could someday turn into a goodbye. And when we have our first kiss with someone and it's magical, we never, ever imagine that someday that could turn into a last kiss.

我知道自己是无可救药的浪漫主义者，我觉得你们也是，因为你们来到了我的演出现场。我们这种无可救药的浪漫主义者的弱点在于，我们爱上某人并向某人问好时，在那奇妙的一刻，不会想到某天彼此会迎来告别。当我们第一次亲吻，在那奇妙的一刻，也绝对不会想到某天那会成为我们的最后一吻。

——巡演纪录片《泰勒·斯威夫特：爱的告白世界巡回演唱会》（*Taylor Swift: Speak Now World Tour Live*），2011年11月21日

No matter what love throws at you, you have to believe in it. You have to believe in love stories and prince charmings and happily ever after. That's why I write these songs. Because I think love is fearless.

不管爱情投你以何物，你都得相信爱情。你得相信爱情故事、相信有白马王子、相信相爱的人终会幸福地生活在一起。这是我写这些

歌的初衷。因为我认为爱情意味着无所畏惧。
　　　　　——专辑《放手去爱》歌词本内页，2008年11月11日

When I find that person that is right for me, he'll be wonderful. And when I look at that person, I'm not even gonna be able to remember the boy who broke up with me over the phone in 25 seconds when I was 18.

要是我找到了那个对的爱人，他一定无与伦比。我看着他时，绝不会想起18岁那年，用一通25秒的电话甩了我的那个男孩。
　　　　　——美国脱口秀节目《艾伦秀》，2008年11月11日

With my experience with, like, nice guys and not-nice guys, the ones that are not nice are the ones who try to label themselves as a "nice guy."

从我的经历来看所谓的好男孩和坏男孩，那些标榜自己是"好男孩"的往往并不表里如一。
　　　　　——美国乡村音乐电台节目《鲍比·伯恩秀》
　　　　　（*The Bobby Bones Show*），2013年10月11日

I am getting to a point where the only love worth being in is the **love worth singing about.**

我越来越觉得，唯一值得拥有的爱情是那种**值得歌唱的爱情**。
　　　　　——《滚石》杂志，2013年8月1日

I just figure if guys don't want me to write bad songs about them **they** shouldn't do bad things.

我觉得如果有人不想我在歌里控诉他们行为不端,**他们就该好好安分守己。**

——美国电视节目 *Dateline*,2009年5月31日

If you're debating whether you want to break up with a guy or not, I always ask myself the simple question of "Do you want more or not?" When they leave and they go home to their house, do you wish they would turn around and come back to yours? And "I don't know" usually equals no in almost any scenario.

如果在犹豫是否要和某人分手,我通常会问自己一个简单的问题:"你还想和他在一起吗?"他离开后回到他的家,你还希望他掉头回到你家吗?几乎任何场景下,"我不知道"大多都等同于否定的答案。

——*Elle*(加拿大版),2012年11月19日

My experiences in love have taught me difficult lessons, especially my experiences with crazy love. The red relationships. The ones that went from zero to a hundred miles per hour and then hit a wall and exploded. And it was awful. And ridiculous. And desperate. And thrilling. And when the dust settled, it was something I'd never take back.

过往的恋情带给我很多惨痛的教训,特别是那些我经历过的疯狂的爱情。那些热烈如赤红般的恋情,宛如驾驶一辆从零飙速至每小时100英里的跑车,然后撞向墙壁,最终归于爆炸。这种爱情虽然糟

糟透顶、荒谬至极、绝望之至，却也令人兴奋不已。当一切尘埃落定，它再也不会为我所有。

——专辑《红》歌词本内页，2012年10月22日

Right now the way that I feel about love is that it lives somewhere between hope and fear... You have the hope that this could turn out to be different than it's ever turned out before, and then you have the fear that it's gonna turn out like it always has before.

我当下觉得爱情处于希望与恐惧的中间地带……你希望这段恋情走向不同于过往恋情的结局，又害怕它最终还是会重蹈覆辙。

——All for the Hall慈善音乐会，2010年9月23日

I'd never been in a relationship when I wrote my first couple of albums, so these were all projections of what I thought they might be like. They were based on movies and books and songs and literature that tell us that a relationship is the most magical thing that can ever happen to you. And then once I fell in love, or thought I was in love, and then experienced disappointment or it just not working out a few times, I realized there's this idea of happily ever after which in real life doesn't happen. There's no riding off into the sunset, because the camera always keeps rolling in real life.

写前两张专辑的时候，我还没正式恋爱过，所以我写的都是自己对恋爱的想象。这些歌曲的创作基于一些电影、书籍、歌曲和文学作品，它们告诉我们恋爱是个体身上可能发生的最奇妙之事。但当我爱上某人，或觉得自己恋爱了，经历过失望或恋情失败了，不过几次我就意

识到,"从此幸福地生活在一起"并不适用于现实生活中的爱情。一切从来不会以(两人携手)奔向落日结束,因为现实生活还在上演。

——*Elle*,2015年5月7日

I have a lot of rules placed on my life, and I just choose not to apply rules to love.

我的生活里有许多条条框框,**面对爱情我只想无拘无束。**

——英国访谈节目《乔纳森·罗斯秀》
(*The Jonathan Ross Show*),2012年10月6日

I think I am smart unless I am really, really in love, and then I am ridiculously stupid.

我想我还算聪明,除非我深陷爱情,那时我就会变得**无可救药般的愚蠢。**

——*Vogue*,2012年1月16日

["Mine"] is a song that is about, kind of, my tendency to run from love. It's been sort of a recent tendency, and I think it's because, for me, every really direct example of love that I've had in front of me has ended in goodbye, and has ended in breakups and things like that… This song is sort of about finding the exception to that and finding someone who would make you believe in love and realize that it could work out.

歌曲《我的》基本上写的是我对爱情的逃避态度。我近来有这种倾

向，因为我眼前所有活生生的爱情，无一不以告别和分手之类的结局告终……这首歌讲的就是寻找爱情中的例外，找到那个让你相信爱情，相信爱情会有美满结局的人。

——与粉丝们的直播聊天，2010年7月20日

I'm not really that girl who dreams about her wedding day. It just seems like the idealistic, happy-ever-after [moment]. It's funny that my wedding references have all been like "Marry me, Juliet," and on my "Speak Now" I'm ripping one to shreds.

我不是那种憧憬结婚的女孩。婚礼像是一个理想化的、好像两人从此就会幸福地生活在一起的时刻。有趣的是，我（在歌曲中）描写的婚礼都是那种"嫁给我吧，朱丽叶"式的，或是在歌曲《爱的告白》里把婚礼搅得天翻地覆式的。

——美国杂志《公告牌》(Billboard)，2010年10月15日

Over the years, I think, as you get more experience under your belt, as you become disappointed a few times, you start to kind of think of things in more realistic terms. It's not, you meet someone and that's it, you know. If they like you and you like them, well, it's gonna be forever, of course. I don't really look at love like that anymore. I think the way I see love is a little more fatalistic, which means to me that when I meet someone and we have a connection, the first thought I really have is, "When this is over, I hope you think well of me."

这几年来，我觉得随着经历渐长，随着自己经历过几次失望，我开

始从更加现实的角度看待事物。从你们的相遇开始,爱情就注定了结局。只要你们互相喜欢,就能天长地久。这些已经不是我看待爱情的方式了。爱情于我像是某种宿命,我遇见某人,我们产生了牵绊,我脑海中的第一个想法是:"当一切结束,我希望你对我抱有善意。"

——歌曲《狂野的梦》("Wildest Dreams")解说,出自专辑《1989》(大机器电台发布特辑版),2018年12月13日

If you felt something, it was worth it and it happened for a reason. And for me, when I play songs that are happy songs but I don't really know that person anymore, I still feel happy. Like, it's celebrating that it existed at one point, you know?

过往的感受弥足珍贵,它不会无缘无故地出现。于我而言,演唱快乐的歌时,就算我不记得歌曲所写的那个人了,我还是会感到快乐。这就像是在为那个曾经快乐的时刻庆祝,你明白吗?

——美国VH1频道音乐节目 *Storytellers*,2012年11月11日

A letdown is worth a few songs. **A heartbreak is worth a few albums.**

一次失意写就数首歌曲。**一次心碎成就数张专辑。**

——*Elle*,2010年3月4日

You can have the most pointless relationship, and, if you write a great song about it, **it was worthwhile.**

你可能会经历毫无意义的恋情,但要是能从中写出一首好歌,**这段**

恋情就是有意义的。
　　——乡村音乐网站 Digital Rodeo 视频，2009 年 4 月 15 日

When you're truly heartbroken you're never like, "Yes! I can parlay this into something!" You're like, "I wanna stay in bed for five years and just eat ice cream." But I don't know, I don't think that I've ever, like, celebrated a breakup like, "Now I've got new material!" But it just kind of ends up happening that way.

真正心碎时，你不会处于"太好了！我要借此大做文章！"的状态。你会想："我要在床上躺上 5 年，我只想吃冰激凌。"我从未庆祝过某次分手，从未在那样的时刻庆幸"现在我有新素材了！"我只是最终把分手写进了歌里而已。
　　——美国电台节目《埃尔维斯·杜兰和早间秀》
　　（*Elvis Duran and the Morning Show*），2011 年 7 月 22 日

I heard from the guy that most of *Red* is about. He was like, "I just listened to the album, and that was a really bittersweet experience for me. It was like going through a photo album." That was nice. Nicer than, like, the ranting, crazy e-mails I got from this one dude. It's a lot more mature way of looking at a love that was wonderful until it was terrible, and both people got hurt from it—but one of those people happened to be a songwriter.

专辑《红》大部分歌曲里写的那个人说："我刚听了这张专辑，对我来说真是苦乐参半。感觉就像翻了一遍相册。"这评价挺好的。比我从另一个人那里收到咆哮的、疯狂的电子邮件要好得多。他以更

加成熟的方式看待这段初时甜蜜却结出苦果的感情,这段感情里的恋人两败俱伤——只不过恰好其中一人是词曲作者。

——美国杂志《纽约》(New York),2013年11月25日

When we're trying to move on, the moments we always go back to aren't the mundane ones. They are the moments you saw sparks that weren't really there, felt stars aligning without having any proof, saw your future before it happened, and then saw it slip away without any warning.

我们试图走出一段恋情时,令人难以自拔的往往不是过往那些平淡无奇的时刻。我们难以忘怀的,是你曾看到虚幻的火花,感受到海市蜃楼般铺陈开来的星辰,是当你看到了未来而它却没有任何征兆地消失殆尽。

——专辑《红》歌词本内页,2012年10月22日

When you get your heart broken, or you lose someone from your life, or when you're trying to recover from a breakup, it's almost like the same kind of struggle that someone goes through trying to beat addiction. It's not one habit you're breaking—it's every single minute of the day you're breaking a habit. And it's exhausting.

若你正经历心碎,或是失去了生命中的某人,又或是想走出一段逝去的恋情,你所经历的煎熬就像要克服上瘾的习惯一样。重点不是你要摆脱这个习惯——而是每时每刻你都在为此痛苦挣扎。这让人心力交瘁。

——格莱美听享会,2015年10月9日

My girlfriends and I are plagued by the idea, looking back, that [some boys] changed us. You look back and you think: I only wore black in that relationship. Or I started speaking differently. Or I started trying to act like a hipster. Or I cut off my friends and family because he wanted me to do that. It's an unfortunate problem.

我和我的女性朋友们都被这样一个想法困扰着：回望过往，某些男孩改变了我们。回顾过去，会意识到：我在那段恋情里只穿黑色，或者我讲话的方式变得不一样了，或者我努力变得时髦起来，又或者我如男友所愿与亲友断绝了来往。这实在可悲可叹。

——英国《卫报》(*Guardian*)，2012年10月18日

I think the worst part about a breakup sometimes—if one could choose a worst part—would possibly be if you get out of the relationship and you don't recognize yourself because you changed a lot about yourself to make that person like you. Which I *never* do—I *always* do… I wrote ["Begin Again"] about the idea that you could remember who you used to be, and you could kind of remember that by meeting someone new who makes you feel like it's OK, like everything about you is great.

有时候我觉得失恋最糟糕之处——如果能选的话——可能在于当恋情走向终点，你也丢掉了自我，因为你为了赢得对方的欢心已经改变了太多。我从不想这样做——但又总是身不由己……我在歌曲《重新开始》里写的，就是你可以记起曾经的自己，如果新邂逅的某人让你觉得一切还不错，让你重拾信心，你或许就能重拾自我。

——美国VH1频道音乐节目 *Storytellers*，2012年11月11日

["We Are Never Ever Getting Back Together"] kind of makes a breakup sound like a party. You know, there are so many different ways a breakup could sound, but one of the ways is like, "Yes! Celebration! We're done!"

歌曲《我们再也回不去了》把分手描绘成了一场派对。写失恋的方式很多,其中一种就是高呼:"好!庆祝吧!我们分手了!"
——美国娱乐网站Extra,2012年10月23日

You always kind of have that person, that one person, who you feel like might interrupt your wedding and be like, "Don't do it, because we're not over yet." I think everybody has that one person who kind of floats in and out of their life, and, like, the narrative's never truly over.

总有这么一个人,你觉得他/她可能会打断你的婚礼,说:"别结婚,我们还没结束呢。"我觉得每个人生命中都有这样一个时而出现时而消失的人,就好像你们的故事永远没有终结。
——美国电视节目《早间新闻》(*The Morning Show*),
2014年12月29日

My previous albums [before *1989*] have always been sort of like, "I was right, you were wrong. You did this; it made me feel like this." Kind of a sense of righteous, like, right and wrong in a relationship. And what happens when you grow up is you realize that the rules in a relationship are very, very blurred, and that it gets very complicated very quickly, and there's not always a case of who was right and who was wrong.

我在《1989》之前的专辑里总是传递出："我是对的，你是错的。你的行为让我产生了这种感觉。"我像是抱有一种正义感，好像感情存在分明的是非之别。历经成长后你会意识到，相恋时哪有明晰的规则可循，感情复杂多变，爱人间没有绝对的是非对错之分。

——美国电视节目《瑞安·西克莱斯特访谈秀》
（*On Air with Ryan Seacrest*），2014年10月31日

In the last couple of years the story has been that I'm, like, a serial dater, and I, like, have all these boyfriends and we're traveling around the world and everything's great, until I get overemotional and crazy and obsessive and then they leave. And I'm devastated, and then I write songs to get emotional revenge because I'm psychotic. And, you know, that character, if you think about it, if that's actually how I was, is such a complex, interesting character to write from the perspective of [in "Blank Space"]... If you make the joke first and you make the joke better, then it's kind of like it's not as funny when other people call you a name.

过去几年间，传言中我总是在不停约会，我男友无数，我们一起环游世界，一切都很美好，直到我开始变得情绪化，行事疯狂偏执，最终被男友们抛弃。我备受打击，因此精神错乱，开始写歌进行情感报复。但是如果你细想一下他们描绘的这个人，如果我真如他们所述，这个人物其实极其复杂有趣，就像歌曲《空白格》里的女主角一样值得一写……要是你本人先以此戏谑，要是你的戏言足够高明，别人再拿你开涮时就没那么有意思了。

——美国电视节目《早间新闻》，2014年12月29日

People say that about me, that I apparently buy houses near every boy I like—that's a thing that I apparently do. If I like you I will apparently buy up the real-estate market just to freak you out so you leave me. Like that makes sense, like that's something you should do.

人们说显而易见，我在每个喜欢的男孩附近都买了房子——事实确实如此。我要是喜欢你，就会买下整个房地产市场；你害怕极了，自然就会离我而去。好像这样做就讲得通，好像我就该这么做一样。

——美国杂志《名利场》，2013年3月15日

I can't deal with someone who's obsessed with privacy. People kind of care if there are two famous people dating. But no one cares *that* much. If you care about privacy to the point where we need to dig a tunnel under this restaurant so that we can leave? I can't do that.

我没法和对隐私问题斤斤计较的人相处。人们关注两个名人的约会，但又不是特别在乎。如果你过分执着于保护隐私，我们是不是得在餐厅里挖条地道才能离开？我做不到。

——*Vogue*，2012年1月16日

They always go to the same fabricated ending that every other tabloid has used in my story, which is, "She got too clingy," or "Taylor has too many emotions, she scared him away." Which has honestly never been the reason for any of my break-ups. You know what has been the reason? The media. You take something very fragile, like trying to get to know someone, and it feels like walking out into the middle of a gladiator arena with someone you've just met.

他们总是用各种小报上编排我的故事东拼西凑出我（恋情）的结局，将一切归于"她太黏人了"，或是"泰勒太情绪化了，她把对方吓跑了"。以上真的从来都不是导致我分手的原因。那原因是什么呢？是媒体。我小心翼翼地试着去了解某人，那感觉就像和一个刚认识的人站上了角斗场的中心[1]。

——英国时尚周刊 *Glamour*，2015 年 4 月 24 日

["I Know Places"] is a song about how other people will really ruin a relationship if they get a chance to, and how it might be the best way to go about starting a relationship to keep it as secret as possible, just because it's very fragile. And I think that this was the song that I wrote about sort of how covert it would have to be in order for me to ever make something work eventually.

歌曲《藏身之地》写的是有些人会瞅准机会摧毁一段感情，而感情又实在不堪一击，所以可能开始一段恋情最好的方式，就是尽可能地将其保密。我写这首歌就是想表达，为了让恋情走下去，你必须尽力为其寻找藏身之地。

——歌曲《藏身之地》解说，出自专辑《1989》（大机器电台发布特辑版），2018 年 12 月 13 日

---

1 本书内容口语化，英文原文存在前后主语不一致之处，为使中文语句表意通顺，部分语句在翻译时作了主语统一或主语弱化处理。

《爱情故事》：恋情、心碎与名誉

I really didn't like the whole serial-dater thing. I thought it was a really sexist angle on my life. And so I just stopped dating people, because it meant a lot to me to set the record straight— that I do not need some guy around in order to get inspiration, in order to make a great record, in order to live my life, in order to feel okay about myself.

我很讨厌说我不停约会的说法。这算是从性别歧视的角度评判我的生活。为了证明那些说法都是无稽之谈，为了证明我不需要从男人那里获取灵感，为了制作一张优秀的专辑，为了活出自我，为了达成自洽，我决定不再约会。
　　——《时尚先生》杂志（*Esquire*），2014年10月20日

I'll say, "Things are great" but what's interesting is the first thing people say to you is, "Don't worry, you'll find someone."

我说，"一切都很好"。但有趣的是，人们见到你的第一句话却是："别担心，你会找到另一半的。"
　　——英国《太阳报》（*The Sun*），2014年10月27日

If you're the girl that needs a boyfriend, and then once she loses that boyfriend needs to replace him with a different boyfriend, it's just this constant stream of boyfriends all the time. And I just don't feel like I ever want to be that girl. I want to be the girl who, like, when she falls in love, it's like a big deal and it's a rare thing.

如果你是那种需要男友的女孩，一和男友分手就马上交新男友，你

就会持续不断地换男朋友。我不想成为这种女孩。我想成为那种重视并珍视爱情的女孩。

——美国脱口秀节目《艾伦秀》，2011年10月19日

I'm not actively looking, because you don't find anything when you're looking for it, but I think what I would mostly be looking for in a guy... is someone who sees me in my actual dimensions: 23 years old, five-foot-ten, people close to her call her "Tay," was really insecure in middle school. Like, a guy who wants to know the stories of who I was before this, and the things that aren't on my Wikipedia page and the things that didn't happen on an awards show—a guy who just wants to know the girl.

（对于真爱，）我并不汲汲以求，因为明白那强求不来，但我理想中的爱人……他能看到真实的我：23岁，身高5英尺10英寸[1]，亲近之人称她"Tay"，中学时整日惶惶不安。他会想要了解我的过去，想了解维基主页、颁奖典礼之外的我——他在意的仅仅是我本身。

——美国杂志《名利场》，2013年3月15日

If someone doesn't seem to want to get to know me as a person but instead seems to have kind of bought into the whole idea of me and he approves of my Wikipedia page? And falls in love based on zero hours spent with me? That's maybe something to be aware of. That will fade fast. You can't be in love with a Google search.

---

[1] 5英尺10英寸约等于1.78米。

如果某人并不想了解我本人，对我的认识止于想象，并且对维基主页描述的我深信不疑，与我素昧平生就爱上了我？可能得注意一下这种情况。因为那种爱恋会转瞬即逝。你不可能和谷歌搜索结果相爱。

——*Vogue*，2012年1月16日

Boys only want love if it's torture and a constant chase. Men want love if it's real, right, healthy and consistent.

男孩只为彼此折磨、你追我赶的爱情着迷。男人追求的爱情，须得真情实感、情投意合、感情健康且始终如一。

——英国《太阳报》，2014年10月27日

When I'm getting to know someone, I look for someone who has passions that I respect, like his career. Someone who loves what he does is really attractive. In high school, I used to think it was "like sooooo cool" if a guy had an awesome car. Now none of that matters. These days I look for character and honesty and trust.

了解一个人时，我会着重发掘他让我产生敬意的热爱所在，比如他对事业的热爱。热爱自己所做之事的人很有魅力。高中时期，如果一个男生有辆很棒的车，我会觉得那"超酷"。如今这都无关紧要了。性格、诚实、信任是我如今最看重的个人品质。

——英国时尚周刊*Glamour*，2010年10月5日

I don't think love is ever gonna be perfect. And I think that when you actually are in a long relationship and you have to sustain it and work at it, I think that's a very real thing. And it's not all pretty and sparkly and fairy tale-esque and, you know, it doesn't really have the stamp of, like, Prince Charming. But I think that he would listen to you at the end of a hard day and I think that he'd be there for you and feel like a teammate.

我认为不存在完美的爱情。如果你身处一段长期的恋爱关系中,你得维护这份感情,为这份感情做出努力,这是非常现实的事情。爱情并不总是光鲜亮丽、甜如童话,你的爱人也不会笼罩着白马王子的光环。但他会在结束一天的辛苦工作后倾听你的心声,会像队友一样永远站在你身侧。

——美国电台节目《埃尔维斯·杜兰和早间秀》,
2011年7月22日

Real love doesn't mess with your head. Real love just is. Real love just endures. Real love maintains. Real love takes it page by page.

真爱不会扰人心绪。真爱就是如此,矢志不渝、历久弥新、细水长流。
——Vogue,2016年4月14日

If love is worth it, if it's that good that it's worth fighting for, **then you know that it's the right love.**

如果一份爱情值得你为其付出,值得你为其奋斗,**你会明了那就是对的爱。**

——歌曲《爱情故事》解说,出自专辑《放手去爱》
(大机器电台发布特辑版),2018年12月13日

《爱情故事》：恋情、心碎与名誉

Two new year's Eves ago I found myself in the midst of a very, like, incredible 3 a.m. moment, where you feel like you're invincible and you end up, like, jumping in a pool in the winter. And you feel super untouchable in that moment, and then the next morning you feel very fragile. And you're like, "This is love, this is what love really is." Like, we all want to find someone to kiss at midnight. That's cool or whatever, but who's gonna want to hang out with you the next day when you're like, "Advil or nothing"? So ["New Year's Day"] is a song about finding real love and finding someone to hang out with on New Year's Day.

前年的跨年夜，我发觉自己身处一个奇妙的时刻，那时是凌晨3点，觉得自己所向披靡，甚至能一头扎进冬季的泳池里。那一刻觉得自己坚不可摧，但来日清晨，又变得脆弱不堪。我会想："这就是爱情，这就是爱情的本质。"我们都想有个能在午夜拥吻的爱人。那确实很酷，但第二天你纠结"吃不吃止痛药"时，谁还会陪在你身边呢？歌曲《新年日》讲的就是找到真爱，找到那个新年日还愿意陪着你的人。

——泰勒·斯威夫特NOW秘密演出，2018年6月28日

When you say a relationship is public, that means I'm going to see him do what he loves, we're showing up for each other, other people are there and we don't care. The opposite of that is you have to go to an extreme amount of effort to make sure no one knows that you're seeing someone.

一段公开的恋情，意味着我会去看他做自己热爱的事，我们出席彼此的场合，即便他人在场也毫不在乎。与此相反的地下恋情，就是

你得费尽心思，确保没人知道你要去见某人。

——《时代周刊》，2023年12月6日

There's a camera, like, a half-mile away, and you don't know where it is, and you have no idea when the camera is putting you in the broadcast, so I don't know if I'm being shown 17 times or once. I'm just there to support Travis. I have no awareness of if I'm being shown too much and pissing off a few dads, Brads, and Chads.

镜头可能离我有半英里远，我不知道镜头在哪里，也不知道自己什么时候会出现在转播中，所以我并不清楚自己在镜头里出现了17次还是1次。我去看橄榄球赛只是为了支持特拉维斯。我没注意自己是不是总是出现在现场的镜头里，也没在意是不是惹恼了某些父亲、布拉德和查德[1]。

——谈及现身橄榄球比赛，《时代周刊》，2023年12月6日

---

1 泰勒与特拉维斯·凯尔斯（Travis Kelce）恋爱后，自2023年9月起经常出席观看男友所在球队的橄榄球赛。球赛现场经常转播她在包厢里为男友加油的一举一动，这"惹恼"了不少铁杆球迷，他们认为泰勒在球赛转播中出现的镜头太多。本条为泰勒在《时代周刊》"2023年年度人物采访"中的回应。而她调侃性的文字游戏"dads, Brads, and Chads"随后在福克斯一档模仿秀节目中被用作父子三人的名字，三人身着特拉维斯的87号球衣，面对镜头恳求参加时代巡回演唱会的母亲回家。

帝国缔造者

《空白格》：
音乐之内

Songwriting has always been the number one thing... **If I didn't write, I wouldn't sing.**

写歌是我的头等大事……**如果我不写歌，我就没法唱歌。**
　　　　　　　——美国电视节目 *CBS This Morning*，2014年10月29日

I didn't want to just be another girl singer. I wanted there to be something that set me apart. **And I knew that had to be my writing.**

我不想成为一名平平无奇的女歌手。我想变得与众不同。**而能让我与众不同的就是写歌。**
　　　　　　　——美国杂志《娱乐周刊》，2007年7月25日

Music is the only thing that's ever fit me like that little black dress you wear every single time you go out. Other things fit me for certain seasons, but music is the only thing that I would wear all year round.

音乐就是时常伴我左右的万能小黑裙，是为我量身定制之物。有些事

物只在特定的季节里与我相伴，而音乐则是全年都伴我左右的唯一。
　　　　　　　　——《时尚先生》杂志，2014年10月20日

When I'm writing an album, my world kind of becomes a big storyboard. And everyone in it becomes a character or has the potential to become a character.

创作专辑时，我的世界就变成了一块巨大的故事板。我身边的每个人，要么是故事中的角色，要么有成为故事中角色的潜力。
　　　　　　——与粉丝的线上聊天及Google+ Hangout互动，
　　　　　　　　　　　　　　　　　　2012年8月13日

When I was 12 years old and I started writing songs, I hadn't been in relationships! I would just think about the movies I had watched and the most memorable scenes and when they're standing in the rain and this girl had no idea that this guy had feelings for her this entire time and she thought that he liked that other girl, but really he liked her. And there's a moment that happens in movies that I try to capture in songs. It's cinematic; it's emotional.

12岁开始写歌时我还没谈过恋爱！我那时会回想自己看过的一些电影，有些难忘的电影场景里，两人站在雨中，女孩对男孩一直喜欢自己这件事毫不知情，她一直以为男孩已经心有所属，但事实上他中意的那个人就是女孩。我想在歌里描绘的，就是这些电影里的某个时刻，那种电影般的、情感丰沛的时刻。
　　　　　——美国VH1频道音乐节目 *Storytellers*，2012年11月11日

I've always known that [writing] was the main pillar holding up my career. I've always known it was the main pillar of kind of my sanity as well.

我一直明白写作是支撑我事业的重要支柱。**它也是我保持理智的重要支柱。**
　　　　　　——《时代周刊》世界百大人物晚宴，2019年4月23日

A lot of people look at me and are just like, "You're 16. How many boyfriends have you had?" And I haven't had that many boyfriends at all. I just like to take examples of what my friends are going through or examples of what the couple next door is going through. And songwriting is a lot more observing than it is experiencing, in some cases.

很多人看到我都会打趣道:"你现在16岁了。一共交往过几个男朋友?"我真的还没谈过几个男朋友。我写歌时喜欢以朋友或者隔壁情侣的经历举例。写歌有时候更多源于观察，而非亲身经历。
　　　　　　　　　　　　——雅虎网，2006年10月24日

It's not... heartbreak that inspires my songs. It's not love that inspires my songs. It's individual people that come into my life. I've had relationships with people that were really substantial and meant a lot to me, but I couldn't write a song about that person for some reason. Then again, you'll meet someone that comes into your life for two weeks and you write an entire record about them.

我歌曲的灵感……不来源于失恋，也不来源于爱情。我的灵感来自

我生活中的每个人。某些交往过的人对我而言意义重大，但出于一些原因，我没法把他写进歌里。而另一种情况是，我和某人的交集只有两周时间，却为他写了一整张专辑。
　　——美国新闻电台节目 *All Things Considered*，2012年11月2日

I've always looked at writing as sort of a protective armor, which is weird because... writing about your life [is] usually likened to vulnerability. But I think that when you write about your life, it gives you the ability to process your life. I use it as a way of justifying things that happened to me, whether they're good or bad. You know, I like to honor the good times and really process the bad times when I write.

我一直将写作视为保护自己的盔甲，这挺奇怪，因为……源于生活的写作常常被视为脆弱的体现。但我觉得，写自己的生活恰恰可以获得掌控生活的能力。我用写作诠释发生在我身上的一切，好事坏事都是如此。写作的时候，我一面珍藏那些美好，一面坦然应对失意。
　　——《时代周刊》世界百大人物晚宴，2019年4月23日

When you are missing someone, time seems to move slower and when I'm falling in love with someone, time seems to be moving faster. So I think, because time seems to move so slow when I'm sad, that's why I spend so much time writing songs about it. It seems like I have more hours in the day.

思念某人时觉得度秒如年，爱上某人时又觉得时间转瞬即逝。我想，也正因为自己悲伤时觉得时间过得如此缓慢，才有大把的时间

将失意写成歌曲。就好像一天多出来几个小时一样。

——美国杂志《公告牌》，2012年10月19日

I love writing songs because I love preserving memories, **like putting a picture frame around a feeling you once had.**

我爱写歌，因为我喜欢保存记忆，**写歌就像为某时某刻的感觉封上相框。**

——*Elle*（英国版），2019年2月28日

Getting a great idea with song writing is a lot like love. You don't know why this one is different, but it is. You don't know why this one is better, but it is. It sticks in your head and you can't stop thinking about it.

写歌时蹦出个好点子很像爱情。你不知道为什么这个点子那么不同，它就是如此不同。你不知道为什么这个点子更好，它就是更好。它盘踞在你的脑海里，让你无法思考其他事物。

——美国达美航空杂志*Sky*，2012年11月

My advice to first-time songwriters would be, know the person you're writing the song about. First know that. And then write a letter to them, like what you would say if you could. Because, you know, that's why I listen to music, is because it says how I feel better than I could, and it says what I wish I'd said when that moment was there.

我给新手词曲作者的建议，就是你要知道自己歌曲的目标受众是

谁。首先明确受众。然后给他们写信，写你想对他们说的话。因为音乐能比我更好地表达我的感受，能说出我在某个时刻想要诉之于口的话语，这就是我听音乐的原因。

——与粉丝的直播聊天，2010年7月20日

I used to think that if you leave out details that people could relate more. But I don't think that's the case, because I think that it's really the more you let people in, the more they feel let in, and the more they feel like we all share something.

我曾认为（写歌时）不透露过多细节，听者就可以将歌曲联系到自己身上。如今我觉得事实并非如此，你只有让听者更深入地沉浸曲中，他们才会觉得自己置身其中，才会与歌曲产生更强烈的共鸣。

——美国娱乐网站 Extra，2012年2月15日

Songs for me are like a message in a bottle. You send them out to the world and maybe the person who you feel that way about will hear about it someday.

歌曲是我封在漂流瓶里的信息。我将它们投向茫茫人海，也许有天那个曲中人能听到我的心意。

——美国网站"每日野兽"（Daily Beast），2012年10月22日

My favorite song of all time is "You're So Vain" by Carly Simon. I think that the imagery of that song, ... like "You walked into the party like you were walking onto a yacht"—like, that is the best opening line I've heard in so long. And, you know, I love that for its imagery, but then there are songs that are so simple, like "Apologize" by OneRepublic. It's just very, very kind of plainly said, and you can't believe that someone hadn't written that before.

我最喜欢的歌是卡莉·西蒙[1]的《你是如此自傲》。我觉得这首歌的意象……比如歌词"你走进派对现场，就像跨上一艘游艇"——这是我听过最好的歌词首句。我喜欢这首歌营造的意象，但也喜欢那些叙事简单的歌曲，比如共和时代[2]的歌曲《抱歉》。这首歌非常、非常平铺直叙，你简直不能相信之前从未有人写过这种类型的歌。
——南非电视节目 *Top Billing*，2014年11月7日

One of my favorite things about female writers, about writers in general, about people who take what happens to them and they process it and they put it out into the world, is if you write, you can turn your lessons into your legacy.

女性作家、整个作家群体以及那些将亲身经历加工后公之于世的创作者们，这些人最让我喜爱的一点，就是他们通过写作将此前的教训化为日后的宝藏。
——《时代周刊》世界百大人物晚宴，2019年4月23日

The writing I love the most places you into that story, that room, that rain soaked kiss. You can smell the air, hear the sounds, and feel your heart race

---

1 卡莉·西蒙（Carly Simon）：美国创作女歌手，也是第一位同时拥有格莱美奖、金球奖和奥斯卡奖的艺人。
2 共和时代（OneRepublic）：美国流行摇滚乐队，发行"Apologize""Counting Stars"等多首广为传唱的歌曲，曾获iHeartRadio音乐奖年度组合/团体等奖项。

as the character's does. It's something F. Scott Fitzgerald did so well, to describe a scene so gorgeously interwoven with rich emotional revelations, that you yourself have escaped from your own life for a moment.

我最喜爱的写作作品能将我置身于那个故事中，让我进入故事里的房间，见证那个被雨水浸湿的吻。你能闻到空气中的味道，听到四周的声响，你的心脏也跟着角色的心脏一起砰砰跳着。弗朗西斯·斯科特·菲茨杰拉德[1]在这方面的造诣炉火纯青，他笔下的场景里交织着浓烈的情感暗流，引人入胜的描绘能让读者得以片刻逃离现实生活。

——*Elle*（英国版），2019年2月28日

I think these days, people are reaching out for connection and comfort in the music they listen to. We like being confided in and hearing someone say, "this is what I went through" as proof to us that we can get through our own struggles.
We actually do NOT want our pop music to be generic. I think a lot of music lovers want some biographical glimpse into the world of our narrator, a hole in the emotional walls people put up around themselves to survive.

我认为当下人们正从自己听的音乐中寻求联结与慰藉。我们喜欢被人全然信赖，喜欢听别人诉说"这是我经历的一切"，以此说服自己也能渡过眼前的难关。
我们并不希望流行音乐变得千篇一律。我觉得很多乐迷都喜欢音乐

---

[1] 弗朗西斯·斯科特·菲茨杰拉德（Francis Scott Fitzgerald）：美国作家，代表作《了不起的盖茨比》《人间天堂》等。

中的个人故事。人们为了生存竖起情感的围墙，这些个人故事就是围墙上的缺口，让乐迷得以一窥叙述者的个人世界。

——*Elle*（英国版），2019年2月28日

I try to write lyrics about what's happening to me and leave out the part that I live in hotel rooms and tour buses. It's the relatability factor. **If you're trying too hard to be the girl next door, you're not going to be.**

我尽量在歌词里写自己的生活近况，不去提发生在酒店房间和巡演巴士里的事。我想引起人们的共鸣。**但如果你执着于表现得像邻家女孩那样平易近人，结果只会适得其反。**

——《纽约时报》，2008年11月7日

I think it's the writer in me that's a little more obsessed with the meaning of the song than the vocal technique. All that stuff is like math to me. Overthinking vocals and stuff—I never want to get to that point.

于我而言，代表作家的那部分自我更痴迷于歌曲的内涵，而非声乐上的技巧。声乐技巧对我来说就像数学。为声乐之类思虑过多——我永远不会那样做。

——《洛杉矶时报》(*Los Angeles Times*)，2008年10月26日

Since I was 12, I would get an idea, and that idea is either a fragment of melody and lyric mixed in, [or] maybe it's a hook. Maybe it's the first line of a song. Maybe it's a background vocal part or something, but it's like the first piece of a puzzle. And my job in writing the song and completing it is filling in all the rest of the pieces and figuring out where they go.

12岁起,我的脑海里总会冒出些点子,要么是一段和了旋律的歌词,(要么)可能是歌里抓耳的"hook"[1]。有时是一首歌的首句歌词,有时是背景声部或者其他,但总之,这个点子是我写歌的第一块拼图。我后续创作、完成这首歌曲,就是把剩下的拼图拼好,为每一块拼图找到自己的位置。
——美国新闻电台节目 *All Things Considered*,2012年11月2日

There are mystical, magical moments, inexplicable moments when an idea that is fully formed just pops into your head. And that's the purest part of my job. It can get complicated on every other level, but the songwriting is still the same uncomplicated process it was when I was 12 years old writing songs in my room.

有时,完全成型的想法跃入我的脑海,那种时刻玄妙莫测、无法言明。那是我工作中最纯粹的一部分。其他事各有各的复杂之处,但从我12岁时在房间里写歌起,创作歌曲就一直是件简单纯粹的事。
——《时尚芭莎》(*Harper's Bazaar*),
2018年7月10日

I've gotten a lot of questions about songwriting, about the process, about, you know, what happens when you get an idea. The answer is, the first

---

[1] hook指歌曲中的一小段歌词或短句,其目的是让听众在听到这首歌时更加难忘。一个好的hook可以通过运用强烈的旋律、节奏或抒情短语来达到这一目的。

thing I do is I grab my phone, and I either sit it on the edge of the piano or put it right down on my bed in front of my guitar, and I play whatever melody slash gibberish comes to my brain first.

人们会问我很多关于写歌的问题，比如写歌的过程是什么样的？我是怎样得到灵感的？我的回答是，我写歌的第一件事就是拿起手机，要么把它放在钢琴边上，要么就干脆放在床上的吉他跟前，然后把脑海里最先想到的旋律或只言片语弹唱出来。

——雅虎网在线直播，2014年8月18日

Creativity is getting inspiration and having that lightning bolt idea moment, and then having the hard work ethic to sit down at the desk and write it down.

创造力就是获取灵感，抓住那个电光石火般的灵感瞬间，然后凭借勤奋刻苦的工作态度，坐在书桌前把它写下来。

——*Vogue*，"泰勒·斯威夫特快答73问"，2016年4月19日

When I get an idea, it happens really fast, and I need to record it really fast into whatever I have, either a cell phone or write it on something. And so I was walking through an airport and I got an idea and I needed to write it on something, and I knew there were paper towels in the bathroom. So, ran into the bathroom, started writing it down, ran back out to the terminal, and finished the song, only to realize it was the men's bathroom that I had run into.

我想到新点子时，一切都发生得很快，所以我得用手头现有的东西把它记录下来，要么记在手机里，要么写在某个地方。有一次，我在机场有了灵感，得找个东西把它写下来，我知道洗手间里有那种厚纸巾。于是我就跑进洗手间里把那个点子写了下来，又跑回航站楼把那首歌写完，直到那时我才意识到，自己刚才跑进去的是男洗手间。

——美国脱口秀节目《杰·雷诺秀》(The Jay Leno Show)，
2009年12月4日

The moment in the day when I get the most ideas is when I'm about to go to sleep because, from the time I wake up till that moment, I'm thinking about things nonstop. I'm thinking about what I need to get done that day, I'm thinking about, you know, what decisions I need to make that are gonna affect everything. So before I go to bed, that's the one time when I'm just thinking about ideas, and stuff usually hits me then.

一天之间，我灵感最多的时候就是临睡之前，因为从醒来到临睡前的这段时间里，我一直在不停思考。思考当日要完成的事，思考那些牵一发而动全身的决定。所以睡前就是我唯一能思考新点子的时候，我通常能在这时想到些什么。

——乡村音乐网站 Digital Rodeo 视频，2009年4月15日

I start all of my co-writing sessions with girl talk. I walk in and I go, "I have to tell you what I'm going through right now" and I spend 25 minutes talking about the guy that I met four months ago and how things were fine and then he lied about this and I freaked out.

我所有的合创歌曲会议都以女生闲聊的话题开始。我走进会议室，说"我得跟你讲讲我正在经历什么"。然后，在接下来25分钟的时间里，讲我4个月前遇到的男人，讲我们的恋情开始时进展得如何顺利，讲后来他对我撒了谎，我因此陷入了崩溃情绪中。

——美国杂志《公告牌》，2012年10月19日

There is a stressful and joyful element to making an album. For me, I'm either incredibly stressed or overjoyed, and the way that usually goes is that if I've just written a song, I'm the happiest you will ever see me. But if I haven't written a song in a week and a half, I am more stressed than you will ever, ever see me at any other point.

制作专辑是一段压力与喜悦并存的过程。对我来说，要么压力过大、要么欣喜异常。通常情况下，刚写完一首歌时，我会处于最快乐的状态中。但要是我一周半内还没写完一首歌，我就会处于绝无仅有的、最最焦虑的状态中。

——美国杂志《娱乐周刊》，2010年8月27日

I like to put the songs, like all the demos that I make and all the guitar vocals, on either, like, a CD or my iPod or something. The ones that I skip over, if I don't feel like listening to them in the car, that's how you know it's not gonna go on a record.

我喜欢把自己的音乐样带和吉他弹唱在内的全部歌曲，都保存在光碟和iPod之类的地方。我把那些自己都不想在车里听的歌跳过，这

样就知道哪些歌不会被收录进专辑里了。
　　　　——美国热门乡村歌曲电台107.3 94.9，2012年10月26日

If I'm putting together an album and half of my brain is like, "This is so great!" there's another half of my brain that's poking holes in every part of it going, "What are people who hate you gonna say about this song? Are they gonna like it? You need to write a song so good even people who hate you get it stuck in their head."

如果我在为专辑选曲，我的一半大脑会想："这太棒了！"另一半大脑则会处处找茬："讨厌你的人会怎么评价这首歌？他们会喜欢这首歌吗？你得写首好到就算讨厌你的人也忘不掉的歌。"
　　　　——*Vogue*（澳大利亚版）封面拍摄幕后，2015年10月18日

It's always really difficult to pick a first single, I feel like, for my albums because I try to make an album that's so kind of vast in its scope of things that it's kind of hard to pick which is gonna be a representative that goes out first. Because there isn't ever one song that could just sum up what the album is.

我觉得为自己的专辑选首发单曲通常都很艰难，因为我尽力丰富拓宽专辑的内涵，这就很难选出一首代表歌曲作为首发单曲。因为哪首歌都不能完全囊括整张专辑的内容。
　　　　——美国广播节目《扎克·桑秀》（*Zach Sang Show*），
　　　　　　2019年4月29日

["Tim McGraw"] is really about how people can be affected by country music. It's about a couple who falls in love, and their song's a Tim McGraw song. And even when they're apart, every time they hear that song it takes them back to that place, and it almost haunts them.

歌曲《蒂姆·麦格劳》实际写的是乡村音乐给人们带来的影响。歌里写的那对相爱的情侣,将蒂姆·麦格劳[1]的一首歌作为两人的主题歌。即使他们分隔两地,每次听到这首歌,歌曲就会把他们带回故地,这首歌几乎一直萦绕在他们心头。

——雅虎网视频,2006年10月24日

I really wanted to make sure it was the right choice, so I took that word "fearless" and I applied [it] to each one of the things that my songs deal with: getting your heart broken, having to face the fact that you're not going to be with the person you thought you were going to be with, someone apologizing to you over and over again for something they're never going to stop doing, having faith that maybe someday things will change—all of those things I thought had a fearless element to them.

我很想确保给专辑取这个名字是正确的选择,所以我选了"无畏"这个词,并将它融入专辑每首歌的主题中:伤心欲绝;不得不面对无法和想长相厮守的人走下去的事实;某人一次次道歉却不会真正改过自新;坚信某天事情会迎来转机——无畏是贯穿全部主题的

---

[1] 蒂姆·麦格劳(Tim McGraw):美国乡村音乐男歌手,其歌曲和专辑曾多次登上各大乡村音乐榜榜首,为乡村音乐领域做出了卓越贡献。

要素。

——美国乡村音乐网站The Boot，2008年12月19日

I don't want to write a song that's so obviously trying to achieve a sort of girlpower goal, or a "believe in yourself" goal. **I tend to write about the kind of nuisances of life.**

我不想写那种明显想彰显女性力量的歌，也不想写那种鼓励大家"相信自己"的歌。我更多地书写生活中遇到的麻烦琐事。

——Vogue（英国版），2014年11月

["You Belong With Me"] is a song that I wrote about a guy that, he was one of my friends. And I walked by and he was talking on the phone with his girlfriend and she was screaming at him, just yelling at him, and so loud that I could hear her voice coming through the phone, which is never good... And I felt so bad for him, because it turned out that she was yelling at him because he said that he would call her back in 10 minutes and instead he called her back in 15... I walked by and I started singing to myself, "You're on the phone with your girlfriend, she's upset."

歌曲《你应该和我在一起》里写的男孩是我之前的一个朋友。我有次从他身边走过，他正和女朋友打电话。那个女孩在电话里冲着他叫喊，简直是大喊大叫，声音大到我能听到她在电话那头的声音，这不太好……我为这个朋友感到抱歉。后来发现他女朋友冲他喊叫的原因是因为他说10分钟内回电话，但过了15分钟才回……我从

他身旁走过,自己唱着:"你在跟女友打电话,她很生气。"[1]
——英国音乐访谈节目 *The Hot Desk*,2009年5月

I made an album called *Fearless* that ended up being kind of the breakthrough record that was the first time I had songs on pop radio and, like, worldwide hits and things like that. And so *Speak Now* chronicled my life after that and adjusting to that, and love and life and priorities and balancing things and all the feelings that go along with that and being 19 and 20 at the time.

我创作的专辑《放手去爱》后来成了一张具有突破性的专辑,我的歌第一次在流行音乐电台上播放,第一次成为全球热门歌曲。专辑《爱的告白》写的就是我在那之后的生活和对这种生活的适应,它记录了我19至20岁时的爱情、日常生活、珍视之事,记录了我如何平衡一切,以及我感受到的一切。
——第54届格莱美年度颁奖典礼彩排,2012年2月9日

I think if I had to put a color to *Speak Now*, it would be purple. I think that there's just something kind of... honest and true about that record that kind of, to me, seems purple. And *Fearless*, to me, is golden because it was, you know, the first time that anyone really recognized my music outside of America, and to me that was like a golden rush of something new. My first album, I think, would be blue.

---

[1] 歌曲《你应该和我在一起》首句歌词。

如果要为专辑《爱的告白》选个颜色,我会选紫色。我觉得这张专辑中包含的……诚实与真实,对我来说是类似紫色的存在。而专辑《放手去爱》对我来说是金色的,因为那是我的音乐第一次被美国以外的听众认可,就像追逐新鲜事物的淘金热一样。而我的第一张专辑,应该是蓝色的。

——环球音乐韩国网站视频,2012年10月23日

I had a lot of people who would say, "Oh, she's an 18-year-old girl. There's no way that she actually carried her weight in those writing sessions." And that was a really harsh criticism I felt because, you know, there was no way I could prove them wrong other than to write my entire next record solo. So I went in and I made an album called *Speak Now*. There is not one single cowriter on the entire thing.

很多人会说:"哦,她只是个18岁的小姑娘。她不可能在歌曲创作中有多少话语权。"这对我来说是非常犀利的批评,因为要想证明他们所言为虚,我只能自己独立完成下一张专辑的创作。所以我就这么做了,创作了一张名为《爱的告白》的专辑。我一个人写了这张专辑里的所有歌曲。

——纪录片《泰勒·斯威夫特——名誉之路》
(*Taylor Swift—Road to reputation*),2018年9月28日

["Speak Now"] was inspired by one of my friends who was telling me about her childhood sweetheart crush guy who, you know, they were kind of together in high school and then they went their separate ways. And it was kind of understood that they were gonna get back together. And then

so she one day comes in and tells me, "He's getting married."…
Later on I just was wrapping my mind around that idea of how tragic it would be if someone you loved was marrying somebody else. And then later I had a dream about one of my ex-boyfriends getting married, and it just all came together that I needed to write this song about interrupting a wedding.

歌曲《爱的告白》的灵感来自我的朋友，她曾跟我说起自己的青梅竹马，他们高中时短暂相恋，之后就分道扬镳了。那时大家都觉得他们终会走到一起。但后来某天她告诉我："他要结婚了……"
我后来一直在想，所爱之人另娶他人，该是何等伤感。随后我又梦到某个前男友要结婚了，这一切最终促使我写下了这首关于打断婚礼的歌。
——歌曲《爱的告白》解说，出自专辑《爱的告白》
（大机器电台发布特辑版），2018年12月13日

This one really means a lot to me because this is for a song called "Mean" that I wrote. And there's really no feeling quite like writing a song about someone who's really mean to you and someone who completely hates you and makes your life miserable and then winning a Grammy for it.

这个奖项[1]对我意义重大，因为这座奖属于我写的歌曲《卑鄙》。某人待你非常刻薄，对你厌恶至极，让你的生活痛苦不堪，然后你据此写了一首歌，还得了格莱美，这感觉无与伦比。
——第54届格莱美年度颁奖典礼，2012年2月12日

---

[1] 2012年，泰勒凭歌曲《卑鄙》获得第54届格莱美最佳乡村歌手奖项。

I'm used to being called too something. From my first album, I've been called either, you know, "This is too pop," "This is too rock." I had a song called "Mean" that people said was too bluegrass, too country, which I thought was funny. And I kind of had this revelation that I don't mind it if people are calling my music too something. It's people saying that all my songs are starting to sound the same—that's the big fear.

我已经习惯别人说我做什么事做得太过了。从第一张专辑开始，就总有人说我，"这首歌太流行了""这首歌太摇滚了"。我有首歌叫《卑鄙》，人们说这歌太蓝草音乐[1]、太乡村音乐了，这些观点挺有意思的。我意识到自己并不怎么在乎别人说我的音乐太过如何。要是人们说我的歌听起来千篇一律——那才是我该害怕的事。

——美国VH1频道音乐节目 *Storytellers*，2012年11月11日

Red started out, I was making country music. And I was getting the ideas exactly the same way I always did, and they were coming to me in the same ways. And then, a few months in, they started coming to me as pop melodies, and I could not fight it, and I just embraced it.

专辑《红》创作初期，我想把它做成乡村音乐。我构思的方式和往常一样，获取灵感的方式也一如既往。但几个月后，灵感为我带来的都是充满流行元素的旋律。我无法抗拒，索性欣然接受。

——纪录片《泰勒·斯威夫特——名誉之路》，
2018年9月28日

---

1 蓝草音乐（Bluegrass Music）：乡村音乐的另一个分支，节奏硬而快，强调器乐使用。

《空白格》：音乐之内

I love the color red for the title because, if you correlate red with, you know, different emotions, you come up with the most intense ones. On this side you've got, like, passion and falling in love, and that intrigue and adventure and daring. And then on the other side you've got, like, anger and jealousy and frustration and betrayal.

用红色为专辑《红》命名深得我心，因为如果把红色和各种情绪联系在一起，与之匹配的都是那些最为强烈的情绪。一面是满腔热忱、坠入爱河，是秘密相爱、大胆冒险和勇往直前；另一面则是怒气冲冲、心生妒忌，是灰心丧气和横遭背叛。

——英国电视节目 *MTV News*，2012年10月6日

I want there to be something on the album for anyone who's going through anything. And those are tough bases to cover, but I try to be really diverse with the amount of emotions that I'm covering because I want someone who's falling in love for the first time to have a song that they relate to. I want someone who's lonely, who misses her ex-boyfriend, I want her to relate to it. I want the guy that just met someone new and he's absolutely in love, I want him to have a song.

我希望自己的专辑能让处在不同境遇里的大家都有所感触。虽然很难把一张专辑做得如此丰富，但我尽量让专辑更具多样性，涵盖不同的情绪。我想有一首能让正在初恋中的人产生共鸣的歌，也想有一首能让在孤独中思念前男友的女孩产生共鸣的歌，还想有一首能让对某人一见钟情的男孩产生共鸣的歌。

——歌曲《留下来》（"Stay Stay Stay"）解说，出自专辑《红》（大机器电台发布特辑版），2018年12月13日

You feel differently every day. You're never the same exact person two days in a row. I mean, it's like, you've got so many different things that make up someone's personality and that make up a particular emotion. And with my songs I just try to capture a tiny glimpse of one nuance of an emotion, and that can usually be stretched out into three and a half minutes.

你每天都有不同的感受。今日的你绝不是昨日的你。我的意思是，一个人的性格和某种特定的情绪都由许多事物共同决定。我写歌时只想细致入微地捕捉某种情绪碎片，然后将它扩展成一首3分钟半的歌曲。

——歌曲《重新开始》解说，出自专辑《红》（大机器电台发布特辑版），2018年12月13日

I like to balance out the amount of happy songs, breakup songs, sentimental songs, I-miss-you songs, angry songs. I don't want to try and harp on the same emotion too much because **I feel like if you make the "angry" album, that's going to lose people.**

我尽量平衡专辑里表达不同情绪的歌曲数量：快乐的歌、分手的歌、感性的歌、思念的歌、愤怒的歌。我不想刻意放大或赘述某种情绪，**因为如果整张专辑里的歌都以"愤怒"为基调，听众们是不会买账的。**

——*Elle*，2009年6月15日

We were in the studio and this guy walked in who was a friend of my ex's.

He introduced himself and made some comment about how he heard that I was gonna get back together with my ex. And after he left, I was talking about it with Max [Martin] and Shellback, and I was just like, "And we are never, ever, ever getting back together!" I picked up a guitar, Max was like, "We should write that"—it just kind of happened.

我们当时在录音室里,然后我前男友的某个朋友走了进来。他自报家门,说听说我准备和前任复合,并对此评论了几句。他走后,我跟马克斯和希尔贝克谈起这事,说:"我们再也再也再也回不去了!"我拿起吉他,马克斯说:"我们应该把它写成歌"——然后就有了这首歌[1]。

——iHeartRadio音乐节后台,2012年9月22日

There are elements of darkness in our everyday life. There are elements of kind of these darker emotions, and we have to just figure out how to get through them or shine a light on them or look at them a different way, just in order to survive and be happy and be content. But in my songwriting, a lot of the time I'll have kind of a darker message with a lighter, happier beat or melody and just juxtapose them because I like the way that that feels.

我们的日常生活中有黯淡的时刻,以及一些低落的情绪。为了生存、为了保持愉悦、为了心怀满足,我们得设法熬过这些时刻,设法照亮那些黯淡之处,或者换个角度看待它们。创作歌曲时,很多

---

[1] 此处指歌曲《我们再也回不去了》。

时候我都会为黯淡的内容配上明亮欢快的节拍或旋律,我喜欢这种组合带来的感觉。

——美国电视节目 *Big Morning Buzz Live*,2014年10月27日

I tried to make ["I Knew You Were Trouble"] sound sonically how that feeling was when I felt it, which was chaotic and loud and out of control and intense... I didn't want to think too hard about staying in the lines. I **wanted it to sound as crazy as it felt.**

我尽力让歌曲《我知道你是大麻烦》的听感重现自己当时的所感,混乱、喧嚣、失控而激烈……我不想过多遵循创作规则,**我想让这首歌重现那种疯狂。**

——《芝加哥论坛报》(*Chicago Tribune*),2012年10月18日

The wild, unpredictable fun in making music today is that anything goes. Pop sounds like hip hop; country sounds like rock; rock sounds like soul; and folk sounds like country—and to me, that's incredible progress. I want to make music that reflects all of my influences, and I think that in the coming decades the idea of genres will become less of a career-defining path and more of an organizational tool.

现如今,音乐创作的狂野和难测都来源于一切皆有可能。流行乐听来像嘻哈乐;乡村音乐有摇滚乐的听感;摇滚乐听来像民俗音乐;民俗音乐又有乡村音乐的听感——在我看来,这是了不起的进步。我想在制作音乐时体现自己受到的所有影响,并且,我觉得在接下来的几十年间,流派这个概念对职业道路的限制会越来越少,它更

多会成为架构音乐的工具。

——《华尔街日报》(Wall Street Journal)，2014年7月7日

I was also attached to being a country artist at that point. Really, like, you build these relationships with radio and with the community, and it's sacred. We labeled *Red* a country album, and it came out, and it was universally agreed on that the songwriting was great, but it was also noted that it was a little bit multiple personality.

那时候我还是个乡村歌手。与乡村电台和整个乡村音乐界建立的关系非常神圣。我们把《红》标为乡村专辑，专辑问世后，大家对歌词创作一致赞扬，但也有人指出，这张专辑的曲风有些多样。

——纪录片《泰勒·斯威夫特——名誉之路》，
2018年9月28日

We don't make music so we can, like, win a lot of awards, but you have to take your cues from somewhere if you're gonna continue to evolve. You have a few options when you don't win an award. You can decide, like, "Oh, they're wrong. They all voted wrong." Second, you can be like, "I'm gonna go up on the stage and take the mic from whoever did win it." Or, third, you can say, "Maybe they're right. Maybe I did not make the record of my career. Maybe I need to fix the problem, which was that I have not been making sonically cohesive albums. I need to really think about whether I'm listening to the record label and what that's doing to the art I'm making."

我们创作音乐不是为了多多得奖，但要是你想继续做下去，就得广

纳意见。没能获奖时你有几个选择。一是断言:"哦,他们错了。他们都投错了。"二是心想:"我要上台夺下获奖者手里的麦克风。"第三个选择,你可以承认:"也许他们是对的。也许我还没创作出职业生涯里最好的专辑。也许我需要解决专辑听感不连贯的问题。我得好好考虑一下是否听取了唱片公司的意见,以及这对我现在制作的音乐有什么影响。"

——格莱美听享会,2015年10月9日

I think that if you're chasing a trend, by the time you put that music out, the trend is going to be over and there's going to be sort of a new wave of what's working. And I think I'd much rather kind of be part of a new wave and create something new rather than try to chase what everyone else is doing at the time.

我觉得(做音乐)要是总追逐潮流,等发行所谓的潮流音乐时,恐怕前浪早已退去,后浪已经登场。我更想成为后浪的一部分,与其和他人一起涌向一时的潮流,不如尝试创新。

——英国电台KISS FM,2014年10月9日

There's a mistake that I see artists make when they're on their fourth or fifth record, and they think innovation is more important than solid songwriting. The most terrible letdown as a listener for me is when I'm listening to a song and I see what they were trying to do. Like, where there's a dance break that doesn't make any sense, there's a rap that shouldn't be there, there's like a beat change that's, like, the coolest, hippest thing this six months—but it has nothing to do with the feeling, it has nothing to do with the emotion, it has nothing to do with the lyric.

我发现很多歌手在创作自己的第四张或第五张专辑时都会犯一个错误，就是将创新凌驾于稳扎稳打的歌曲创作之上。作为一个听者，听歌时我最失望的就是歌手的意图太过刻意。比如，歌里出现了一段毫无意义的舞曲，出现了一段不必要的说唱，出现了一段最近半年间很酷、很时髦的节奏变化——但这都与（歌曲要表达的）感情无关，与情绪无关，与歌词也无甚关联。

——美国杂志《纽约》，2013年11月25日

When you're five albums in—and I've been fortunate enough to sell a lot of albums so far— you don't have anyone to challenge you.
My label's never going to say to me, "Oh this album isn't different enough artistically, you really need to be stretching yourself."
You have to do it yourself. You have to push yourself because at this point a lot of people are just going to tell you that whatever you do is good enough.

发行5张专辑后——很幸运这些专辑至今的销量都不错——已经没人会质疑我了。
唱片公司不会对我说："这张专辑在艺术层面上还不够与众不同，你得多拓展一下自己。"
但我自己要有这种意识。我得自己逼自己，因为在当下这个节点，很多人只会一味肯定我所做的一切。

——英国《太阳报》，2014年10月27日

I really like to explore the edges of what I'm allowed to do. And I don't like to think that there are ceilings for what we're allowed to do musically. I think that if you don't play using different instruments, if you don't paint using different colors, you're making the choice to stay the same.

我很喜欢探索自己所能做到的极限。我觉得音乐上没有限制我们能力的天花板。如果你做音乐拒绝使用不同的乐器，如果你作画拒绝尝试不同的色彩，你就是在原地踏步。
　　——美国VH1频道音乐节目 *Storytellers*，2012年11月11日

I'm just so grateful that country music has let me paint with so many different colors, the fact that they have let me stretch musically and they've been so incredibly encouraging. You know, when I go out all over the world, I know that behind the scenes, back in America, country music is cheering me on and excited that I'm going to Asia and Europe. And that feels really good because it feels like, you know, that's always going to be home base and it's always gonna be what I'm so proud of.

我很感激乡村音乐界一直不断包容我尝试新事物，他们允许我拓展自己的音乐，并给予我极大的鼓励。到世界各地演出时，我知道在幕后，在美国，乡村音乐界正为我欢呼，为我即将踏足亚洲和欧洲而激动不已。这种感觉很美好，因为乡村音乐界永远是我的大本营，永远是我引以为豪的地方。
　　——2012年加拿大乡村音乐协会奖颁奖典礼后台，
　　　　2012年9月9日

It feels amazing to have so much control over my career and so much creative control over what the record looks like, how it sounds, what songs end up making the album. **I'm very lucky, you know, to get to have** all those choices up to me.

充分掌握自己事业的感觉非常棒,在创作层面掌控专辑的视觉呈现、整体听感及专辑选曲的感觉也非常棒。**我很幸运自己能掌控这一切。**
——美国堪萨斯州音乐电台 Mix 93.3,2012年10月26日

I like to take two years to make an album, so the first year is a lot of experimentation. And it's just sort of like, I'll try out all kinds of different things, and write this kind of song and that kind of song. And after a while you start to naturally gravitate towards one thing. And that's what happened with [1989], and the thing I naturally gravitated towards was sort of like late 80s– infused synth-pop.

我喜欢以两年为周期来制作一张专辑,第一年里我会做各种各样的实验。这种实验就是我会尝试各种不同的事物,写各种各样的歌曲。一段时间后,你自然就会专注到一件事情上去。专辑《1989》的制作就是这样,当时20世纪80年代的合成器流行乐自然而然地吸引了我的全部注意。
——英国广播电台 BBC Radio 1,2014年10月9日

When I knew the album had hit its stride, I went to Scott Borchetta and said, "I have to be honest with you: I did not make a country album. I did not make any semblance of a country album." And of course he went into a state of semi-panic and went through all the stages of grief—the pleading, the denial. "Can you give me three country songs? Can we put a fiddle on 'Shake It Off'?" And all my answers were a very firm "no", because it felt disingenuous to try to exploit two genres when your album falls in only one.

专辑《1989》的制作步入正轨时,我去找斯科特·波切塔,对他说:"我必须对你说实话:我这次没做乡村音乐专辑。这张专辑跟乡村音乐一点关系都没有。"当然,他简直惊慌失措,经历了悲伤情绪的所有阶段,一面恳求(不要完全转向流行乐),一面拒绝(接受这个事实):"你能给我写三首乡村歌曲吗?我们能在《统统甩掉》里加点小提琴吗?"我的回答都是非常坚定的"不行",因为在明确只有一种风格的专辑里,强行加入两种音乐风格只会让人觉得虚伪。

——美国杂志《公告牌》,2014年12月5日

What My fans in general were afraid of was that I would start making pop music and I would stop writing smart lyrics, or I would stop writing emotional lyrics. And when they heard the new music they realized that that wasn't the case at all.

我的歌迷们普遍害怕的是,我要是开始做流行音乐,就不会再写精巧的歌词,或者不会再写感性的歌词。但听到新音乐后他们就会打消这些顾虑。

——《芭芭拉·沃尔特斯:2014年十大魅力人物》[1],
2014年12月15日

---

1 《芭芭拉·沃尔特斯:2014年十大魅力人物》(*Barbara Walters Presents: The 10 Most Fascinating People of 2014*):名单包括演员斯嘉丽·约翰逊(Scarlett Johansson)、脱口秀主持人奥普拉·温弗瑞(Oprah Winfrey)等。

《空白格》：音乐之内

Somebody once told me that you truly see who a person is when you tell them something they don't want to hear... To the country music community, when I told you that I had made a pop album and that I wanted to go explore other genres, you showed me who you are with the grace that you accepted that with.

有人曾告诉我，人的真实本性会在逆耳之言面前显露无遗……而当我告诉乡村音乐界，我做了一张流行乐专辑，我想探索其他音乐风格时，你们得体地接受了，向我展示了你们的优雅本性。

——第50届美国乡村音乐学院奖[1]年度颁奖典礼，
2015年4月19日

I think what I loved about country music, and what I will always love about it, is that it is such a storytelling genre. You start a story, you tell the second part of the story, and then you finish the story at the end of the song, and you feel like you've been on a lyrical journey. And that is a part of my songwriting that's never gonna leave.

我觉得乡村音乐是一种非常会讲故事的音乐流派，无论过去还是未来，这种特质一直令我着迷。歌曲开头为故事开篇，接下来讲述故事的第二部分，然后在歌曲结尾收述故事的结局，听者会觉得好像循着歌词经历了整个故事。讲故事是我在歌曲创作中永远不会丢掉的东西。

——加拿大电视节目 *Tout le monde en parle*，2014年9月28日

---

[1] 美国乡村音乐学院奖（Academy of Country Music Awards，ACM Awards）：美国乡村和西部音乐学院于1964年在洛杉矶创立的重要奖项，为美国三大乡村音乐奖之一。

There's a song called "Love Story" that I wrote when I was 17. I'm going to be playing that as long as I'm playing concerts. And I can go back and I can connect to that song—because of the stories I've heard from fans saying, "We walked down the aisle to that song," or how special I feel it was when that was our first No. 1 worldwide hit. But "Tim McGraw," that song I don't really connect to as much. I connect to it in the form of nostalgia, but that was a song about a first love. I'm in a very different place in my life right now, and I think you can only hope to grow so much, emotionally, that you can't necessarily connect to wide-eyed 15-year-old ideas of love anymore.

17岁时我写了一首叫《爱情故事》的歌。后来凡是开演唱会，我都会表演这首歌。它让我回到过去，它和我紧紧相连——因为我从歌迷那里听到过的故事，比如"我们听着这首歌走过过道"；而且它是我第一首登顶全球热歌榜的单曲，对我来说独一无二。但歌曲《蒂姆·麦格劳》与我的联结就没有这么紧密了。于我而言，它是怀旧情愫，因为这首歌写的是初恋。我现在的经历与以前大不相同，只能期待自己在情感上快速成长，而不一定能再与15岁时对爱情的懵懂想法产生共鸣。

——美国新闻电台节目 *All Things Considered*，2014年10月31日

When you're making pop, you can make a hook out of different elements that I wasn't able to do previously, and that has been thrilling for me as a songwriter. You can shout, speak, whisper—if it's clever enough, it can be a hook.

制作流行音乐时，你可以用以前没用过的不同元素创作hook部分，作为词曲作者，我对此非常兴奋。你可以大喊、讲话、低语——**只要够巧妙，就能做hook。**

——美国杂志《公告牌》，2014年10月24日

I like to look at albums as being sort of statements. Visually, sonically, emotionally, I like them all to have their own fingerprint. This time [on *1989*] I'm kind of just doing whatever I feel like. I felt like making a pop album, so I did. I felt like being very honest and unapologetic about it, so I did. I felt like moving to New York—I had no reason to, it wasn't for love or business—so I did. I felt like cutting my hair short, so I did that, too. All these things are in keeping with living my life on my own terms.

我喜欢将专辑视为某类宣言。我希望专辑在视觉效果、听觉感受、情感表达上都保有自己的特点。这张专辑（《1989》）制作期间，我基本上在随心所欲做事。想做一张流行音乐专辑，就做了。对这张专辑想开诚布公、毫无保留，也这样做了。想搬到纽约——虽然没什么理由，不是为了爱情，也不是为了事业——就搬去了。我想把头发剪短，最终也剪短了。所有一切都是为了随我自己的心意而生活。

——美国杂志《公告牌》，2014年10月24日

I wanted to start [*1989*] with ["Welcome To New York"] because New York has been an important landscape and location for the story of my life in the last couple of years. I dreamt about moving to New York, I obsessed over moving to New York, and then I did it. And the inspiration that I found in that city is kind of hard to describe and hard to compare to any other force of inspiration I've ever experienced in my life. It's like an electric city.

我想将《欢迎来纽约》作为专辑《1989》的开篇歌曲，因为过去几年间，纽约一直是我人生故事中浓墨重彩的景观和地点。我曾梦想着搬到纽约，我对此魂牵梦萦，最终也如愿以偿。这座城市给予我的灵感有些难以名状，也很难与我人生中获得的其他灵感之力作比。这座城市令人心潮澎湃。

——歌曲《欢迎来纽约》解说，出自专辑《1989》
（大机器电台发布特辑版），2018年12月13日

I would like to clarify that the line is actually "Got a long list of ex-lovers." I'm very lucky that that line and my song ["Blank Space"] was misunderstood all over the world and had, like, eight weeks at number one.

我想澄清一下，这句歌词其实是"我有一长串前任名单"[1]。全世界有很多听众都听错了这句歌词，误解了《空白格》这首歌。但我很幸运，这首歌最终在排行榜上连续8周位列第一。

——2015年iHeartRadio音乐奖[2]颁奖典礼，2015年3月29日

This group of producers is a lot smaller than it was on *1989*. I picked

---

1 当时很多听众都将《空白格》的歌词"Got a long list of ex-lovers"听成了"the lonely Starbucks lovers"或"star-crossed lovers"，泰勒在发表最佳歌词奖的获奖感言时以此开了个玩笑。
2 iHeartRadio音乐奖（iHeartRadio Music Awards）：由美国在线广播电台iHeartRadio主办的音乐颁奖典礼。

people who I worked with on *1989*, but I felt like they would be versatile enough to kill *1989* and make something new.

(专辑《名誉》)的制作团队要比《1989》的制作团队小得多。我从《1989》的专辑制作团队里选了几位来制作新专辑，我觉得这些制作人多才多艺，足以超越《1989》并有所创新。

——《名誉》专辑秘密试听会，2017年10月

This one was different because I kind of built it out from the concept of a reputation. So there are a lot of kind of like, "I'm angry at my reputation" moments. There are [moments] like, "I don't care about my reputation. I'm fine, OK! I don't care!" And then there are these moments where it's very like, "Oh my God, what if my reputation actually makes the person that I like not want to get to know me?"

这张专辑的不同之处在于，我将它建构在名誉这个概念之上。所以专辑里有很多与名誉有关的时刻，比如，有描写"我为自己的名誉愤怒"的时刻；有描写"我不在乎自己的名誉。我很好，没关系！我一点儿都不在乎！"的时刻；还有描写"天啊，要是我喜欢的那个人因为我的名誉对我避而远之该怎么办？"的时刻。

——泰勒·斯威夫特NOW秘密演出，2018年6月28日

[*reputation* is] legitimately an album about finding love throughout all of the noise. And so it starts with the noise and how that all makes you feel, and how it makes you feel when people are saying things about you that you feel like aren't true, and living your life sort of in defiance of that, in defiance of your reputation.

专辑《名誉》是一张真正意义上在喧嚣中寻找爱情的专辑。因此它以喧嚣及其带来的感受为开头,描述人们传你谣言时的感受,描述在生活中无视那些谣言、无视自己的名誉。

——纪录片《泰勒·斯威夫特——名誉之路》,
2018年9月28日

"... Ready For It?" introduces a metaphor that you may hear more of throughout the rest of the album, which is like this kind of crime and punishment metaphor, where it talks about, like, robbers and thieves and heists and all that... The way that it's presented in "... Ready For It?" is basically like finding your partner in crime, and it's like, "Oh my God, we're the same, we're the same, oh my God! Let's rob banks together, this is great!"

我在歌曲《准备好了吗?》引入了一个隐喻,在专辑《名誉》中你会多次听到这个关于犯罪和惩罚的隐喻,它讲的是强盗、小偷和抢劫之类的事……在歌曲《准备好了吗?》中,这个隐喻主要表现为找到了你的犯罪同伙,就像是:"哦,天啊,我们是一类人,是一丘之貉,天啊!我们一起抢银行吧,这太棒了!"

——《名誉》专辑秘密试听会,2017年10月

Track five is kind of... legendary [on each record]... like, "Oh, I know I'm gonna like track five. Like, track five's the emotional, vulnerable song."

曲目五……在每张专辑中都是传奇性的存在……就像是:"哦,我知

道自己会喜欢曲目五。那是（专辑里）情感最丰沛、最脆弱的歌"。
——《名誉》专辑秘密试听会，2017年10月

There's an effect that you may hear on the vocals throughout the rest of [*reputation* after "Don't Blame Me"] that is recurring, and it's a vocoder... It's a vocal effect where you sing and the vocoder splits your voice into chords, and you can play your chords—your voice—on a keyboard... So that's what you'll hear in the beginning and throughout ["Delicate"], and then you'll hear it several times [on the rest of the album]. We tried it in the studio and I thought it sounded really emotional and really vulnerable and really kind of, like, sad but beautiful.

专辑《名誉》中，你可能注意到曲目《别怪我》之后的人声中都有一种反复出现的效果，那就是声码器……这是一种人声效果，你唱歌时声码器能将声音分割成和弦，然后你就可以在键盘上演奏这些和弦，也就是你的声音。你能在歌曲《易碎》的开头和全曲中听到这种效果，在专辑的其他歌曲中还会听到数次。我们在录音室里试了几次，我觉得这种声效听起来非常动情、非常脆弱、非常凄美。
——《名誉》专辑秘密试听会，2017年10月

I always wanted to structure a song where each individual section of the song sounded like a move forward in the relationship... I wanted, like, the verse to seem like its own phase of a relationship, the prechorus to sound like its own phase of a relationship, and the chorus to sound like its own phase of a relationship. And I wanted them to all have their own identity but seem like they were getting deeper and more fast-paced as the song went on. So, finally, I was able to achieve that in ["King of My Heart"].

我一直都想创作这样一首歌，歌曲的每个部分听起来就像恋爱中的每一步……比如，我希望主歌听起来像恋爱初期，导歌听起来像恋爱中的转折，副歌则来到了一段恋情中最为刻骨铭心的部分。我想让每个部分既各具辨识度，又能随着歌曲的展开不断深入，节奏不断变快。终于，我在歌曲《心的主宰》中做到了。
——《名誉》专辑秘密试听会，2017年10月

[reputation] is sort of like a catharsis, where, like, after I wrote it, I was like, "Hhh, OK, wow. OK, so that's done." But I had to say all of it, because **I was feeling a lot of feelings.**

《名誉》有点像是一种宣泄，写完这张专辑后，我长舒了一口气："啊，好了，好了，写完了。"但我必须都说出来，因为**我当时真的感触良多。**
——泰勒·斯威夫特NOW秘密演出，2018年6月28日

There's a common misconception that artists have to be miserable in order to make good art, that art and suffering go hand in hand. I'm really grateful to have learned this isn't true. Finding happiness and inspiration at the same time has been really cool.

有一种普遍的错误观念，就是伟大的艺术源于艺术家的苦痛，艺术与痛苦并驾齐驱。我很庆幸自己认识到事实并非如此。同时获得快

乐和灵感真的很酷。

——*Elle*，2019年3月6日

This new music is much more playful and actually inward facing. Like, when you get into this album, it's much more about me as a person—no pun intended with the song title ["ME!"]. But it's kind of taking those walls, taking that bunker down from around you.

新专辑（《恋人》）更俏皮有趣，实际更面向自我。深入听这张专辑，其内容更多关于我本人——我不是在双关歌曲《我！》的歌名[1]。这张专辑像是将我周遭的围墙和四周的掩体统统推倒。

——美国广播电台 Beats 1，2019年5月1日

"Me!" is a song about embracing your individuality and really celebrating it and owning it. And, you know, I think that with a pop song we have the ability to get a melody stuck in people's heads, and I just want it to be one that makes them feel better about themselves, not worse.

歌曲《我！》写的是拥抱自己的个性，为其庆祝并将其发扬光大。我认为流行歌曲有能力让一段旋律在人们脑海中根深蒂固，而我希望萦绕在人们脑海里的旋律，能让大家自我感觉更好，而非更糟。

——2019年美国国家橄榄球联盟选秀，2019年4月25日

---

[1] 本条出自2019年泰勒的采访，采访中主持人多次问及新专辑的"彩蛋"，此处泰勒意在打趣前一句"more about me as a person"中的"me"和单曲"ME!"虽为同一个词，但无言外之意。而后文提到的"围墙""掩体"，对应专辑《名誉》时期泰勒不接受采访和媒体刺探的态度，仿若在自己周遭筑起围墙。

In isolation my imagination has run wild and this album [folklore] is the result, a collection of songs and stories that flowed like a stream of consciousness. Picking up a pen was my way of escaping into fantasy, history, and memory. I've told these stories to the best of my ability with all the love, wonder, and whimsy they deserve.

新冠疫情隔离期间，我的想象力天马行空，歌曲和故事如意识流般从脑海中涌出，最终汇成了专辑《民间故事》。提起笔，我就能逃进虚构故事，逃进历史和记忆中去。这些故事值得我将所有的爱与奇思妙想倾注其中，也值得我尽自己的最大所能将其好好讲述出来。

——照片墙，2020年7月23日

To put it plainly, we just couldn't stop writing songs. To try and put it more poetically, it feels like we were standing on the edge of the folklorian woods and had a choice: to turn and go back or to travel further into the forest of this music... In the past I've always treated albums as one-off eras and moved onto planning the next one as soon as an album was released. There was something different with folklore. In making it, I felt less like I was departing and more like I was returning. I loved the escapism I found in these imaginary/not imaginary tales. I loved the ways you welcomed the dreamscapes and tragedies and epic tales of love lost and found. So I just kept writing them.

简单来说，我们停不下创作的脚步。更诗意一些的表达是，我们站在民间故事森林的边缘，面临着如下选择：转身离去还是继续深入探索这座音乐森林……过去我将每张专辑都视为一个个限定的时代，前一张专辑一发行就会马不停蹄地筹划下一张专辑。《民间故事》则不同。制作这张专辑的时候，我觉得自己不是在远离什么，而是在回归某处。我爱这些虚构／非虚构故事中蕴藏的逃避感，爱那些欣然接纳幻景、悲剧、逝去与复得的爱情史诗故事的种种方式。所以我就这样继续写了下去。

——照片墙，2020年12月10日

My world felt opened up creatively. There was a point that I got to as a writer who only wrote very diaristic songs that I felt it was unsustainable for my future moving forward... So what I felt after we put out *folklore* was like "Oh wow, people are into this too, this thing that feels really good for my life and feels really good for my creativity... it feels good for them too?"

在创作层面，我感觉自己的世界开阔了起来。从前我是那种非常依赖从日常生活中取材的词曲作者，并且一度觉得这种创作模式对自己的未来发展来说缺乏可持续性……专辑《民间故事》发行后，我发觉："哇，听众们也喜欢这种（取材于虚构故事的）音乐，这对我的生活和创造力都有好处……听众们也会有更好的听感吗？"

——苹果音乐，2020年12月15日

[*Midnights*] is a pretty dark album, but I'd say I had more fun making it than any album I've ever made. Because I don't think that art and suffering have to be holding hands all the time. I think you can write songs about pain or grief or suffering or loss... But I think with time and with the more albums I put out, making albums and making things and writing things feels like a way to sort of suck the poison out of a snakebite.

《午夜》是一张颇为暗色调的专辑,但对我来说,这张专辑的制作却是我最快乐的一次专辑制作体验。因为我认为艺术不总是与痛苦并驾齐驱的。我觉得当然可以写关于痛苦、悲伤、苦难或失去的歌……但随着时间流逝,随着我发行了越来越多的专辑,制作新专辑、创作与写作就像是从被毒蛇咬伤的患处吸出毒素。

——美国脱口秀节目《吉米今夜秀》(*The Tonight Show Starring Jimmy Fallon*),2022年10月24日

It's always been really, really important for me, personally, to one day own my work, to own my music, own my art.

于我而言,持有自己的作品、音乐及艺术的所有权,一直以来都非常、非常重要。

——时代巡回演唱会,伊利诺伊州芝加哥,2023年6月4日

Sometimes you need to talk it over (over and over and over) for it to ever really be... over. Like your friend who calls you in the middle of the night going on and on about their ex, I just couldn't stop writing. This will be the first time you hear all 30 songs that were meant to go on *Red*. And hey, one of them is even ten minutes long.

有时候你得在(一遍一遍、翻来覆去的)倾诉中才能完全消化掉心碎。就像你的朋友半夜给你打来电话,滔滔不绝地讲述他们的前

任，我则完全停不下手中的笔。这将是大家首次听到为专辑《红》创作的全部30首歌曲。并且，其中有一首歌的时长长达10分钟。

——宣布专辑《红（重制版）》发行，照片墙，
2021年6月18日

I first made *Speak Now*, completely self-written, between the ages of 18 and 20. The songs that came from this time in my life were marked by their brutal honesty, unfiltered diaristic confessions and wild wistfulness. I love this album because it tells a tale of growing up, flailing, flying and crashing... and living to speak about it.

我在18至20岁时创作了专辑《爱的告白》，专辑中的歌都由我独立写成。那段时期创作的歌曲都极度坦诚，用毫无修饰的日记式歌词剖白自我，充溢着炽烈而惆怅的渴望。我爱这张专辑，因为它讲述的故事，是成长、挣扎、飞翔又坠落，而我最终幸存，在此讲述一切。

——宣布专辑《爱的告白（重制版）》发行，推特，
2023年5月5日

Midnights is a collage of intensity, highs and lows and ebbs and flows. Life can be dark, starry, cloudy, terrifying, electrifying, hot, cold, romantic or lonely. Just like *Midnights*.

《午夜》是一幅拼满了激烈情绪、得意失意和潮起潮落的剪贴画。生活可以暗无天日、繁星满天或阴霾密布，可以令人心潮澎湃、或冷或热、满怀浪漫或心生孤独，一如专辑《午夜》。

——推特，2022年10月20日

Surprise! I think of *Midnights* as a complete concept album, with those 13 songs forming a full picture of the intensities of that mystifying, mad hour. However! There were other songs we wrote on our journey to find that magic 13.

… I'm calling them 3 a.m. tracks. Lately I've been loving the feeling of sharing more of our creative process with you, like we do with From The Vault tracks. So it's 3 a.m. and I'm giving them to you now.

给大家个惊喜！我将《午夜》构想为一张完整的概念专辑，专辑里的13首歌描绘出在那神秘、疯狂的午夜时分激荡的所有强烈感觉。但不止于此！选定这奇妙的13首曲目之前，我们还写了一些其他歌曲。……我将这些歌称为凌晨3点曲目。我最近很喜欢和大家分享我们的创作历程，就像之前和大家分享私藏版曲目[1]的创作一样。现在已经是凌晨3点了，这些歌曲也要和你们见面了。

——推特，2022年10月21日

Watching [Kendrick Lamar] create and record his verses on the "Bad Blood" remix was one of the most inspiring experiences of my life. I still look back on this collaboration with so much pride and gratitude, for the ways Kendrick elevated the song and the way he treats everyone around him. Every time the crowds on The Eras Tour would chant his line "you forgive, you forget, but you never let it… go!", I smiled. The reality that Kendrick would go back in and re-record "Bad Blood" so that I could

---

[1] 重录专辑不仅收录了原版专辑的所有曲目，而且收录了创作于原专时期的其他歌曲，这些新增曲目被称为"私藏版曲目"（From The Vault Tracks）。

reclaim and own this work I'm so proud of is surreal and bewildering to me.

看肯德里克·拉马尔录制混音版《敌对》里的歌曲段落，是我生命中最具启发意义的经历之一。我对这次合作始终倍感自豪、满怀感激，既因为肯德里克在很多方面都提升了这首歌的品质，也因为他待人接物极尽友善。每次在时代巡回演唱会上，观众们唱起他的部分"你原谅，你忘却，但你从未……释然！"，我都会微笑。我简直不敢相信肯德里克愿意重回录音室录制歌曲《敌对》，让我能重新拥有这首令自己骄傲之作的版权，像做梦一样。

——谈及歌曲《敌对（重制版）》（合作歌手：肯德里克·拉马尔），
推特，2023年10月27日

The 1989 album changed my life in countless ways, and it fills me with such excitement to announce that my version of it will be out October 27th. To be perfectly honest, this is my most FAVORITE re-record I've ever done because the 5 From The Vault tracks are so insane. I can't believe they were ever left behind. But not for long!

专辑《1989》在很多方面都改变了我的生活，我怀着无比激动的心情宣布，我的重录版本《1989》即将于10月27日发行。坦白说，这是我目前最喜欢的一张重录专辑，因为其中收录了5首非常棒的私藏版歌曲。不敢相信它们之前竟被搁置了。但它们不久后就会和大家见面！

——照片墙，2023年8月10日

One of my favorite parts of directing is the prep phase: writing a treatment, a shot list, & working with an animator to storyboard it out ahead of time.

导演工作中我最喜欢的部分之一就是前期准备阶段：撰写导演阐述[1]和分镜剧本，然后和动画设计师一起提前准备好故事板。
　　——谈及歌曲《柳》（"willow"）的音乐录影带制作，推特，
2020年12月15日

I was really happy when [Aaron Dessner] kind of pushed me forward like, "Nope, do the thing that makes you uncomfortable." Because I think that's what makes it a song that really, to me, stands out.

我很高兴（艾伦·德斯纳）能推着我前行，他说："不行，你得去做自己舒适圈之外的事。"因为我觉得只有这样，才能写出真正出色的歌。
　　——谈及歌曲《骗局》（"hoax"）的创作，纪录片《民间故事：长池录音室》（folklore: the long pond studio sessions），
2020年11月25日

A good song **transports you to your truest feelings** and translates those feelings for you.

---

[1] 导演阐述（director treatment）：又称导演创意阐述、导演摘要，为影片、节目等创作，包含重要情节、人物、架构等信息。

一首好歌不仅能让你**切身体会到自己当初最真切的情感**，还能为你诠释这些情感是为何物。

————纳什维尔创作人奖[1]颁奖现场，2022年9月20日

I would love to tell you that this is the best moment of my life, but I feel this happy when I finish a song, or when I crack the code to a bridge that I love, ... or when I'm rehearsing with my dancers or my band... For me, the award is the work. All I want to do is keep being able to do this. I love it so much.

我想对大家说，这是我人生中最美好的时刻，但其实每当我写完一首歌或者构思出喜欢的桥段时……每当我和舞者或乐队成员们一起排练时……我感受到的快乐与此刻无异。对我来说，工作就是褒奖。继续工作就是我的唯一所求。我非常热爱自己的工作。

————格莱美年度专辑奖项获奖致辞，第66届格莱美颁奖现场，2024年2月4日

I categorize certain songs of mine in the Quill style if the words and phrasings are antiquated, if I was inspired to write it after reading Charlotte Brontë or after watching a movie where everyone is wearing poet shirts and corsets.

我将自己那些遣词造句较为"老派"复古的歌曲归为"羽毛笔之

---

[1] 纳什维尔创作人奖（Nashville Songwriter Awards）：由纳什维尔创作人协会颁发，2022年纳什维尔创作人奖颁奖典礼上，泰勒获颁"十年创作艺人"（Songwriter-Artist of the Decade）奖项。

歌"，一同属于羽毛笔之歌的，还有那些读完夏洛特·勃朗特[1]的书后创作的歌，以及看完一部剧中角色都穿着诗人衫[2]和束腰的电影后创作的歌。

——谈及自己的歌曲分类方式，纳什维尔创作人奖颁奖现场，
2022年9月20日

Fountain pen style means a modern storyline or references, with a poetic twist... The songs I categorize in this style sound like confessions scribbled and sealed in an envelope, but too brutally honest to ever send.

"墨水笔之歌"记述的故事线和事物则更加现代，并伴有诗意的转折……这类歌曲听起来就像潦草写下的告白，我将它封进信封，但因内容太过直白而从未寄出。

——谈及自己的歌曲分类方式，纳什维尔创作人奖颁奖现场，
2022年9月20日

Glitter gel pen lyrics don't care if you don't take them seriously because they don't take themselves seriously. Glitter Gel Pen lyrics are the drunk girl at the party who tells you that you look like an angel in the bathroom.

"珠光笔之歌"根本不在乎是不是得到了旁人的认真对待，因为它

---

1 夏洛特·勃朗特（Charlotte Brontë）：英国作家，代表作《简·爱》《谢利》，与妹妹艾米莉·勃朗特（Emily Brontë）和安妮·勃朗特（Anne Brontë）在英国文学史并称"勃朗特三姐妹"。

2 诗人衫（poet shirt）：也称海盗衬衫，版型宽松，袖子为袖管长及手腕，袖口处蓬起再收紧的主教袖，常饰有宽大的褶边。

们自己也没把自己当回事儿。这类歌曲就像派对上喝得醉醺醺的女孩，在洗手间里对你说，你看起来就像个天使。

　　——谈及自己的歌曲分类方式，纳什维尔创作人奖颁奖现场，
2022年9月20日

Writing songs is my life's work and my hobby and my never-ending thrill.

写歌是我毕生的事业，是我的热爱所在，是我永不枯竭的乐趣来源。
　　——纳什维尔创作人奖颁奖现场，2022年9月20日

There's so much pressure going into putting new music out. If I don't beat everything I've done prior, it'll be deemed as, like, a colossal failure.

发行新音乐要面临非常大的压力。新音乐作品如果没能超越以前的作品，好像就会注定一败涂地。
　　——纪录片《美利坚女士》，2020年1月23日

Everybody in music has their own sort of niche specialty thing that they do that, you know, sets them apart from everybody else. And my storytelling is what it is for me.

音乐从业者都有自己的独到本领，这能让他们从众人中脱颖而出。而我的独到之处就是讲故事。
　　——纪录片《美利坚女士》，2020年1月23日

These songs maybe started out being about something that happened to me or in my life; maybe it's something that I wrote about a fictional character I created one day when I was bored. But my dream is that when they go into your world, they become about your life.

这些歌可能最初取材于我的亲身经历或生活见闻，可能来源于我某日无聊时创造出的虚构人物。但我的梦想是，当这些歌进入你们的世界，会成为你们生活的一部分。

——时代巡回演唱会，佛罗里达州坦帕，2023年4月17日

I remember people would come up to me and they'd be like "So you've put out, like, five albums that you haven't done tours for. So what's your plan? Like, what are you going to do? You're going to just do a show with, like, all the albums in it and what, it'll be like a three-and-a-half-hour-long show?" And I was like "Yeah, it's going to be called The Eras Tour. See you there."

我记得人们会来问我："你已经发行了5张专辑[1]，但在此期间还没举办过一场巡演。所以你的计划是什么？你打算怎么办？你会不会办一场囊括所有专辑、演出时长三个半小时的巡演？"我回答道："没错，它就叫时代巡回演唱会。我们巡演见。"

——巡演纪录片《泰勒·斯威夫特：时代巡回演唱会》，
2023年10月13日

When I dreamed up the idea of The Eras Tour, I thought it would be really

---

1　这5张专辑指2019至2022年发行的《恋人》《民间故事》《永恒故事》《放手去爱（重制版）》和《午夜》。

fun to sort of go back through all these different phases I've had musically because it's been a little bit of everything. You've been so kind to me in letting me explore genres and step outside boxes that are created for us in the music industry and that's only because of you that I get to do that. So, thank you.

萌生出时代巡回演唱会的想法时,我就在想,如果能回顾自己经历的所有音乐时期,一定会很有趣,因为这差不多就是在回顾我迄今为止的音乐历程。你们待我一向慷慨,让我去探索不同的音乐流派,让我跳出音乐界为音乐人设下的条条框框,因为有你们,我才能做到这些。所以,感谢大家。

——巡演纪录片《泰勒·斯威夫特:时代巡回演唱会》,
2023年10月13日

Every day I would run on the treadmill, singing the entire set list out loud. Fast for fast songs, and a jog or a fast walk for slow songs. Then I had three months of dance training, because I wanted to get it in my bones. I wanted to be so over-rehearsed that I could be silly with the fans, and not lose my train of thought.

每天我都会一边在跑步机上跑步,一边大声地完整唱一遍巡演歌单。唱快歌时快跑,唱慢歌时就慢跑或快走。然后我进行了为期三个月的舞蹈训练,我想让动作成为自己的肌肉记忆。我希望自己准备得特别充分,那样就可以(在台上)和粉丝们一起犯傻,而不至于忘记接下来的一连串动作。

——谈及筹备时代巡回演唱会,《时代周刊》,
2023年12月6日

I think you'll see that you absolutely are main characters in this film. Because that's what made the tour magical. That's what made it different than anything I've ever done in my life. Your attention to detail. Your preparation. Your passion. Your intensity. You cared so much about these shows, and that made all the difference for us.

大家会看到，你们是这部电影的主角。因为是你们让这场巡演变得如此梦幻，是你们让这场巡演成为我生命中的独一无二。你们关注细节、悉心准备、热情满满、活力四射。你们如此在乎这一场场演出，这对我们来说至关重要。
——在巡演纪录片《泰勒·斯威夫特：时代巡回演唱会》首映式上给粉丝的寄语，2023年10月11日

Happy Pride Month, everyone! You know, on this tour I get to look out into the most stunningly beautiful, brilliant crowds of people who are living their authentic lives. Who are loving who they want to love, who are identifying how they identify, and allies who support them in that and celebrate them in that. It's the most beautiful experience for me to look out into the crowds on this tour. I'm looking out tonight, I'm seeing so many incredible just individuals who are living authentically and beautifully and this is a safe space for you, this is a celebratory space for you.

大家"骄傲月"快乐！在这次巡演中，我注意到一群遵循本心而活、无比美丽夺目的人。他们爱自己想爱的人，认同自己的身份，还有支持他们、赞美他们的盟友。能在巡演中见到这群人是我最美妙的经历。今晚，我向人群中望去，看到这么多无与伦比的个体真切而

美好地生活着，这里是你们的安全之地，也是你们的庆祝之地。
　　——时代巡回演唱会，伊利诺伊州芝加哥，2023年6月2日

Since I was a teenager, I've wanted to own my music, and the way to do it was to rerecord my albums... The way that you have embraced that, the way you have celebrated that, you really decided that it was your fight too, and that you were 100% behind me, and if I cared about it, you cared about it. I will never stop thanking you for that.

自青少年时期，我就想拥有自己的音乐，重新录制专辑就是为了拿回自己的音乐版权……对此，你们不仅欣然接受，还为我庆祝，并且发自内心地认定这也是你们的战斗，你们全心全意地支持我，将我在乎的东西放在心上。我对此感激不尽。
　　——时代巡回演唱会，加利福尼亚州洛杉矶，2023年8月8日

I'd written so much tortured poetry in the past 2 years and wanted to share it all with you, so here's the second installment of *TTPD: The Anthology*. 15 extra songs. And now the story isn't mine anymore... it's all yours.

过去两年间我写了许多充满苦痛的诗歌，我想把它们分享给大家，这就是专辑《苦难诗社》的第二篇章《苦难诗社：选集》[1]，其中包含15首新歌。现在这些故事已不属于我……它们属于你们。
　　　　　　　　　　　　　　——推特，2024年4月19日

---

1 《苦难诗社：选集》(*THE TORTURED POETS DEPARTMENT: THE ANTHOLOGY*)：发行于2024年4月19日专辑《苦难诗社》正式发行后不久。

《不朽》:
泰勒最伟大的传奇故事——与粉丝共谱

I've always made music so that I could feel camaraderie with my fans—not in a way that was trying to kind of cater to any male fantasy. And that wasn't on purpose, that's just been what has felt natural to me.

我创作音乐是为了维系和粉丝间的友情,而非试图迎合任何男性幻想。我并非刻意为之,一切都是自然而然,发自本心。

——"泰勒·斯威夫特1989",2014年10月27日

When I was younger and I would write songs in my bedroom, the first thing I would feel was fear, because I was afraid that no one would ever hear it. I can't thank the fans enough, because I don't have to feel that way anymore.

小时候我在卧室里写歌,当时我的第一感觉就是恐惧,因为我怕没人听我写的歌。我对歌迷们感激不尽,因为现在我不再感到那种恐惧了。

——美国乡村音乐电视奖2010年年度艺人,2010年12月3日

You can have, like, a bad day right up until the point where you go onstage, but the second you hear the screams of like 20,000 people, you're like, "This day isn't that bad. It's gonna be OK."

上台前,你可能刚度过了糟糕的一天,但一听到两万多名观众的呐喊,你会觉得:"今天也没那么糟。一切都会好起来的。"
　　——美国乡村音乐电台94.9 *The Bull*,2011年6月20日

I want these songs to go out into the world and become whatever my fans want them to be. I want them to picture their ex-boyfriend, not mine. And I know there's going to be a media guessing game whenever I put out music, but that does not mean that I have to confirm or help them with it.

我希望自己的歌走向世界,由歌迷们自由解读。我希望他们听歌时联想到的不是我的前任,而是自己的前任。我知道我每次发行新歌,媒体都会对歌曲内容大肆猜测,但那并不意味着我要证实他们的推测,或者给他们提供正确的引导。
　　——美国电视节目《早间新闻》,2014年12月29日

That's the difference between a singer and a performer. **A singer sings for themselves and a performer performs for everyone else.**

歌手和表演者的区别在于,**歌手为自己而唱,表演者为观众而表演。**
　　——音乐选秀节目《美国之声》[1],2014年11月3日

---

[1] 2014年11月,泰勒担任音乐选秀节目《美国之声》(The Voice)第七季顾问导师。

I really just thought that I was writing about my life, but what I really didn't understand was that the second I put it out, it was gonna be playing in other girls' bedrooms and playing in the cars of people I had never met before. And when that happens... I think you start to realize that as human beings, all we really want is a connection with someone else. And I think that music is that ultimate connection. You know, what if you've got no connection with anybody else? You can always turn to music and you can know that somebody else has gone through it and that you're not alone.

我曾经真的以为我只是在写自己的生活，我当时还没有意识到，歌曲一发行，就会在其他女孩的卧室里播放，就会在与我素不相识之人的车里播放。这些发生后……我开始意识到，作为人类，我们真正渴求的正是与他人的联系。我觉得音乐就是这种终极联系。如果你与所有人都失去了联系，你可以永远投身于音乐，然后明了曾经也有人经历过这一切，你并非孑然一身。
——歌曲《隐形的爱》（"Invisible"）解说，出自专辑《泰勒·斯威夫特》（大机器电台发布特辑版），2018年12月13日

Performing live, I usually go through all the emotions that I went through when I was writing the song onstage because that's the state of mind you have to be in. And so sometimes it does get really emotional onstage... It's really wonderful to feel those feelings in front of an entire crowd of people who you feel like have your back because you know the reason they're there is they've felt that way too.

现场表演时，我通常会在台上重历一番写歌时经历的所有情绪，因

为表演需要你处在那种状态中。所以有时候我会在台上变得非常情绪化……在一群完全支持你的人面前经历那些情绪，是一种很奇妙的体验，因为你知道观众们之所以在此，是因为他们与你感同身受。

——美国脱口秀节目《蕾切尔·雷秀》(*Rachael Ray Show*)，
2011年1月3日

I've also been a fan, and I've been sitting in the last row of an arena watching my favorite artist not play the song I wanted to hear. And I think there has to be a genuine respect for the position that fans are in, when they have all these memories that are attached to these songs that you put out maybe five years ago. And maybe you're sick and tired of playing it, but if they want to hear it, I'm gonna play it.

我也是一名歌迷，我也曾坐在场馆的最后一排，看着我最爱的歌手没有唱我想听的歌。5年前发行的那些歌可能承载了歌迷们的很多回忆，所以我觉得必须尊重这种情况。也许我已经疲于或厌倦于演唱某首歌，但只要歌迷们想听，我就愿意唱。

——美国VH1频道音乐节目 *Storytellers*，2012年11月11日

I feel like this song has two lives to it in my brain. In my brain, there's the life of this song where this song was born out of catharsis and venting and trying to get over something and trying to understand it and process it. And then there's the life where it went out into the world and you turned this song into something completely different for me. You turned this song into a collage of memories of watching you scream the words to this song, or seeing pictures that you post to me of you having written the words to this song in your diary, or you showing me your wrist, and you have a tattoo of the lyrics to this song underneath your skin. And that is how you have changed the song "All Too Well" for me.

我觉得这首歌（《回忆太清晰》）在我脑海里有两种生命：第一种生命诞生于宣泄情绪，试着克服、理解并处理某些情绪的需要；第二种生命在于这首歌发行后走向世界，歌迷们赋予了这首歌截然不同的意义，将这首歌变成了一幅记忆拼贴画，在画里你们或尖叫着唱出歌词，或发布在日记里写下歌词的照片，又或是给我看纹了歌词的手腕。你们就这样以种种方式，改变了《回忆太清晰》对我的意义。
——巡演纪录片《泰勒·斯威夫特：名誉巡回演唱会》，2018年12月31日

People always talk to you about marriages and relationships, and they say relationships take work, and you have to keep surprising each other... I think the most profound relationship I've ever had has been with my fans. That relationship takes work, and you have to continue to think of new ways to delight and surprise them. You can't just assume that because they liked one of your albums, they're going to like the new one, so you can make it exactly the same as you made the last one. You can't just assume that because they were gracious enough to make you a part of their life last year, that they're gonna want to do the same thing this year. I think that core relationship needs to be nurtured.

关于婚姻和感情，有些老生常谈的观点，感情需要经营，彼此要营

造新鲜感……而我最深厚的感情是同粉丝们建立的情谊。这份感情也需要经营，你得不断想些新点子，让粉丝满意，保持新鲜感。你不能理所应当地认为，他们喜欢你的某张专辑，就会同样为你的新专辑买账，而你不用为此做出任何创新。你也不能理所应当地认为，自己有幸成为他们去年生活里的一部分，今年就还将占据一席之地。在我看来，这份珍贵的感情需要滋养。

——雅虎网，2014年11月6日

When I meet my fans, it's not like meeting a stranger. It's sort of like saying hello to someone that I already know is on the same page with me.

见到歌迷不像见到陌生人。和歌迷打招呼，就像和志同道合之人打招呼。

——"美国乡村音乐协会音乐节：乡村摇滚之夜"新闻发布会，2011年8月9日

There's more of a friendship element to it than anything else. Maybe it's a big-sister relationship. Or it's a *Hey, we're the same age*— and we were both 16 when my first album came out, and we've both grown up together.

（我与粉丝间的关系）更多是一种友情，或是一种姐妹情谊，又或是一种"嗨，我们是同龄人"的关系——第一张专辑发行时，我们都是16岁，现在我们一起长大了。

——《纽约时报》，2013年11月25日

You might think a meet-and-greet with 150 people sounds sad, because maybe you think I'm forced to do it. But you would be surprised. A meaningful conversation doesn't mean that conversation has to last an hour. A meet-and-greet might sound weird to someone who's never done one, but after ten years, you learn to appreciate happiness when it happens, and that happiness is rare and fleeting, and that you're not entitled to it.

你可能认为和150个人开见面会听起来有点悲伤，因为觉得我是被迫做这事的。但你会大吃一惊。交谈的意义不由它持续的时间决定。对没开过见面会的人来说这事可能有点奇怪，但出道10年后，我已经学会及时珍惜幸福，幸福千载难逢又转瞬即逝，我无权一直拥有。

——*GQ*，2015年10月15日

At every single fan meet and greet that we do every night, I have groups of girls that come up to me with their cell phones and are like, "Look what my ex-boyfriend just texted me." And I love that they're my friends, and I love that we understand each other. And we're allowed to understand each other because I'm allowed to make the kind of music that I want to make.

每晚举办的每场粉丝见面会上，都会有成群的女孩拿着手机来到我跟前，说："看我前男友刚给我发的信息。"我很乐意和她们成为朋友，也很开心我们彼此理解。而我们能互相理解则得益于我能随心所欲地创作自己的音乐。

——大机器唱片集团派对，2011年1月28日

I wasn't trying to make people dress a certain way, but seeing girls coming to my shows wearing sundresses and cowboy boots and curling their hair is one of my favorite experiences ever because I remember when I was weird for dressing the way that I dressed and I was weird for having curly hair.

我并未有意引导大家的着装方式,但我人生中最棒的经历之一,就是看到女孩们穿着无袖背心裙,蹬着牛仔靴,卷着头发来看我的演出,因为我还记得当初觉得自己的这种着装和卷发很奇怪。

——时尚杂志《嘉人》(*Marie Claire*),2009年6月22日

One thing about my fans is they really love to dress up. In costume. As characters from my music videos. And you look out into the crowd and you see that person dressed up from [the] "You Belong With Me" video, that person dressed up from "Love Story," that person randomly dressed up like a banana, I don't know why... I think it's hilarious, so they just keep dressing up in crazier and crazier costumes, which makes me then make music videos where we dress up in crazier and crazier costumes.

我的歌迷们有个特点,就是他们非常热衷于打扮——盛装打扮——打扮成我音乐录影带里的角色。你向人群中放眼望去,看到这个人打扮成《你应该和我在一起》录影带里的角色,那个人的着装来自《爱情故事》,还有随意打扮成香蕉的歌迷,虽然我也不知道这是为什么……我觉得这很搞笑,然后来看演出的歌迷们穿的服装就愈发疯狂起来,这也让我音乐录影带里角色的着装愈发疯狂。

——线上音乐平台Vevo认证视频,2012年10月29日

We like to reward people who are in the back rows, or people who didn't think they had a chance to say hi to me at the show, people who brought signs and dressed up and make puffy-paint T-shirts and go crazy. It's almost like a spirit award. We round them up and we bring them backstage for a party after the show.

我们喜欢给后排的观众制造惊喜,给那些觉得自己没机会在演出中和我打招呼的人惊喜,还有那些带着标语、盛装打扮、穿着彩绘T恤衫、举止疯狂的人。这就好比一种精神奖励。我们把大家组织起来,带到后台参加演出后举办的派对。

——美国网站"每日野兽",2012年10月22日

When I was younger, I was just obsessed with Broadway shows. As much as I can show these audiences an element of that theatrical nature to a performance, I think that it allows them to escape from their lives a little bit more.

年纪稍小一些的时候,我对百老汇演出非常着迷。我尽可能地向观众们展示表演中的戏剧元素,因为觉得这样能让观众们进一步逃离自己的生活。

——《时代周刊》,2014年11月13日

What I'm battling in this day and age is that every person in the audience probably knows what costumes I'm gonna wear, and they could know the set list if they really wanted to. So I decided to start inviting special guests out. Getting people to say yes to come up onstage was a lot easier than I thought. I'd never want to pressure anybody. I'd never go, "Come on, come on!" But people start to realize before they even got there that if they were to walk out onstage, the crowd's gonna freak out, and they're gonna scream, and it's gonna be an amazing moment for everyone involved.

这段时期里我要面临的问题是，观众们可能都知道我要穿什么样的演出服装，并且如果他们真想知道演出曲目，也总有办法知道。所以我决定邀请特别嘉宾，让他们答应上台比我想象的要简单得多。我不想给任何嘉宾施加压力，也不会苦苦哀求他们，说："拜托了，拜托了！"但大家在登台前就会意识到，他们上台后观众们会欣喜若狂、会放声尖叫，这对在场的每个人来说都是无与伦比的体验。
——巡演纪录片《泰勒·斯威夫特：1989世界巡回演唱会》，
2015年12月20日

I did this thing called the *1989* Secret Sessions a few months ago, way before the album came out. I had spent months picking fans on Instagram, Tumblr, Twitter—people who had been so supportive and had tried and tried to meet me... And in every single one of my houses in the U.S. and my hotel room in London, I would invite 89 people over to my living room, play them the entire album, tell them the stories behind it. And I'd say, you know, you can share your experience, but please keep the secrets about this album a secret.

几个月前，我组织了几场《1989》专辑秘密试听会，就在专辑《1989》发行前夕。我花了几个月的时间从照片墙、汤博乐和推特上挑选歌迷——选那些一直支持我，一直想见我的歌迷……我在美国的所有居所里，在伦敦的酒店房间里，为每场试听会邀请的89

位歌迷播放整张专辑，向他们讲述这张专辑背后的故事。我对他们说，你们可以分享这次经历，但请保守与这张专辑有关的所有秘密。

——美国新闻电台节目 *All Things Considered*，2014年10月31日

When I pick people to send packages to, I go on their social-media sites for the last six months and figure out what they like or what they are going through. Do they like photography? I'll get them a 1980s Polaroid camera. Do they like vintage stuff? I'll go to an antiques place and get them 1920s earrings… When you actually get to know them on a person-by-person basis, you realise what you're doing is special and sacred and it matters.

决定给哪些粉丝寄包裹时，我会浏览他们过去半年间的社交媒体主页，试着弄清他们想要什么，或者正在经历什么。喜欢摄影吗？我会送一台20世纪80年代的宝丽来相机。喜欢古着吗？我会去古董店里买几副20世纪20年代的耳饰……当你开始去一个一个了解粉丝们，会觉得自己所做的事既特殊、神圣，又非常重要。

——英国《每日电讯报》，2015年5月23日

The easter egg hunts, when they stop being fun for my fans I'll stop doing them, but they seem to be having fun with them. And I think that with music, I'm always trying to expand the experience from just being an audio one. Like, if I can turn it into something that feels symbolic or seems like a scavenger hunt or seems like some kind of brain game that feels like it's more, then I think that's something to keep in mind as a goal for me. Like, I just want to entertain them on as many levels as I possibly can.

关于埋彩蛋这事，要是我的歌迷们开始觉得兴致缺缺，我就不会继续做了，但他们目前好像仍然乐在其中。在音乐方面，我一直尽力将体验范围从听觉体验拓展到更为广泛的维度。比如，如果我能让音乐给人以象征意义，或者把它变成寻宝游戏或某种脑力游戏，那么这就是我应该牢记于心的目标。我只是想最大限度上为歌迷们带去快乐。

——美国广播电台 Beats 1，2019 年 5 月 1 日

My fans make fun of me—it's really cool. They have all these Gifs of me making an idiot of myself or tripping and falling on stage. They bring humour back into it for me. I get too serious sometimes... and they bring me back to like, "OK, I'm not really doing anything that difficult. I just need to calm down."

我的歌迷们会拿我取笑——这挺酷的。他们手里有各种各样我犯傻、在台上被绊倒或摔倒的动图。他们让我重拾幽默。有时候我太严肃了……他们让我回过神来，释怀道："好吧，我其实没在做什么难事，我只需要冷静下来。"

——英国《每日电讯报》，2015 年 5 月 23 日

My struggle is trying to maintain a normal outlook, a normal attitude, and a normal mindset amongst these abnormal circumstances. So one thing I do is I go online and I kind of look at my fans' pages on their Instagrams and their Twitter, and their Tumblr pages, and I just kind of like look at what their life is like. And it kind of returns this normalcy to my very weird life.

我的难处在于，要在不同寻常的（生活）情景里维持正常的面貌、态度和心态。我会上网看歌迷们的照片墙和推特主页，看他们的汤博乐主页，看看他们的生活是什么样的。这让我反常的生活重归正常。
　　　　　　——英国广播电台BBC Radio 2，2014年10月9日

Everything I did was for [my fans], and I didn't need to try and get every headline or try to get the cover of this or the cover of that. Like, I just needed to think of ways to reach out to them in ways I hadn't even thought of before. So the relationship between me and my fans really actually strengthened throughout the course of *reputation*, and that was what made it something that I think I'll look back on and find to be one of the most beautiful times of my life, was when I realized that, like, it's me and it's them, and that's what makes this fun for me.

我当时做的一切都是为了我的歌迷们，我没必要去争取拿下每个头条，或者去争取登上这样那样的封面。我要做的就是想出一些新方式和大家多接触。可以说整个《名誉》专辑期间，我和歌迷间的关系变得十分稳固，这也是我回首过往，觉得这是自己生命里一段美好时光的原因。因为我意识到，是我，是歌迷们，让一切充满乐趣。
　　　　　　——美国广播电台Beats 1，2019年5月1日

[The re-recording process is] going to be fun, because it'll feel like regaining a freedom and taking back what's mine. When I created [these songs], I didn't know what they would grow up to be. Going back in and knowing that it meant something to people is actually a really beautiful way to celebrate what the fans have done for my music.

重录过往专辑将是个有趣的过程，因为这让我感觉自己正在重获自由，正在拿回属于自己的东西。当初写这些歌时，我并不知道它们以后会成为什么。重录这些歌，知道这些歌对人们来说意味着什么，实际上是在以一种非常美妙的方式庆祝歌迷们为我的音乐带来的一切。

——美国杂志《公告牌》，2019年12月11日

There is an element to my fan base where we feel like we grew up together. I'll be going through something, write the album about it, and then it'll come out, and sometimes it'll just coincide with what they're going through.

我的粉丝们有个特点，感觉我们是一起成长的。我会经历一些事，把它们写到专辑里，专辑发行后，有时候就正好与粉丝当下的经历契合。

——纪录片《美利坚女士》，2020年1月23日

[Fans] had to work really hard to get the tickets. I wanted to play a show that was longer than they ever thought it would be, because that makes me feel good leaving the stadium... I know I'm going on that stage whether I'm sick, injured, heartbroken, uncomfortable, or stressed. That's part of my identity as a human being now. If someone buys a ticket to my show, I'm going to play it unless we have some sort of force majeure.

粉丝们费尽周折才得到巡演门票。我想为大家献上一场时长上史无前例的演出，因为只有这样，离场时我才能心安……我清楚无论自己是生病受伤、伤心难过，还是心力交瘁，都要上台演出。这已经成为我当下自我认知的一部分。只要有人买了我的演出门票，除非遇到不可抗力，我都会上台表演。

——谈及时代巡回演唱会，《时代周刊》，2023年12月6日

Thank you for the adventure of a lifetime. May it continue...

感谢大家与我共历这场毕生难忘的冒险。愿我们一直在冒险的路上……

——时代巡回演唱会欧洲场次完结帖文，照片墙，2024年4月21日

《一切皆变》：
日新月异的音乐行业

Every choice you make in a management meeting affects your life a year-and-a-half from now. I know exactly where I'm going to be next year at this time. That's because I'm sitting there in those management meetings every single week and scheduling everything and approving things, or not approving things, based on what I feel is right for my career at this point.

我在管理层会议上做的每个决定，都会影响我接下来一年半的生活。当下，我很清楚明年此时将身在何方。因为我每周都要参加管理层会议，根据当前对自己职业生涯的判断，制定行程、批准或否决某些提议。

——美国杂志《公告牌》，2011年12月2日

There are some artists who are completely right-brained, impulsive, artistic, but who don't understand the business side of things. Then there are artists who are all business, but aren't really intuitive or plugged into an artistic outlet. Ryan [Tedder] and I can sit working on a song, but then, on our lunch break, we'll be talking about tour dates, scheduling, which venues are the best to play.

有些完全属于右脑型[1]的艺人，他们意气用事、才华横溢，但对商业运作一窍不通；而有些艺人虽精于商业运作，直觉却不够敏锐，还缺乏艺术造诣。瑞恩[2]和我可以一起创作歌曲，但在午休时间，我们还会一起探讨巡演日期，制定行程，讨论表演的最佳场地。

——英国《星期日泰晤士报》(Sunday Times)，2014年10月26日

You can be accidentally successful for three or four years. Accidents happen. **But careers take hard work.**

运气可能造就三四年间的一时得意。这不足为奇。**但要成就一番事业，必得兢兢业业做事。**

——GQ，2015年10月15日

It's true that I've never had a burning desire to rebel against my parents. But in other respects I think I have rebelled. I mean, I rebelled against my record label when they wanted to shelve me, and I've rebelled against people trying to push me around in the recording studio. To me, that's always been much more exciting than going out and getting drunk.

我确实从未强烈渴望过反抗我的父母。但在其他方面，我也曾叛逆

---

1 一般认为，右脑型人情感丰富、直觉敏锐、创造力强，擅长表达和艺术创作，而左脑型人逻辑缜密、分析能力强，擅长计算、推理等。
2 瑞恩·泰德（Ryan Tedder）：美国摇滚男歌手，共和时代乐队主唱。

过。比如，我反抗过想要搁置我的唱片公司[1]，反抗过录音室里试图欺负摆布我的人。于我而言，这些事要比出门喝得酩酊大醉刺激得多。

——英国《每日电讯报》，2009年4月26日

I'm very well aware that the music industry is changing and it will continue to change. And I am open to that change. I am open to progress. I am not open to the financial model that is currently in place. I really believe that we in the music industry can work together to find a way to bond technology with integrity.

我非常清楚，音乐行业正处于变革中，变革也是音乐界未来发展的趋势。我乐意接受这种变革，也乐意拥抱进步。但我无法接受现行的资金运作模式。我深信，只要音乐业内的诸位共同协作，就能找到兼顾科技革新与艺术操守的方法。

——2014年公告牌女性音乐奖颁奖典礼，2014年12月12日

Music is art, and art is important and rare. Important, rare things are valuable. Valuable things should be paid for. It's my opinion that music should not be free, and my prediction is that individual artists and their labels will someday decide what an album's price point is. I hope they don't underestimate themselves or undervalue their art.

音乐是艺术，艺术是珍稀的要物。珍稀的要物意味着它们保有价

---

1 此处指美国广播唱片公司，泰勒曾与其签订发展合约。

值。保有价值的事物值得为其付出报酬。我认为音乐不应是无偿之物，独立艺术家及其唱片公司总有一天能掌握专辑的标价权。我希望他们不要妄自菲薄，也不要低估自己艺术的价值。

——《华尔街日报》，2014年7月7日

I just really hope we can teach a younger generation the value of investment in music rather than just the ephemeral consumption of it. I think that there has to be a way for streaming or any future ways that we access music to fairly compensate the writers, musicians, and producers of that music.

我衷心希望，我们能让年轻一代的音乐人意识到投身音乐的价值所在，而非盲目追求音乐带来的短时效益。我认为流媒体及未来的音乐服务必须找到解决方法，保证我们在享受音乐的同时，其创作者、音乐家和制作人能得到相应的报酬。

——2014年公告牌女性音乐奖颁奖典礼，2014年12月12日

For anyone who wants to create music, for any little kid who's taking piano lessons right now, I want them to have an industry to go into.

我希望每个想要从事音乐创作的人，每个此时此刻正在上钢琴课的**孩子，都能享受良好、规范的行业氛围。**

——美国广播电台Beats 1，2015年12月13日

With Beats Music and Rhapsody, you have to pay for a premium package in order to access my albums. And that places a perception of value on what I've created. On Spotify, they don't have any settings or any kind of qualifications for who gets what music. I think that people should feel that there is a value to what musicians have created, and that's that.

在流媒体平台 Beats Music[1] 和 Rhapsody[2] 上,用户需要升级至高级套餐才能收听我的专辑。这让我觉得自己创作的音乐是有价值的事物。而声破天平台上却没有类似的设置,用户可以随心所欲地收听一切音乐。我认为人们应该意识到音乐家们的创作具有价值,仅此而已。

——《时代周刊》,2014 年 11 月 13 日

Everything new, like Spotify, all feels to me a bit like a grand experiment. And I'm not willing to contribute my life's work to an experiment that I don't feel fairly compensates the writers, producers, artists, and creators of this music.

声破天平台等一切新鲜事物,对我来说都有点像一场大规模的实验。我认为在这场实验中,音乐的作者、制作人、艺人及创作者都无法从中取得相应的报酬,因而不愿把毕生心血投入其中。

——雅虎网,2014 年 11 月 6 日

I didn't think that it would be shocking to anyone [not to release *1989*

1　Beats Music:原苹果旗下流媒体音乐平台,于 2015 年 11 月 30 日关闭服务。
2　Rhapsody:流媒体音乐平台,是美国最早的大型音乐服务商之一,2016 年开始以 Napster 品牌名提供服务。

on Spotify]. With as many ways as artists are personalizing their musical distribution, it didn't occur to me that this would be anything that anyone would talk about. But I could never have expected so many text messages, emails and phone calls from other artists, writers and producers saying thank you.

我觉得不在声破天上架专辑《1989》不是件什么稀奇事。毕竟艺人们各有多种多样的音乐发行方式，我的这一决定实在不值一谈。但我从未想到，会有这么多艺人、作者和制作人通过信息、电子邮件和电话向我表示感谢。

——美国杂志《好莱坞报道》，2014年12月17日

I'm sure you are aware that Apple Music will be offering a free 3 month trial to anyone who signs up for the service. I'm not sure you know that Apple Music will not be paying writers, producers, or artists for those three months.
I find it to be shocking, disappointing, and completely unlike this historically progressive and generous company.

大家都知道，苹果音乐将为其平台注册用户提供3个月的免费试用服务。但不知大家是否知晓，在这3个月的试用期内，苹果音乐不会向音乐创作者、制作人及艺人支付任何报酬。
这项颇为震惊、令人大失所望的条款，与该公司历来引领进步、慷慨大方的行事风格相去甚远。

——致苹果音乐的公开信，2015年6月21日

The contracts [with Apple Music] had just gone out to my friends, and one of them sent me a screenshot of one of them. I read the term "zero percent compensation to rights holders." Sometimes I'll wake up in the middle of the night and I'll write a song and I can't sleep until I finish it, and it was like that with the letter [to Apple Music].

我的朋友们刚拿到与苹果音乐的合同,就有人给我发了一张合同的截图,上面写着:"版权持有人所获报酬为零。"有时候,我会半夜醒来写歌,写完之前都无心睡眠,致苹果音乐的公开信也是这样写完的。

——美国杂志《名利场》,2015年8月11日

Apple treated me like I was a voice of a creative community that they actually cared about. And I found it really ironic that the multi-billion-dollar company reacted to criticism with humility, and the start-up with no cash flow [Spotify] reacted to criticism like a corporate machine.

苹果公司视我为创作者们的代表,对我倍加重视。讽刺的是,面对批评,这家市值数十亿美元的公司表现得如此谦逊,而尚无现金流的初创公司声破天却像台企业机器。

——美国杂志《名利场》,2015年8月11日

What people who are forecasting the downfall of the music industry don't think about is that there is a still a huge percentage of the country who drive their kids to school every day and play a CD and listen to it with their kids—there's a CD in the CD player in their car. So I understand that the industry's changing and a lot of people are streaming. However, there are a lot of people who aren't.

那些预测音乐行业已行至穷途末路的人并未意识到，全国范围内还有相当数量的人会在每天驾车送孩子上学的路上播放碟片，和孩子们一起听音乐——他们车上的光盘播放器里还有碟片。我知道音乐界正处于变革时期，很多人正在收听流媒体音乐。但事实不能以此一概而论。

——美国新闻电台节目 *All Things Considered*，2014年10月31日

Target has always been an amazing partner. They really invest in an artist, and I think that they invest in the idea of an album. You know, people like to talk about album sales going downhill and all that, but with partnerships like Target and with, you know, partners like that, they put the album at the forefront of what they do and they really celebrate it, which is what I love.

塔吉特[1]一直以来都是位了不起的合作伙伴。他们真正为艺人投资，也为专辑的理念投资。虽然人们喜欢谈论（实体）专辑销量下降等话题，但与塔吉特等伙伴合作时，他们会将专辑作为一切工作的前提，为专辑庆祝，而这正是我热爱塔吉特之处。

——《红》塔吉特豪华版专辑发行派对，2012年10月22日

I've been very optimistic and enthusiastic about the state of the music industry, and thankfully so have my fans. And they proved that they're ready

---

1 塔吉特公司（Target）：美国第二大零售商，与泰勒多次合作发行专属版唱片。

and willing to invest in music and pay their hard-earned money to buy music. And I think it made an incredible statement, especially in this time in music.

我一直对音乐行业的现状抱有乐观和热情，幸运的是，我的歌迷们也是如此。他们已经证明自己愿意并已准备好为音乐投资，用其辛苦所得购买音乐作品。我觉得这是意义非凡的宣言，对此时此刻的音乐界来说尤为如此。

——《早安美国》(*Good Morning America*)，2014年11月11日

We all have to step up and make albums that are good, top to bottom, if selling albums is still important. It is to me, but a lot of artists have already given up on that. I have friends who just think it's not attainable, which I feel is a very defeatist way to look at life.

如果销售专辑仍然重要，业内人士都应行动起来，制作出任何方面都品质优良的专辑。这对我来说很重要，但很多艺人已经放弃这条路了。我有些朋友认为这是天方夜谭，我觉得这是在以失败主义的目光看待生活。

——英国《每日电讯报》，2015年5月23日

I think that the way that the music industry is changing so quickly, we can learn something from every big release, anything that connects with people... I think that what we need to start doing is catering our release plans to our own career, to our own fans, and really get in tune with them. I've been on the internet for hours every single night figuring out what these people want from me.

我认为当今音乐行业如此日新月异，我们可以从每次大型（音乐作品的）发行活动中，从与人们产生联结的事物中吸取经验……我们现在要做的，就是根据各自事业和粉丝的具体情况制定发行计划，做到真正与之同频。我每晚都要在网上泡几个小时，就是为了弄清人们对我的期望。

——美国新闻电台节目 *All Things Considered*，2014年10月31日

If you look at... how people used to gather around a record player to listen to music, it was such a social event. And now these days we have, I think, a responsibility to try and turn music back into a social event... I think it's really kind of exciting that we have so many outlets now to make a song back into something that people not only listen to, but kind of assign to their memories and talk about with their friends.

如果你回想一下……过去人们围在唱片机前听音乐，那简直算得上是一种社交活动。而如今，我觉得我们有责任努力让音乐重新变回一种社交活动……我觉得令人兴奋的点在于，现在有多种方式让歌曲不仅为人们所听，还能融入听者的记忆，成为他们与朋友交谈的话题。

——澳大利亚电台节目《凯尔与杰基·欧秀》
（*The Kyle & Jackie O Show*），2019年4月29日

My generation was raised being able to flip channels if we got bored, and we read the last page of the book when we got impatient. We want to be caught off guard, delighted, left in awe. I hope the next generation's artists will continue to think of inventive ways of keeping their audiences on their toes, as challenging as that might be.

我们这一代人的成长过程中，无聊了就切换频道，没耐心了就翻开书的最后一页看结局。我们追求猝不及防、欣喜若狂和惊叹不已的感觉。我希望下一代艺人也能继续想些新颖的方法，让观众们时刻准备迎接新鲜的刺激，尽管这是个充满挑战的目标。

——《华尔街日报》，2014年7月7日

It's really important to me to see eye to eye with a label regarding the future of our industry. I feel so motivated by new opportunities created by the streaming world and the ever changing landscape of our industry... I also feel strongly that streaming was founded on and continues to thrive based on the magic created by artists, writers, and producers.

我非常重视与唱片公司就着眼于音乐行业的未来达成共识。流媒体服务和日新月异的音乐界带来了许多新机遇，我为此倍受鼓舞……我还强烈地感受到，艺人、创作者和制作人的奇思妙想是流媒体的立身之本，是其蓬勃发展的关键所在。

——照片墙，2018年11月19日

As part of my new contract with Universal Music Group, I asked that any sale of their Spotify shares result in a distribution of money to their artists, non-recoupable... I see this as a sign that we are headed towards positive change for creators—a goal I'm never going to stop trying to help achieve.

我在与环球音乐集团签订的新合同中，请求集团将其所有出售声破天股份的所得，以不可扣除的方式返还给旗下艺人……我将此视为我们一同携手，向为创作者们带来积极改变迈进的信号——而这也是我将一直为之奋斗的目标。

——照片墙，2018年11月19日

I spent 10 years of my life trying rigorously to purchase my masters outright and was then denied that opportunity… God, I would have paid so much for them! Anything to own my work that was an actual sale option, but it wasn't given to me.

10年来，我一直积极争取直接买回自己的专辑母带，但我的请求后来遭到了拒绝……天啊，我本想花大价钱买下它们！任何能让我拿回自己母带的条件我都会予以考虑，但我连这样的条件都没拿到。

——谈及专辑母带被卖给斯库特·布劳恩，美国杂志《公告牌》，
2019年12月11日

I was so knocked on my ass by the sale of my music, and to whom it was sold.

自己的音乐被卖掉令我不知所措，得知买主是谁更如晴天霹雳。

——《时代周刊》，2023年12月6日

With the Scooter thing, my masters were being sold to someone who actively wanted them for nefarious reasons, in my opinion.

在我看来，我的专辑母带版权被卖给了斯库特，就是卖给了一直以来对它们虎视眈眈、企图占有的人。

——谈及前6张专辑母带被卖给斯库特·布劳恩，
《时代周刊》，2023年12月6日

This is probably one of my last opportunities as an artist to grasp onto that kind of success. So I don't know, like, as I'm reaching 30, I'm like, "I want to work really hard while society is still tolerating me being successful."

这可能是我最后几次以艺人的身份取得这样的成功。我也不确定，我快30岁了，我的想法是："趁着社会还能容许我成功，我要加倍努力地工作。"

——谈及制作专辑《恋人》，纪录片《美利坚女士》，2020年1月23日

My dad, my mom, and my brother come up with some of the best ideas in my career.
I always joke that we're a small family business.

我的爸爸、妈妈和弟弟在我的职业生涯中提出了一些绝妙想法。
所以我一直开玩笑说我们是个小型家族企业。

——《时代周刊》，2023年12月6日

《随你怎么说》：

名人与争议

People can think about me any way they want to—as long as they do think of me.

人们怎么想我都行——只要他们还能想起我就好。

——美国杂志《乡村音乐周刊》，
2007年12月3日

You become a brand as soon as you sell one thing, so you can either recognize it and embrace it or you can deny it and pretend it's not happening.

一旦卖出去了某件东西，你就成了一个品牌，所以要么你承认它并接受它，要么就否认它并装作无事发生。

——美国ABC新闻，2012年10月26日

I just try not to get too territorial about what's personal time and what's professional time... This is what I've asked for for my entire life. This is the one thing that I wanted. And the fact that I actually get to do that one thing that I've always wanted—I just don't think I'm ever gonna want to complain about it.

我尽量不把私人时间和工作时间划分得太清楚……这是我的毕生所求，是我梦寐以求之事。如今，我可以做自己一直梦想的事——我没理由再为此抱怨什么。

——《时代周刊》网站视频，2009年4月24日

You can't believe too much of your positive hype, and you can't believe too much of your negative press—**you live somewhere in between.**

你不能太相信关于自己的正面炒作，也不能太在意自己的负面新闻——**你要在两者间寻找立足点。**

——美国杂志《名利场》，2015年8月11日

I just feel like you have to have a perception change when your life shifts into the gear of everybody knows who you are. You have to focus on thinking about it in the perspective of: I'm gonna go shopping right now. It's not gonna take the amount of time that it used to take before people knew who I was. It's gonna take double. And I'm cool with that, because this is what I wanted and I'm one of the lucky people who actually got what they wanted in life.

我觉得，人人都认识你的时候，你得在观念上有所改变。你得集中精力，从以下几个角度思考问题：我现在准备去购物。比起出名前，现在购物要花费更多时间。我得花双倍的时间。我对此很淡定，

因为这就是我想要的,我是真正实现自己梦想生活的幸运儿之一。
——英国音乐访谈节目 The Hot Desk,2009年5月

Playing stadiums... walking down the street... I'd choose playing stadiums. It's a trade-off. There's no way to travel two roads at once. You pick one. And if you don't like the road you're on, you change direction. You don't sit there and go, "Oh, I wish I could have all the good things in the world and none of the bad things." It doesn't work like that.

在体育馆里演出……还是走在街上……我会选在体育馆里演出。这需要权衡。你无法同时涉足两条路,只能选择其中一条。如果你不喜欢脚下的路,换个方向就好。但你不能坐在原地抱怨道:"哦,我希望拥有世间一切好事,所有坏事都离我远远的。"现实不会如此。
——英国杂志《新音乐速递》(New Musical Express),
2015年10月9日

I like to have fun, and I like to be happy, and I like to have a level of spontaneity in my life and just go off on a whim here. And that's the part of my brain that's an artist, and then there's the part of my brain that also understands that there's, like, a harsh reality to every single one of my actions.

我喜欢找乐子、喜欢快乐,生活中喜欢在一定程度上随心而为,做些心血来潮的事。这是我脑中属于艺术家的那部分,还有一部分的我明白自己的每个行为都要面临严酷的现实。
——瑞典与挪威合办脱口秀节目 Skavlan,2012年11月9日

If I know I can't deal with talking to people that day, I just don't go out. I just have to wake up in the morning and say, how am I feeling today? If someone asks for a picture, am I gonna feel imposed upon today because I'm dealing with my own stuff? Am I gonna take my own stuff out on some innocent 14-year-old today and be in a bad mood? Okay, maybe not... Maybe I won't leave the house.

如果我知道自己某天不在能和人交谈的状态里，就不会出门。早上醒来问问自己今天感觉如何？如果有人来要合影，我会不会觉得勉强，因为还在为自己的事烦心？我会不会把烦心事带来的情绪宣泄在14岁的天真孩子身上，会不会心情欠佳？好吧，也许不要……也许还是不出门了吧。

——《时尚先生》杂志，2014年10月20日

I don't know if I'll have kids. It's impossible not to picture certain scenarios and how you would try to convince them that they have a normal life when, inevitably, there will be strange men pointing giant cameras at them from the time they are babies.

我不知道自己是否会有孩子。我会禁不住想象某些场景，想象从婴儿时起，就有奇怪的人扛着硕大的摄像机对准你的孩子，你还得努力让孩子们相信他们拥有正常的生活。

——时尚杂志 *InStyle*，2014年11月

I'm realistic about the fact that millions of people don't have time in their day to maintain a complex profile of who I am. They're busy with their work and their kids and their husband or their boyfriend and their friends. They only have time to come up with about two or three adjectives to describe people in the public eye. And that's okay. As long as those three adjectives aren't *train wreck*, *mess*, *terrible*.

我清楚地认识到，大部分人都没什么时间深入了解我是谁。他们忙于自己的工作和孩子，忙于自己的丈夫或男友，忙于自己的朋友。他们只有想出两三个词的时间来形容公众人物。这没关系。只要那两三个形容我的词不是骇人听闻、一塌糊涂和糟糕透顶就好。

——《时尚先生》杂志，2014年10月20日

There is a little bit of an imbalance where all these people know aspects of your personality. They feel they know you, they know your cats' names and all this stuff. But at the same time, you're meeting them for the first time.

有点不平衡的地方在于，大家了解你性格的方方面面。他们觉得自己认识你，知道你宠物猫的名字等一切信息。但与此同时，你才第一次见到他们。

——美国广播电台Beats 1，2015年12月13日

I do not give an edited version of myself to my friends. [And] anytime I read one of those tabloid articles that says, "A source close to Swift says," it's always incorrect. None of my friends are talking, and they know *everything*.

我不会在朋友面前粉饰真实的自我。每次看到小报文章上写"泰勒身边的消息人士称",全部都是捏造的报道。我的朋友们了解我的一切,但没人泄露任何信息。

——美国杂志《名利场》,2015年8月11日

If you give people one thing to talk about they multiply it by 50, and they make all these sensationalized stories up about you. If you give people zero to talk about, anything multiplied by zero is still zero.

如果你给人们提供一件事作谈资,他们就会对其大肆加工,然后编造出各种各样耸人听闻的故事。如果你不给人们提供任何谈资,他们便没了加工故事的原料。

——英国访谈节目《格拉汉姆·诺顿秀》
(*The Graham Norton Show*),2014年10月10日

You know what I've found works even better than an NDA? Looking someone in the eye and saying, "Please don't tell anyone about this."

你知道什么比保密协议更能让人保守秘密吗?看着他们的眼睛,说:"**请你一定不要告诉任何人。**"

——《滚石》杂志,2014年9月8日

There are a lot of really easy ways to dispel rumors. If they say you are pregnant, all you have to do is continue to not be pregnant and not have a baby. If the rumor is that you have fake friendships, all you have to do is continue to be there for each other. And when we're all friends in fifteen years and raising our kids together, maybe somebody will look back and go, "That was kind of ridiculous what we said about Taylor and her friends."

能轻易击碎流言蜚语的方法有很多。要是他们传你怀孕了,你只需不怀孕,不生孩子。要是谣言说你和朋友是塑料友谊,你们只需要一直陪在彼此身边。等我们做了15年朋友,等我们一起养大彼此的孩子,也许有人想起往事,会说:"之前关于泰勒和她朋友们的传言简直是无稽之谈。"

——Vogue,2016年4月14日

I look at some of my best friends who are doing the most amazing work, creating the most amazing things, setting the best example for women and girls—and because of that they're the biggest targets.
There's a really dark side of humanity and a very dark corner of the internet, and they know that the most value will be if they can take down someone who is really doing good things.

我的一些好朋友们正从事着最了不起的工作,创作最了不起的作品,为成年女性和女孩们树立最好的榜样——她们也因此成了某些人最大的攻击目标。
人性存在至暗之处,网络上也有阴暗的角落,这些攻击者们知道,要是能将这些从事高尚事业的人拽入泥潭,他们就能从中获益。

——英国《太阳报》,2014年10月27日

I think the reason a lot of celebrities feel insecure and want to stop eating altogether is because they see so many pictures of themselves on a daily basis. It's unhealthy how many times you see your own image—it's just constant. When you see something enough, you're going to tear it down to the point where some days you feel like you're not even pretty.

许多名人没有安全感,甚至断食,我觉得根源在于他们每天都要被自己的照片狂轰滥炸。看太多自己的照片不利于健康——何况是持续性地看。自己的形象反复出现在眼前,总有一天你会因为觉得自己不够漂亮而将照片撕碎。

——英国时尚周刊 *Glamour*,2009 年 7 月 1 日

I think as a songwriter you have to be pretty well aware of who you are as a person, but then I think you also have to have one eye on what people think of you and kind of what the general perception is of you out in the world. And, um, in the last couple of years I've noticed there's been sort of a pretty sensational fictionalization of my personal life. I mean, to the point where it's just sort of like, "Wow, that too?"

作为一名词曲作者,你得对自己有非常清晰的洞察,也得关注他人眼中的自己,关注外界对你的整体看法。过去几年间,我注意到自己的私人生活已经被编排得出神入化、耸人听闻,甚至已经到了能让我惊呼"哇,这也能编?"的地步了。

——歌曲《空白格》解说,出自专辑《1989》(大机器电台发布特辑版),2018 年 12 月 13 日

If I could talk to my 19-year-old self, I'd just say, "Hey, you know, you're gonna date just like a normal 20-something should be allowed to, but you're going to be a national lightning rod for slut-shaming."

如果能和19岁的自己说说话,我会说:"嗨,你会像其他20多岁的人一样约会,但你会因为那几次约会背上轻浮放荡的骂名。"

——*Vogue*,"泰勒·斯威夫特快答73问",
2016年4月19日

I don't like seeing slide shows of guys I've apparently dated. I don't like giving comedians the opportunity to make jokes about me at awards shows. I don't like it when headlines read "Careful, Bro, She'll Write a Song About You," because it trivializes my work. And most of all, I don't like how all these factors add up to build the pressure so high in a new relationship that it gets snuffed out before it even has a chance to start.

我不想看自己约会对象的图片集,不想给喜剧演员在颁奖典礼上开我玩笑的机会,不喜欢"小心点兄弟,她要把你写进歌里了"那样的头条标题,因为这都是对我工作的贬损。最重要的是,我不喜欢这一切积土成山,成为巨大的压力,在新恋情的火花尚未燃起前就将其一头压灭。

——《滚石》杂志,2014年9月8日

I just decided I wasn't willing to provide them that kind of entertainment anymore. I wasn't going to go out on dates and have them be allowed to take pictures and say whatever they wanted about our body language. I wasn't going to sit next to somebody and flirt with them for five minutes, because I know the next day he'll be rumored to be my boyfriend. I just kind of took the narrative back.

当时我决心不再让他们抓住任何消遣我的由头。我不出门约会，不让他们拍到我，不给他们随意品评我和约会对象的身体语言的机会。我不再会和邻座的人打趣5分钟，因为我知道第二天他就会成为我的绯闻男友。我不会让他们拿到任何可以借题发挥的素材。

——*Vogue*，2015年2月13日

They can say whatever they want about my personal life because I know what my personal life is, and it involves a lot of TV and cats and girlfriends. But I don't like it when they start to make cheap shots at my songwriting. Because there's no joke to be made there.

他们可以随意对我的私生活评头论足，因为我知道自己真实的私生活里都是电视节目、猫咪和女性朋友。但我不喜欢他们对我的歌曲创作说三道四，因为我的歌曲创作没有任何玩笑可开。

——英国《卫报》，2014年8月23日

I feel like my personal life was really, really discussed and criticized and debated and talked about, to a point where it made me feel kind of almost tarnished in a way, you know? And the discussion wasn't about music, and it broke my heart that I had made an album that I was proud of [*Red*] and I was touring the world and playing to sold-out stadiums, and still they managed to want to only talk about my personal life…
It was at the end of recording [*1989*] that I began to feel like my life was mine again and my music was at the forefront again and I was living

my life on my own terms, and I really no longer cared what people were saying about me. And that was when I started to see people talk less about the things that didn't matter.

我的私生活被不断讨论、不断批评,成为争论的焦点、成为大众的谈资,甚至好像成了我的污点。人们讨论的不是我的音乐,就算我写了一张自己引以为豪的专辑《红》,就算我在全球范围内举行巡演,就算我的巡演场馆里座无虚席,他们只想窥探我的私生活,我觉得很伤心……

直到专辑《1989》录制后期,我才感觉重新掌控了自己的生活,音乐重回我的生活重心,一切都由我做主,我也不再对外界的流言蜚语耿耿于怀。从那时起,我发现人们也不怎么谈论我那些微不足道的事情了。

——歌曲《释怀》解说,出自专辑《1989》
(大机器电台发布特辑版),2018 年 12 月 13 日

I would much rather my personal life be sung about. I think it sounds nicer that way, rather than me talking about it in some magazine article or something.

我宁愿把自己的私人生活唱出来。听起来要比在某些杂志报道里讲述自己的私人生活好得多。

——英国访谈节目《乔纳森·罗斯秀》(*The Jonathan Ross Show*),
2012 年 10 月 6 日

There are so many people in the town where I live, Hendersonville [outside of Nashville], that think they do have a song written about 'em.

You go out into this big world and you go on tour with all these people, and you go back and it's still a small town and they still gossip about it. I think it's one of everybody's favorite things to talk about—who my songs are written about.

我居住在纳什维尔郊区的亨德森维尔，那里的很多人都觉得有些歌写的就是他们。你去闯荡这广阔世界，和许多人一起开巡演，回到这座小城，还是无法免于城里人的八卦。我觉得这是大家最爱谈论的话题之一——我的歌里写的都是谁。

——美国杂志《娱乐周刊》，2007年7月25日

I think that as a songwriter you're supposed to stay open, and you're supposed to stay vulnerable, and you're supposed to feel pain and feel it intensely. As a celebrity, you're kind of encouraged to put up these emotional walls and block out all the voices saying terrible things about you and to you. And so they're mixed messages, and I'm trying to kind of like walk a tightrope in between the two.

我觉得词曲作者应该保持开放敏感的心态，善于捕捉痛苦，放大对痛苦的感知。而作为名人，你最好竖起情绪保护墙，将所有关于你或针对你的恶语中伤挡在墙外。两者的要求截然不同，我试着在这两者间寻求微妙的平衡。

——英国广播电台BBC Radio 1，2014年10月9日

When you put out one song or you're in one movie, what you don't realize is that no matter what, you're a role model, whether you choose to embrace it or whether you choose to ignore it. And I just choose to embrace it because I feel like it's the biggest honor in the world when a mom comes up to me and says, "My eight-year-old daughter listens to your music, and I think that it's so great that she looks up to you."

当你发行一首新歌或参演一部电影，不知不觉间就已经成了一个榜样，不管你对此欣然接受还是置之不理，事实就是如此。我会欣然接受这一身份，因为觉得这是世间莫大的荣幸，特别是有的妈妈来到我面前，说："我8岁的女儿听你的音乐，她很崇拜你，我很高兴。"
——美国脱口秀节目《艾伦秀》，2008年11月11日

If you're kind of just taking accountability and responsibility for your own actions, it's kind of a natural thing that happens where, you know, all of the sudden you have parents coming up and thanking you and you're just sort of like, "You're welcome?"

如果你为自己的行为负责，自然就会有父母突然上前向你道谢，你会惊讶地回答"不客气？"
——"泰勒·斯威夫特1989"，2014年10月27日

I think about what—if I'm lucky enough to have grandkids someday—what they would say if they went back and looked back at pictures and videos and things like that. And I'm sure they'd laugh at me and, like, make fun of my awkwardness and things like that, but I would never want to embarrass them.
And it's interesting because it's like this whole role model question. Like,

are you a role model? Do you think about the little kids in the front row when you're doing all the things you're doing in your life? I think that's an unnecessary pressure to put on yourself, but it's easier when you make it about your own life, your own legacy, when you kind of bring it in-house and you're like, "What if I have a five-year-old someday?"

我在想，要是某天我有幸有了孙辈——如果他们回头看那些（我的）照片、视频之类的东西，他们会说什么？我敢说他们一定会嘲笑我，一定会拿我的尴尬事取笑，但我绝不想让他们难堪。

有趣的是，这涉及榜样问题。你得扪心自问，你算榜样吗？你在生活中的所作所为，有没有特意为小孩子们考虑过？我觉得你大可不必将成为榜样视为压力，当你在生活中践行，让它成为你的宝贵品质；当你与公众换位思考，想一想"要是某天我有个5岁的孩子呢？"，一切就会轻松得多。

——"泰勒·斯威夫特1989"，2014年10月27日

You don't want to feel like you're the national president of the babysitters club, but you do want to try to do good things and make ripples and good echoes in society and culture.

你肯定不至于真的去做全国育儿俱乐部主席来约束自己的行为，但你确实想做些好事，为社会和文化的发展做出贡献，带来良性影响。

——"泰勒·斯威夫特1989"，2014年10月27日

It's a really interesting idea that you wear shorts and all of a sudden it's very edgy. Which, you know, on the bright side gives you room to grow—**I don't have to do too much to shock people.**

穿上短裤人就能变得时髦起来,这个观点很有趣。积极的一面是,它给你提供了换个新面貌的途径——**我不用刻意做些夸张事来震惊他人。**

——《滚石》杂志,2012年10月25日

I knew other people can make partying look cute and edgy but, if I did, people were going to twist it into this tragic America's-sweetheart-goes-off-the-rails-and-loses-her-mind thing. So I just made sure that that could never be written about me, and I don't feel like I missed out.

其他人可以让开派对这事显得可爱又时髦,但我知道要是我也这么做,人们就会将这事扭曲成"美国甜心一反常态丧失理智"的悲剧。所以,我从不做那些落人话柄的事,也不觉得自己错过了什么。

——*Vogue*(英国版),2014年11月

I feel like whatever you say about whether you do or don't [have sex], it makes people picture you naked. And as much as possible, I'm going to avoid that. It's self-preservation, really.

我觉得不管你就有没有发生性关系这事发表何种言论,都会让人们联想到你赤身裸体的样子。我尽力避免这种情况发生。这是自我保护,真的。

——《滚石》杂志,2009年3月5日

I fought the idea of having security for a very long time, because I really value normalcy... I like to be able to take a drive by myself. Haven't done that in six years... The sheer number of men we have in a file who have showed up at my house, showed up at my mom's house, threatened to either kill me, kidnap me, or marry me. This is the strange and sad part of my life that I try not to think about. I try to be lighthearted about it, because I don't ever want to be scared... And when I have security, I don't have to be scared.

我一度觉得自己不需要安全感，因为我真的很想过正常的生活……我很喜欢一个人开车兜风。尽管上一次开车兜风还是6年前……但现在有人出现在我家和我妈妈家，有人威胁我说要杀了我、绑架我或娶我。我们将这些人记录在册，数量之多，令人咋舌。这就是我现在生活中反常又令人沮丧的一面，我试着不去想它。我不想担惊受怕，所以尽量轻松面对……有安全感的时候，就不会担惊受怕了。

——《时尚先生》杂志，2014年10月20日

There was a guy we had nicknamed Aquaman. And I don't want to speak ill of [him], you know—he wasn't well. But he decided that we were married and decided to swim across... the ocean about a mile to get to my house. And then the cops came or something and then he swam all the way back. He should be an Olympic athlete, actually.

我们给这个人取了个绰号叫"水行侠"[1]。我不想说他的坏话，你知道——他有些健康问题。他臆想已经和我结婚，决定游过……大约一英里的海到我家去。后来安保或警察来了，他就又游了回去。他应该去参加奥运会，真的。

——英国广播电台 BBC Radio 1，2015年2月24日

Something that scares me a little bit is how valuable it would be to find something that I've done wrong, or to find something that is problematic about me. You know, I do have moments where I get really scared, like, who's trying to take pictures in my hotel room window? You live your life with the blinds drawn, like, in every room you go into. And that's the part that kind of gets to me sometimes, is, like, every day, like right now, there's someone in TMZ trying to dig through my trash and figure out what I did wrong.

有时候让我有点后怕的是，找出我做了什么错事，或者找出我身上有什么问题，能换取巨大的价值。我也有非常害怕的时刻，比如，谁在努力透过我酒店房间的窗户拍照？你生活的每个房间都要拉下百叶窗。这就是有时让我感到不安的地方。比如，每一天，或者就在此时此刻，TMZ小报的狗仔可能正在埋头苦翻我的垃圾，试图找出我做了什么错事。

——美国广播电台 Beats 1，2015年12月13日

---

1 此处指2013年3月15日凌晨，警方发现一名男性在泰勒的罗德岛住宅附近游泳。这名来自芝加哥的狂热粉丝称："别担心我！我只是游泳去看泰勒！"该男子随后被捕。

《随你怎么说》：名人与争议

I think the dream and the nightmare of being framed comes from, like, I could do nothing wrong, I could sit in my house with the cats all day, and somehow there could be an article about, like, me buying a house in a place I've never been or dating a guy I've never met. But then you take it a step further, and in nightmare world, it's being framed for murder.

我觉得那些和栽赃陷害有关的噩梦来源于，我可能没做错什么事，可能整天都和猫咪待在家里，但不知怎么就有文章写我在某处购置了房产，而我甚至都没去过那地方；或者写我和某位男士约会，但实际上我都没见过那人。然后我自己就进一步借题发挥，在噩梦里就被栽赃成了杀人凶手。

——美国脱口秀节目《艾伦秀》，2014年10月27日

My overall thought process went something like, "Wow, I can't believe I won! This is awesome. Don't trip and fall. I'm gonna get to thank the fans, this is so cool! Oh! Kanye West is here. Cool haircut... What are you doing there?" And then, "Ouch." And then, "I guess I'm not gonna get to thank the fans."

我当时的心路历程[1]大概是："哇，不敢相信我赢了！太棒了！别被绊倒了。我待会要感谢粉丝们，这太酷了！哦！坎耶·韦斯特在这

---

1 此条及随后4条的所指事件，皆为2009年9月13日的MTV音乐录影带大奖颁奖典礼上，坎耶·韦斯特上台打断了泰勒的获奖感言，并抢走了她的话筒。次年，泰勒在MTV音乐录影带大奖上表演了写给韦斯特的歌曲《无辜者》。虽然两人曾短暂（或表面）和好，但又在2016年的歌词争端和卡戴珊录音视频事件中走向冰点，两人的恩怨纠纷持续至今。

里。好酷的发型……你在那里做什么?"然后心想,"哎"。最后,"我估计没机会感谢粉丝们了"。

——美国脱口秀节目《观点》(*The View*),2009年9月15日

It just all happened really fast and it took a second to realize what was going on. I was really confused when it was going down 'cause the crowd started booing and I didn't know why. And I've never been on a stage with the entire crowd booing before. So I was just devastated 'cause I thought I'd done something wrong.

一切发生得太快,一秒钟后我才意识到发生了什么。当时的一切都让我一头雾水,观众们开始发出嘘声,我不知道那是因为什么。而且我从来没在台上遇到观众们集体嘘声的情况。我备受打击,以为自己做错了什么事。

——美国"NBC年度人物"系列节目,2009年11月26日

I try to focus on what people did for me coming to my defense and Twittering their support. That—that's what I try to focus on, because I don't wanna—to have a grudge. I really just appreciate how nice everyone was to me when I had a really, really weird day.

我试着把注意力放在人们为我做的事情上,他们为我辩护,还在推特上支持我。这就是我试图关注的东西,因为我不想——卷入怨恨纠纷中。在度过了非常、非常奇怪的一天后,我很感激大家现在如此友好地对待我。

——美国"NBC年度人物"系列节目,2009年11月26日

The song "Innocent" is about something that really intensely affected me emotionally. And it took awhile to write this one. I was fortunate enough to get the chance to perform this song on the VMAs, and that's the first time that anyone ever heard it. And putting out an album called *Speak Now*, where you're supposed to say what you feel when you know how you feel, I felt that performing that song on that particular awards show was appropriate.

歌曲《无辜者》写的是一件曾经对我情绪影响很大的事。写这首歌花了不少时间。我很幸运有机会在MTV音乐录影带大奖上表演这首歌,那也是大家第一次听到这首歌。我当时发行了一张名为《爱的告白》的专辑,在那张专辑中要诚实地表达自己的所知所感,当时我觉得,在那个特殊的颁奖典礼上表演这首歌挺合适的。

——歌曲《无辜者》解说,出自专辑《爱的告白》
(大机器电台发布特辑版),2018年12月13日

I feel like I wasn't ready to be friends with [Kanye West] until I felt like he had some sort of respect for me, and he wasn't ready to be friends with me until he had some sort of respect for me—so it was the same issue, and we both reached the same place at the same time.

我觉得自己还没准备好和坎耶·韦斯特成为朋友,除非我感觉到他对我抱有些许尊重;他也没准备好和我成为朋友,除非他对我抱有些许尊重——所以我们面临着同一个问题,我们同时来到了相同的境地。

——美国杂志《名利场》,2015年8月11日

A couple of years ago, someone called me a snake on social media, and it caught on. And then a lot of people were calling me a lot of things on social media. And I went through some really low times for a while because of it. I went through some times when I didn't know if I was gonna get to do this anymore. And I guess the snakes [onstage], I wanted to send a message to you guys that if someone uses name-calling to bully you on social media, and even if a lot of people jump on board with it, that doesn't have to defeat you. It can strengthen you instead.

几年前，有人在社交媒体上称我恶毒如蛇[1]，这骂名迅速蔓延开来。随后许多人都在社交媒体上以这样或那样的恶名称呼我。我一度因此跌入低谷。我熬过了很多艰难时光，那时我常怀疑自己是否还能维系自己的事业。我想借（舞台上的）蛇道具告诉大家，倘若有人在社交媒体上辱骂你、霸凌你，即使许多人与之同流合污，你也不一定就因此一败涂地，那反而是你可以借力的东风。

——《名誉》世界巡回演唱会，亚利桑那州格伦代尔，
2018年5月8日

When this album comes out, gossip blogs will scour the lyrics for the men they can attribute to each song, as if the inspiration for music is as simple and basic as a paternity test. There will be slideshows of photos backing up each incorrect theory, because it's 2017 and if you didn't see a picture of it, it couldn't have happened right?...

---

1 此处指韦斯特当时的妻子金·卡戴珊称泰勒在歌词争端中撒了谎，卡戴珊在社交媒体上发布了所谓的证据视频，并以蛇代指泰勒，泰勒因此遭受了大规模网暴。

There will be no further explanation.
There will just be **reputation**.

这张专辑（指《名誉》）面世时，八卦博客会细细揣摩每一首歌的歌词，试图为每一首歌找个匹配的男主角，好像音乐灵感就像亲子鉴定项目一样简单直白。他们会找些照片来佐证每个不实的理论，毕竟现在是2017年，没有照片，就不能算眼见为实，对吗？……
除此再无解释。
除此只剩**名誉**。

——《名誉》杂志，2017年11月10日

[Your reputation] is only real if it stops you from getting to know someone where you feel like you can connect with them in a really real way.

除非名誉成为彼此了解的阻碍，阻碍对方了解名誉之下的真实自我，除此情形之外，名誉皆为虚假之物。

——泰勒·斯威夫特NOW秘密演出，2018年6月28日

In the death of her reputation / She felt truly alive.

名誉尽毁/浴火而生。

——诗歌"她为何消失"，《名誉》杂志，2017年11月10日

When the album starts off, it's much more bombastic. It's more like, "Oh, I don't care about what you say about me! I don't care what you say about my reputation! It doesn't matter! Blah!" But, like, then it hits this point on track five ["Delicate"] where it's like, oh God, what happens when you meet somebody that you really want in your life and then you start worrying about what they've heard before they met you? And you start to wonder, like, could something fake like your reputation affect something real like somebody getting to know you?

专辑《名誉》开头的几首歌有些夸大其词，就像在说："哦，我才不在乎你们怎么说我！我才不在乎你们怎么谈论我的名誉！无所谓！不在乎！"但到了曲目五《易碎》，这首歌表达的就像是："天啊，要是遇到了生命中真正想要在一起的人，就会担心他们在遇见你之前就听说过你的事情，你们后续会是什么走向？"你开始思索，名誉之类的虚假之物，会不会影响某人了解真实的你？

——《名誉》专辑秘密试听会，2017年10月

I was pretty proud of coining the term "There will be no explanation. There will just be reputation."... I didn't try to explain the album because I didn't feel that I owed that to anyone. There was a lot that happened over a couple of years that made me feel really, really terrible. And I didn't feel like expressing that to them. I didn't feel like talking about it. I just felt like making music, then going out on the road and doing a stadium tour and doing everything I could for my fans.

创作出"除此再无解释。除此只剩名誉。"的表达让我颇为自豪……我没向大家解释这张专辑，因为我觉得自己不欠任何人这个解释。这几年间发生了很多让我觉得糟糕至极的事。我不想告诉他们我的感受如何，也不想谈论这些事情。我只想好好做音乐，然后

出发去巡演,竭尽所能为歌迷们做一切我能做到的事。
——美国广播电台Beats 1,2019年5月1日

The whole time that I was writing an album [reputation] based on all the facets of a reputation and how it affects you, what it actually means to you, I was surrounded by friends and family and loved ones who never loved me less based on the fluctuations of public opinion.

专辑《名誉》的整体创作围绕着名誉的各个维度、名誉带来的影响,以及名誉于人有何意义展开。专辑创作期间,亲友和爱人陪伴着我,他们对我的爱从未因舆论波动而减损分毫。
——2018年全美音乐奖[1]颁奖典礼,2018年10月9日

This is the proudest and happiest I've ever felt, and the most creatively fulfilled and free I've ever been. Ultimately, we can convolute it all we want, or try to overcomplicate it, but there's only one question. **Are you not entertained?**

这是我最自豪、最开心的时刻,我从未觉得自己在创作上如此充实、如此自由。最重要的,我们可以创作更复杂的作品,或者试着将创作变得更具挑战性,唯一的问题在于:**你是否乐在其中?**
——《时代周刊》,2023年12月6日

---

1 全美音乐奖(American Music Awards,AMAs):与格莱美奖、公告牌音乐奖一起被称为美国三大音乐颁奖礼。

人生智慧

《爱的告白》：

勇敢发声

When I turn 18, I may do something crazy, **like go out and vote or something.**

等我满18岁了，就去做点疯狂的事，**比如出去投票之类。**
——美国杂志《娱乐周刊》，2007年7月25日

I've never thought about any kind of prejudice about women in country music because I never felt like it affected me. I was fortunate enough to come about in a time when I didn't feel that kind of energy at all, and it was always my theory that if you want to play in the same ballgame as the boys, you've got to work as hard as them.

我没思考过乡村音乐界对女性的偏见问题，因为我从未受其影响。我很幸运自己出道以来没有接触过这些负能量。我个人的理念一直是，如果你想同男性同场竞技，就得在工作上付出同等努力。
——美国杂志《公告牌》，2011年12月2日

I don't really think about things as guys versus girls. I never have. I was raised by parents who brought me up to think if you work as hard as guys, you can go far in life.

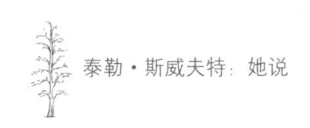

我没怎么思考过男女对立这事,从没想过。我父母从小教育我,只要你足够努力,无论男女,人生路上都能走得长远。

——美国网站"每日野兽",2012年10月22日

You know, Katie Couric is one of my favorite people because she said to me she had heard a quote that she loved [from former secretary of state Madeleine Albright] that said, "There's a special place in hell for women who don't help other women."

凯蒂·柯丽克[1]是我最敬爱的人之一,因为她告诉我,她很喜欢前国务卿马德琳·奥尔布赖特[2]的一句话:"地狱里有个特殊的地方,拒绝帮助其他女性的女人都会去那儿。"

——美国杂志《名利场》,2013年3月15日

I wrote a song called "Mean" about a critic who hated me. I put it out, and all of a sudden, it became an anthem against bullies in schools, which is a refreshing and new take on it. When people say things about me empowering women, that's an amazing compliment. It's not necessarily what I thought I was doing, because I write songs about what I feel. I think there's strength when you're baring your emotions.

---

1 凯蒂·柯丽克(Katie Couric):美国主持人、记者、公益活动家,合作创建了全美娱乐产业基金(Entertainment Industry Foundation)结肠癌研究联盟。
2 马德琳·科贝尔·奥尔布赖特(Madeleine Korbel Albright):1997年1月至2001年1月任美国国务卿,是美国历史上第一位女性国务卿。

歌曲《卑鄙》写的是一名憎恨我的音乐评论家。这首歌发布后，一时间竟成了反抗校园霸凌的主题曲。这种解读令人耳目一新。听到人们说我为女性赋能，我觉得这是很棒的赞美。虽然我写歌时意不在此，当时只是在歌里记录了自己的感想。但我认为，袒露情感能产生力量。

　　——美国网站"每日野兽"，2012年10月22日

I have a lot to learn about politics and feminism—all these huge incredible concepts. I want to end up being really educated about all these big topics that everyone talks about, but, I mean, it's like baby steps, you know? And until I really form an opinion that I feel is educated, I just don't know if I can talk about it.

关于政治和女权主义，我要学习的还有很多——这两个概念太过宏大。我想真正理解这类人人谈论的重大话题，但我现在还在学步阶段。在我思考的观点真正成熟之前，我拿不准要不要谈论它。

　　——*Elle*（加拿大版），2012年11月19日

I feel like at 22 it's my right to vote but it's not my right to tell other people what to do.

我今年22岁，我觉得自己虽然有权行使投票权，但无权告诉别人该怎么做。

　　——美国《大卫深夜脱口秀》（*Late Show with David Letterman*），
　　　　　　　　　　　　　　　　　　　2012年10月23日

In the past I've been reluctant to publicly voice my political opinions, but due to several events in my life and in the world in the past two years, I feel very differently about that now. I always have and always will cast my vote based on which candidate will protect and fight for the human rights I believe we all deserve in this country. I believe in the fight for LGBTQ rights, and that any form of discrimination based on sexual orientation or gender is WRONG. I believe that the systemic racism we still see in this country towards people of color is terrifying, sickening and prevalent.

过去我不愿公开表明自己的政治观点,但在经历了一些事、见证了过去两年间发生的一切后,我现在已经完全改观。我相信在这个国家里,人人都应享有人权,因此无论过去还是将来,我都会把票投给愿意保护人权、愿意为人权奋斗的候选人。我支持维护性少数群体的权利,认为任何基于性取向或性别的偏见都不正当。当前,美国国内针对有色群体的系统性种族主义让人提心吊胆、令人作呕,却仍然大行其道。

——照片墙,2018年10月7日

Invoking racism and provoking fear through thinly veiled messaging is not what I want from our leaders, and I realized that it actually is my responsibility to use my influence against that disgusting rhetoric. I'm going to do more to help. We have a big race coming up next year.

不加掩饰地鼓动种族主义,煽动恐惧情绪,都不是我希望在美国领导人身上看到的行为。我意识到,实际上我有责任利用自己的影响反抗这种政治论调。为此,我要多出些力。明年,我们将迎来一场重要的竞选[1]。

——*Elle*，2019年3月6日

It's very brave to be vulnerable about your feelings in any sense, in any situation. But it's even more brave to be honest about your feelings and who you love when you know that that might be met with adversity from society. So, this [Pride Month] and every month, I want to send out my love and respect to everybody who has been brave enough to be honest about how they feel, to live their lives as they are, as they feel they should be, as they identify. And this is a month where I think we need to celebrate how far we've come. We also need to acknowledge how far we still have left to go.

无论在何种意义和情况下，卸下情感方面的防备都非常勇敢。而更勇敢的是，不顾可能遭受的来自社会方面的阻力，对自己的情感和所爱之人坦诚相待。所以，在这个"骄傲月"[2]和以后每个月，我想向那些在生活中勇敢坦诚自己的情感、勇敢直面自己的本质、遵循自己的感觉、正视自己身份的人致以爱和尊重。在这个月里，我们应该庆祝一路以来取得的一切。我们还要承认，未来任重道远。

——《名誉》巡回演唱会，伊利诺伊州芝加哥，2018年6月2日

I think I was probably 15 the first time I was asked about [feminism]. And

---

1　此处指2020年美国总统大选。接受采访时，泰勒对共和党的执政举措感到失望，更支持民主党的政治主张。

2　2011年，美国前总统布莱克·奥巴马（Barack Obama）将6月设定为性少数群体的"骄傲月"。

so I would just say, "I don't talk about politics. I don't really understand that stuff yet, so I guess I'm just gonna say I'm not [a feminist]." And I wish that when I was younger I would have known that it's simply hoping for gender equality.

我记得大概15岁时，第一次有人问我"女权主义"的问题。我那时说："我不谈论政治。我对政治还一知半解，所以我觉得自己还不算是'女权主义者'。"现在我希望那时的自己能意识到，女权主义其实就是支持性别平等。
　　　　　　　　——"泰勒·斯威夫特1989"，2014年10月27日

I think that when I used to say, "Oh, feminism's not really on my radar," it was because when I was just seen as a kid, I wasn't as threatening. **I didn't see myself being held back until I was a woman.**

我觉得自己过去之所以会说"哦，我没怎么思考过女权主义"，是因为那时大家仅仅把我当作一个孩子，认为我不具备什么威胁性。**直到我成为一名成年女性，才感受到了前行路上的阻力。**
　　　　　　　　——《马克西姆》杂志（*Maxim*），2015年5月11日

I have brought feminism up in every single interview I've done because I think it's important that a girl who's 12 years old understands what that means and knows what it is to label yourself a feminist, knows what it is to be a woman in today's society, in the workplace or in the media or perception. What you should accept from men, what you shouldn't, and how to form your own opinion on that. I think the best thing I can do for them is continue to write songs that *do* make them think about themselves and analyze how they feel about something and then simplify how they feel.

我在每个采访里都会提到女权主义，因为我认为，重要的是让12岁[1]的女孩借此了解女权主义的含义，明白成为女权主义者的意义，理解女性在当今社会、在工作场所、在媒体刻画或公众认知中的处境。你要思考应当从男性那里接受什么，不应当接受什么，以及如何培养自己在这方面的认知。而我能为女孩们做的最大贡献，就是继续写歌，利用歌曲让她们思考自身、分析自己对事物的感受，然后将这些感受升华提炼。

——美国新闻电台节目 *All Things Considered*，2014年10月31日

I don't feel great when I am fed messages, and when I was fed messages as a young girl, that it's more important to be edgy and sexy and cool than anything else. I don't think that those are the right messages to feed girls... My life doesn't gravitate towards being edgy, sexy, or cool... I am imaginative, I am smart, and I'm hardworking. And those things are not necessarily prioritized in pop culture.

被灌输信息的感觉并不好，我年少时他们灌输给我的信息就是没有比变得时髦、性感和酷更重要的事。这并不是应该传递给女孩们的正确信息……我的生活重心不在于追求时髦、性感或酷……我充满想象力，聪明又勤奋。但这些却不是流行文化首要推崇的品质。

——美国电视节目 *CBS This Morning*，2014年10月29日

1　此处年龄为虚指，泛指十几岁的女孩们。

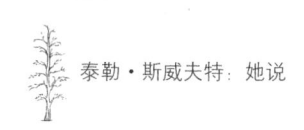

I'm just happy that in 2015, we live in a world where boys can play princesses and girls can play soldiers.

我很开心，2015年，我们生活在一个男孩可以扮演公主，女孩可以扮演战士的世界。
　　——2015年MTV音乐录影带大奖颁奖典礼，2015年8月30日

At some point years and years from now our kids and grandkids will look back on it and say, "Well, you know, look at all the women in office right now. I can't believe there [was] a time when there weren't women presidents."

多年后的某个时刻，我们的子孙后代回首往事时会说："看看现在有多少职场女性，我真不敢相信当年没有女性担任总统。"
　　——美国女性电视频道Lifetime，2008年5月30日

I just struggle to find a woman in music who hasn't been completely picked apart by the media, or scrutinized and criticized for aging, or criticized for fighting aging. It just seems to be much more difficult to be a woman in music and to grow older. I just really hope that I will choose to do it as gracefully as possible.

在音乐行业里，我很难找出一个没被媒体过度指责过的女性，女性不仅会因衰老被过度审视和批评，还会因对抗衰老而遭受批评。在音乐行业，身为女性、年龄渐长都让人举步维艰。我只希望自己可以尽可能从容优雅地老去。
　　——《时代周刊》，2014年11月13日

《爱的告白》：勇敢发声

I open up a magazine and it says, "Who's the hotter mama: J-Lo or Beyoncé?" You don't see, "Who's the hotter dad: Matt Damon or Ben Affleck?" It just doesn't happen. And if we continue this perception that women should be compared to other women and there's a winner and a loser, we're doing ourselves a huge disservice as a society.

我翻开一本杂志，里面写着："哪位妈妈更辣：詹妮弗·洛佩兹[1]还是碧昂斯[2]？"但却不会看到"哪位爸爸更辣：马特·达蒙[3]还是本·阿弗莱克[4]？"根本没有这种内容。如果我们执迷不悟，认为女性就该被互相比较、就该有赢家和输家之分，就是在为整个社会带来巨大危害。

——美国电视节目 *CBS This Morning*，2014年10月29日

One thing that I do believe as a feminist is that, in order for us to have gender equality, we have to stop making it a girl fight and we have to stop being so interested in seeing girls try to tear each other down. It has to be

---

1 詹妮弗·洛佩兹（Jennifer Lopez，昵称J-Lo）：美国女歌手、演员、制片人，曾获世界音乐大奖杰出艺术贡献奖、MTV音乐录影带大奖"迈克尔·杰克逊先锋终身成就奖"（the Michael Jackson Video Vanguard Award）等。

2 碧昂丝（Beyoncé）：美国女歌手，首位前5张个人专辑均获得公告牌200强专辑榜冠军的女歌手，曾获MTV音乐录影带大奖"迈克尔·杰克逊先锋终身成就奖"。

3 马特·达蒙（Matt Damon）：美国男演员，曾获美国金球奖音乐喜剧类最佳男主角，代表作《谍影重重》系列、《火星救援》等。

4 本·阿弗莱克（Ben Affleck）：美国男演员、导演，曾获奥斯卡金像奖最佳影片奖、美国电影电视金球奖最佳导演奖等，代表作《好莱坞庄园》《逃离德黑兰》等。

more about cheering each other on as women.

作为一名女权主义者，我一直坚信的一点是，要想实现性别平等，女性间就该停止竞争，不去凑互相拆台的热闹。作为女性，我们更应为彼此加油鼓劲。

——加拿大电视节目 *Tout le monde en parle*，2014年9月28日

I wouldn't like to think that there's a team of managers or image consultant-type people who are saying, "You need to wear less clothes so you'll sell more albums." But as long as a woman feels like she's expressing her own sexuality or feels empowered looking a certain way onstage, just follow that. I applaud that. But I do think it's harder for women, I honestly do.

我不在乎那群经理或形象顾问说的"你穿得越少，专辑卖得就越多"。只要女性觉得掌握了自身在性方面的话语权，或者觉得在舞台上的某种呈现更有力量，就尽管随心而为吧。我会为其鼓掌。但我也深切意识到，这对女性来说实非易事，真的。

——英国广播电台 BBC Radio 1，2014年10月9日

My friend Ed [Sheeran], no one questions whether he writes everything. In the beginning, I liked to think that we were all on the same playing field. And then it became pretty obvious to me that when you have people sort of questioning the validity of a female songwriter, or making it seem like it's somehow unacceptable to write songs about your real emotions—that it somehow makes you irrational and overemotional—seeing that over the years changed my view.

我的朋友艾德,没人会质疑他是不是自己写歌。职业生涯初期,我以为男性从业者和女性从业者都在同一条起跑线上。但这些年来,显而易见,有人质疑女歌手的创作能力,有人不接受你把自己的真实感受写进歌里——因为觉得那样不够理智还过度情绪化——这些年来目睹的一切让我意识到,大家并不在同一条起跑线上。

——《时代周刊》,2014年11月13日

If a guy shares his experience in writing, he's brave. If a woman shares her experience in writing, she's oversharing and she's overemotional. Or she might be crazy. Or, "Watch out, she'll write a song about you!" That joke is so old. And it's coming from a place of such sexism.

如果男性在写作里分享亲身经历,人们会觉得他勇敢;如果女性在写作里分享亲身经历,人们只会觉得她过度分享、过度情绪化,或者认为她可能疯了,或者发出警告"小心点吧,她会把你写进歌里!"这种玩笑太老掉牙了。实际上这就是性别歧视的典型表现。

——《芭芭拉·沃尔特斯:2014年十大魅力人物》,
2014年12月15日

As the first woman to win Album of the Year at the Grammys twice, I want to say to all the young women out there, there are going to be people along the way who will try to undercut your success or take credit for your accomplishments or your fame. But if you just focus on the work, and you don't let those people sidetrack you, someday when you get where you're going, you'll look around and you will know that it was you and the people who love you who put you there. And that will be the greatest feeling in the world.

作为第一位两度获得格莱美年度专辑奖的女性,我想对在座的各位年轻女性说,这一路上,总会有人贬低你的成就,也会有人将你的成果或声名归功于己。但只要你专心投入工作,不受这些人干扰,某一天你实现了为之奋斗的目标,环顾四周,你会明了,成就自己的是个人努力和爱你的人的支持。而那是世上最美妙的感觉。

——第58届格莱美年度颁奖典礼,2016年2月15日

In 2013, I met a DJ from a prominent country radio station in one of my pre-show meet and greets. When we were posing for the photo, he stuck his hand up my dress and grabbed onto my ass cheek. I squirmed and lurched sideways to get away from him, but he wouldn't let go. At the time, I was headlining a major arena tour and there were a number of people in the room that saw this plus a photo of it happening. I figured that if he would be brazen enough to assault me under these risky circumstances and high stakes, imagine what he might do to a vulnerable, young artist if given the chance.

2013年,在巡演前的一次见面会上,我遇到了一位来自著名乡村音乐电台的DJ[1]。我们摆好姿势准备拍照,就在那时,他把手伸进了我的裙子,抓住了我的屁股。我扭动身体,侧着身子想摆脱他,但他一直没收手。当时,我在举行一场大型巡回演出,见面会的房间

---

1 指丹佛DJ大卫·穆勒(David Mueller),穆勒遭到电台解雇后起诉泰勒诽谤,泰勒反诉其实施性骚扰。

里很多人都看到了这一幕,我们还有一张照片作证。我想,他敢在众目睽睽之下冒着高风险猥亵我,无法想象他要是有机会,会对一个脆弱的年轻艺人做些什么。

——《时代周刊》,2017年12月6日

When I testified, I had already been in court all week and had to watch this man's attorney bully, badger and harass my team including my mother over inane details and ridiculous minutiae, accusing them, and me, of lying... I was angry. In that moment, I decided to forego any courtroom formalities and just answer the questions the way it happened... I'm told it was the most amount of times the word "ass" has ever been said in Colorado Federal Court.

出庭作证前,我已经在法庭上待了一周,不得不眼睁睁地看着他的律师就无谓而荒谬的细枝末节欺负、刁难和骚扰我的团队,包括我的母亲,指责我们撒谎……我很愤怒。那时候我决定抛弃一切法庭礼节,只如实回答问题……据说,这是科罗拉多州联邦法庭上出现"屁股"一词最多的一次庭审。

——《时代周刊》,2017年12月6日

When the jury found in my favor, the man who sexually assaulted me was court-ordered to give me a symbolic $1. To this day he has not paid me that dollar, and I think that act of defiance is symbolic in itself.

陪审团判我胜诉,法庭勒令那个对我实施性骚扰的男人赔偿象征性的1美元罚金。直到今天他都没支付那1美元,我认为这种蔑视的

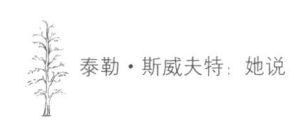

行为本身就具备某种象征意义。

　　　　　　　　　——《时代周刊》，2017年12月6日

This day a year ago was the day that the jury sided in my favor and said that they believed me. I guess I just think about all the people that weren't believed and the people who haven't been believed, or the people who are afraid to speak up because they think they won't be believed. And I just wanted to say I'm sorry to anyone who ever wasn't believed, because I don't know what turn my life would've taken if somebody—if people didn't believe me when I said that something had happened to me. And so I guess I just wanted to say that we have so, so, so much further to go, and I'm so grateful to you guys for being there for me during what was a really, really horrible part of my life.

一年前的今天，陪审团作出了有利于我的判决，说他们相信我。而我想到了那些未曾被相信和尚未被相信的人，还有那些因为觉得没人相信自己便害怕开口的人。我想对那些未曾被相信的人说一句我很遗憾，因为如若某人——如若大家不相信我说自己遭遇了什么事，我不知道自己的人生又会发生什么转折。所以我只想说，我们还有很长的路要走，我非常感激大家在我人生的至暗阶段一直陪着我。

　　　——《名誉》巡回演唱会，佛罗里达州坦帕，2018年8月14日

There is a great deal of blame placed on the victims in cases of sexual harassment and assault... My advice is that you not blame yourself and do not accept the blame others will try to place on you. You should not be blamed for waiting 15 minutes or 15 days or 15 years to report sexual assault or harassment, or for the outcome of what happens to a person after he or she makes the choice to sexually harass or assault you.

性骚扰和性侵案件中,受害者会遭受许多指责……我的建议是不要自责,也不要接受他人对你的指责。无论过了15分钟、15天乃至15年后举报性侵或性骚扰事件,你都不应因此遭受指责,也不应该因为那个对你实施性骚扰或性侵犯的人要付出何种代价遭受指责。

——《时代周刊》,2017年12月6日

Our country's lack of protection for its own citizens ensures that LGBTQ people must live in fear that their lives could be turned upside down by an employer or landlord who is homophobic or transphobic. The fact that, legally, some people are completely at the mercy of the hatred and bigotry of others is disgusting and unacceptable.

Let's show our pride by demanding that, on a national level, our laws truly treat all of our citizens equally.

我们国家缺乏对本国公民的保护,性少数群体因而整日生活在恐惧中,他们的生活可能会被仇视同性恋或变性者的雇主或房东搅得天翻地覆。在法律层面,某些人的仇恨和偏执可以完全摆布一些人的生活,这令人作呕、无法接受。

让我们满怀自豪,要求我们的法律在全国范围内,真正践行人人平等。

——支持《平等法案》[1]的请愿书,2019年5月31日

---

1 《平等法案》(*The Equality Act*)旨在禁止基于性取向和性别认同的歧视,于2019年被民主党掌控的众议院首次通过,但因共和党掌控的参议院否决,未能顺利生效。

Throughout my whole career, label executives and publishers would just say, "Don't be like the Dixie Chicks." And I loved the Dixie Chicks. But a nice girl doesn't force their opinions on people. A nice girl smiles and waves and says thank you. A nice girl doesn't make people feel uncomfortable with her views.

在我的整个职业生涯里，唱片公司的高管和发行商都会说："别学南方小鸡[1]。"但我很喜欢南方小鸡乐队。（他们眼中的）好女孩不会把自己的观点强加于人。好女孩微笑挥手，礼貌道谢。好女孩不会让别人因为自己的观点而不自在。
　　——谈及决定分享自己的政治观点，纪录片《美利坚女士》，
2020年1月23日

I'm trying to be as educated as possible on how to respect people, on how to deprogram the misogyny in my own brain. Toss it out, reject it, and resist it. Like, there is no such thing as a slut. There is no such thing as a bitch. There is no such thing as someone who's bossy, there's just a boss. We don't want to be condemned for being multifaceted.

我尽可能学着尊重他人，尽可能摒弃自己大脑里的厌女症。拒绝厌女、否定厌女、抵制厌女。这世上没有荡妇，没有贱人；只有老板，而没有专横之人。没有人想因为自身的多面性而遭人谴责。
　　——纪录片《美利坚女士》，2020年1月23日

---

[1] 2002年，南方小鸡乐队因就美国发动伊拉克战争发表反战言论遭封杀，2006年复出。

I feel really good about not feeling muzzled anymore. And it was my own doing. I needed to learn a lot before I spoke to 200 million people. But I've educated myself now, and it's time to take the masking tape off of my mouth... like, forever.

我的言论不再受到压制,这种感觉非常好。并且还是我自己的功劳。过去在和两亿人讲话之前,我需要学习很多东西。但现在我已经自学过了,是时候撕下粘在我嘴上的胶带了……永远撕除。

——纪录片《美利坚女士》,2020年1月23日

Racial injustice has been ingrained deeply into local and state governments, and changes MUST be made there. In order for policies to change, we need to elect people who will fight against police brutality and racism of any kind. #BlackLivesMatter

种族歧视在地方和州政府层面根深蒂固,对此**必须**做出改变。为了改变政策,我们必须选举出那些反对警察暴行和任何形式的种族主义的人。#黑人的命也是命

——推特,2020年6月9日

Allow me to be the one millionth person to remind you that tomorrow is your last chance to make your voice heard and to make your vote count. So if you haven't voted yet, please do.

请允许我成为无数个提醒你的人之一,明天是发声和投票的最后机

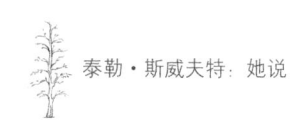

会。所以,如果你还没有投票,就请去投票吧。

——推特,2020年11月2日

Yes!!! fingers crossed and praying that the Senate will see trans and LGBTQ rights as basic human rights.

太好了!!!手指交叉,祈祷参议院能将跨性别者和其他性少数群体的权利视为基本的人权。
　　——谈及美国众议院通过《平等法案》,推特,2021年2月25日

I'm absolutely terrified that this is where we are — that after so many decades of people fighting for women's rights to their own bodies, today's decision has stripped us of that.

我对我们当前的处境感到非常恐惧——数十年来,人们一直在为让妇女群体享有掌控自己身体的权利而奋斗,今天(最高法院)的裁决却剥夺了我们的权利[1]。
　　——谈及美国最高法院关于多布斯诉杰克逊妇女健康组织的裁决,
　　　　　　　　　　　　　　　　　　　　　　推特,2022年6月24日

I've done my research, and I've made my choice. Your research is all yours to do, and the choice is yours to make.

1　2022年6月,美国最高法院在多布斯诉杰克逊妇女健康组织的裁决中,终止了宪法对妇女堕胎权的保护,推翻了1973年罗伊诉韦德案(Roe v. Wade)的裁决,即推翻了妇女是否继续怀孕的权利受宪法上个人自主权和隐私权规定保护的决定。

我已经完成了自己的调查，做出了自己的选择。你的研究要由你完成，你的选择权也在你自己手里。

——谈及2024年美国总统大选，照片墙，2024年9月10日

We can't talk about Pride Month without talking about pain. Right now, and recently and in the recent years, there have been so many harmful pieces of legislation that have put people in the LGBTQIA community at risk, and it's painful for everyone, every ally, every loved one, every person within these communities. That's why I'm always posting "This is when the midterms are, this is when these important, key primaries are." 'Cause we can support as much as we want during Pride Month but [we have to do] our research on these elected officials: "Are they advocates? Are they allies? Are they protectors of equality? Do I want to vote for them?"

谈及"骄傲月"，我们无法避免谈及痛苦。当下，尤其近几年，出台了很多不利于性少数群体的法规，这对性少数群体中的每个人、每位盟友、每位所爱之人，每个性少数群体的成员来说都很痛苦。这也是为什么我时常发帖说："目前正在举行中期选举，目前正在举行重大、关键的初选。"在"骄傲月"里我们可以尽情表示支持，但我们必须自己研究一下这些候选的官员："他们支持性少数群体吗？他们是我们的盟友吗？他们捍卫平等吗？我要投票给他们吗？"

——时代巡回演唱会，伊利诺伊州芝加哥，2023年6月2日

The simplest way to combat misinformation is with the truth.

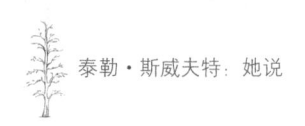

回击误导信息最简单的方式,就是将事实如实以告。

——照片墙,2024年9月10日

I will be casting my vote for Kamala Harris and Tim Walz in the 2024 Presidential Election. I'm voting for [Kamala Harris] because she fights for the rights and causes I believe need a warrior to champion them.

在2024年美国总统大选中,我将把自己的票投给卡玛拉·哈里斯[1]和蒂姆·沃尔兹[2]。投票给卡玛拉·哈里斯,是因为她所为之奋斗的,正是我认为需要一位勇士来奋争的权利和事业。

——照片墙,2024年9月10日

If I get bad press for saying, "Don't put a homophobic racist in office," then I get bad press for that. I really don't care.

如果我因为说"不要让一个仇视同性恋的种族主义者上台"而被媒体恶意报道,那就让他们报道好了。我一点儿也不在乎。

——谈及发声反对玛莎·布莱克本当选田纳西州国会议员[3],
纪录片《美利坚女士》,2020年1月23日

---

1 卡玛拉·哈里斯(Kamala Harris):美国民主党籍政治家,2021年就任美国副总统,是美国首位女性副总统。在2024年的美国总统大选中,不敌唐纳德·特朗普(Donald Trump),落选第47任美国总统。
2 蒂姆·沃尔兹(Tim Walz):美国民主党籍政治家,2018年起担任美国明尼苏达州州长,在2024年美国总统大选中为民主党副总统候选人。
3 2018年,因反对共和党人玛莎·布莱克本(Marsha Blackburn)针对妇女、性少数群体的政策,泰勒发声支持民主党人菲尔·布莱德森(Phil Bredesen)竞选田纳西州国会议员。

I'm sad that I didn't [speak out against Trump] two years ago, but I can't change that. I'm saying right now that this is something that I know is right, and, you guys, I need to be on the right side of history.

我很遗憾自己两年前没有发声（反对特朗普）[1]，但我没法改变过去。我现在说的，是我认为正确的事，我必须站在历史的正确立场上。

——纪录片《美利坚女士》，2020年1月23日

If you can just shift the power in your direction by being bold enough, then it won't be like this forever.

只要足够勇敢，就能将力量为己所用，就能改变当前的局面[2]。

——谈及年轻群体对政治的影响，纪录片《美利坚女士》，2020年1月23日

---

[1] 此处指2016年美国大选，民主党总统候选人希拉里不敌共和党总统候选人特朗普，后者当选第45任美国总统。

[2] 泰勒在田纳西州州长和参议员选举结束后，创作了歌曲《年轻一代》（"Only The Young"），以此鼓舞年轻听众，传达"时代永远属于年轻人，只有年轻一代才可以改变世界"的信念。

《统统甩掉》：
其他人生教训

With the song "Shake It Off," I really wanted to kind of take back the narrative, and have more of a sense of humor about people who kind of get under my skin—and *not let* them get under my skin. There's a song that I wrote a couple years ago called "Mean," where I addressed the same issue but I addressed it very differently. I said, "Why you gotta be so mean?" from kind of a victimized perspective, which is how we all approach bullying or gossip when it happens to us for the first time. But in the last few years I've gotten better at just kind of laughing off things that absolutely have no bearing on my real life.

创作歌曲《统统甩掉》是不想给别人编排我的机会，对那些惹恼我的人回以一丝幽默——不让他们得逞。几年前我写了一首叫《卑鄙》的歌，其中也提到了同样的问题，但我处理问题的方式与现在截然不同。我当时从受害者的角度质问道："你为什么要这么卑鄙？"第一次遭人欺凌或被人非议时，我们都会这样处理问题。但这几年来，对于那些与自己的生活无关紧要的事，我学会了一笑置之。

——美国新闻电台节目 *All Things Considered*，2014年10月31日

You can get everything you want in life without ever feeling like you fit in. You know, selling millions of records doesn't make me feel cool. Like, it makes me feel proud, and like I have a lot of people on my side and I've worked really hard. But, you know, I don't think it's the most important thing in life to fit in. I think it's the most important thing in life to dance to the beat of your own drum and to look like you're having more fun than the people who look cool.

即使不合群,你也可以在生活中得到自己想要的一切。卖出几百万张专辑并没有让我觉得自己很酷。它只是让我骄傲,让我知道有很多人支持我,而我也在一直努力工作。而且我觉得,生活中最重要的事不是努力变得合群,而是跟着自己的节奏起舞,你会过得比那些表面上很酷的人还要开心。

——歌曲《统统甩掉》音乐录影带拍摄幕后,2014年9月11日

I feel like dancing is sort of a metaphor for the way you live your life. You know how you're at a house party and there's a group of people over there just talking and rolling their eyes at everyone dancing? And you know which group is having more fun.

我觉得跳舞有点像生活方式的隐喻。比如家庭聚会上你在跳舞,而有些人只顾着聊天,还冲着跳舞的人翻白眼。而你知道做哪种人更自在。

——英国《卫报》,2014年8月23日

You have to not only live your life in spite of people who don't understand you, you have to have more fun than they do.

你不仅要过好自己的生活，无视那些不理解你的人，**还要比那些人活得更加自在。**

——美国ABC新闻，2014年8月19日

When somebody criticizes you or says something behind your back, those words that they said about you, it's like you feel like those words are written all over your face, all over you. And then those words start to become echoes in your own mind. And then there's a real risk that those words could become a part of how you see yourself. The moment that you realize that you are not the opinion of somebody who doesn't know you or care about you, that moment when you realize that is like you're clean.

有人批评或说你坏话时，你会觉得自己脸上、浑身上下都写满了那些中伤你的话语；然后，这些话语会不断在你的脑海中回响，并且极易入侵你对自我的认知。但当你意识到，那些素昧平生之辈和漠不关心之辈口中捏造的你根本不是自己时，那一刻，你会彻底释怀。

——巡演纪录片《泰勒·斯威夫特：1989世界巡回演唱会》，
2015年12月20日

I hope you know that who you are is who you choose to be, and that whispers behind your back don't define you. You are the only one who gets to decide what you will be remembered for.

我希望你明白，你由自己的选择造就，别人的窃窃私语无法定义你

是谁。你才是那个决定自己该留给别人什么印象的人。
———专辑《1989》歌词本内页，2014年10月27日

Their words will cut / but your tears will dry.

恶语伤人/但泪有尽时。
———*Vogue*（英国版），2017年12月6日

Despite our need to simplify and generalize absolutely everyone and everything in this life, humans are intrinsically impossible to simplify. We are never just good or just bad. We are mosaics of our worst selves and our best selves, our deepest secrets and our favorite stories to tell at a dinner party.

尽管在生活中我们需要简要概括每一个人和每一件事，但人类本质上无法被简要定义。人没有全然的是非黑白之分。我们是一幅幅马赛克拼贴画，由最糟糕的自己和最好的自己，由最深的秘密和最喜欢在晚宴上讲的故事拼成。
———《名誉》杂志，2017年11月10日

When I was growing up and I was in school, I hated my hair. I have really curly hair... Everybody had straight hair, and I wanted straight hair so bad. And I always tried to straighten it, and I spent, like, hours in the morning trying. And then I woke up one day and I realized that just because something is different than everybody else doesn't make it bad.

在我的成长过程中，我上学时很讨厌自己的头发。我的头发非常卷……每个人都是直发，我非常渴望拥有一头直发。于是我试着拉直自己的头发，早上花上数小时把头发弄直。某天我醒来，意识到有和别人不一样的地方也不是件糟糕的事。

——美国杂志《17岁》封面拍摄幕后，2008年5月5日

If you think about human nature, our favorite pair of shoes is the one we bought yesterday. Our favorite thing is the newest thing that we have. And if you think about the thing that we've seen the most and for the longest period of time, [it's] our reflection in the mirror, so obviously that's gonna be our least favorite thing.

要是你思考一下人类的本性，会发现我们最喜欢的鞋子是昨天新买的那双。最喜欢的事物是刚刚到手的东西。再思考一下，我们见过最多最久的事物是镜中自己的影像。显然，这就是我们最不喜欢的东西。

——英国脱口秀节目 Loose Women，2009年2月18日

One of my best friends is this pageant queen... Everybody wants to be her, all the guys want to date her. And I wrote ["Tied Together With A Smile"] the day that I found out she had an eating disorder. You know, it's kind of a halting point in your life when you realize that something that you thought was so strong, you find out that it isn't strong at all.

我有位好朋友是选美皇后……大家都想成为她，所有男孩都想和她约会。有一天，我发现她竟然患有饮食障碍症，于是写下了歌曲

《面带微笑》。在那个人生节点,你意识到有些事物虽然看似坚不可摧,实则外强中干。

——歌曲《面带微笑》解说,出自专辑《泰勒·斯威夫特》(大机器电台发布特辑版),2018年12月13日

I learned to stop hating every ounce of fat on my body. I worked hard to retrain my brain that a little extra weight means curves, shinier hair, and more energy. I think a lot of us push the boundaries of dieting, but taking it too far can be really dangerous. There is no quick fix. I work on accepting my body every day.

我后来学着不再憎恨身上的每一盎司[1]脂肪。我努力重塑自己的大脑,努力让自己相信,多一点体重,意味着多一些曲线,头发光泽一些,精力多一些。我们很多人都在挑战节食的极限,但过度节食真的很危险。没有什么速效减肥法。我每天都在努力接受自己的身体。

——*Elle*,2019年3月6日

The people who strike me as beautiful are the people who have their own thing going on... Unique and different is the next generation of beautiful. You don't have to be the same as everybody else. In fact, I don't think you should.

那些惊艳我的人各有自己的美丽之处。独一无二和与众不同是下一代的美丽标准。你不必追求和他人一模一样。其实我觉得你不该变

---

[1] 1盎司约等于28.35克。

得和他人一样。

——《封面女郎》(*CoverGirl*) 商业拍摄幕后，2010年4月22日

For me, beauty is sincerity. I think that there are so many different ways that someone can be beautiful. You know, someone [can be] so funny that it makes them beautiful, no matter how they look, because they're sincere in it.
Or somebody's, like, really emotional and, like, moody and thoughtful and stoic, but that makes them beautiful because that's sincerely who they are. Or you look out into the crowd and you see someone so happy that they're smiling from ear to ear, and that sincerity comes through.

于我而言，真诚就是美丽。美丽的方式千千万。有人可能很幽默，不管他们外表如何，幽默都让他们变得美丽，因为他们很真诚。
或者有人很情绪化，他们喜怒无常、善解人意、坚忍从容，这些人也很美丽，因为他们在真诚地做自己。或者你向人群中望去，某个非常开心的人正笑得合不拢嘴，从他们身上也流露出真诚。

——YouTube 频道 YouTube Presents，2011年9月1日

I think it's healthy for your self-esteem to need less internet praise to appease it, especially when three comments down you could unwittingly see someone telling you that you look like a weasel that got hit by a truck and stitched back together by a drunk taxidermist. An actual comment I received once.

我觉得为了自尊心的健康着想，少用网上的赞美满足自己的自尊心。想象一下你在三条评论下面无意中看到某人的评论，说你看起

来像一只被卡车撞过、又被喝得烂醉的动物标本剥制师缝好的黄鼠狼。这是我曾经收到的一条真实评论。

——Elle，2019年3月6日

Bravery happens to different people in different ways. And I think that it can be as simple as saying what you mean. It can be as simple as being honest about who you are or who you love. And I think that, you know, it doesn't have to be some courageous act where there's a movie score in the background. I think bravery can happen in little tiny doses every day.

勇敢因人而异、表现不同。我觉得简单来说，直抒胸臆是一种勇敢，坦然面对真实的自我和所爱之人也是一种勇敢。勇敢不一定体现在那些配着电影背景音乐完成的英勇举动中，勇敢可能就蕴藏在日常的细枝末节里。

——美国娱乐网站Extra，2014年1月31日

Being fearless is realizing that life is unpredictable, and it's all in how you deal with that. It's all in how you deal with what's thrown at you and what's given to you and what's taken away from you. And I think that being fearless is not being unafraid or bulletproof or something like that. I think being fearless is being scared of things but living your life and taking chances anyway.

无所畏惧就是意识到生活无法预测，意识到一切都取决于你的所作所为。一切都取决于你如何应对生活中的意外、馈赠和失去。我觉

得无所畏惧的人并非不会恐惧,也不是刀枪不入。无所畏惧的人虽然也会害怕,但无论如何都会过好自己的生活,抓住每一个机遇。

——美国系列电视节目 *My Date With...*,2009 年 11 月 13 日

Every day I try to remind myself of the good in the world, the love I've witnessed and the faith I have in humanity. We have to live bravely in order to truly feel alive, and that means not being ruled by our greatest fears.

每天我都会提醒自己那些世间的美好、见证过的爱和对人类的信心。要想真切地活着,我们必须勇敢生活,不让我们最深的恐惧支配自己。

——*Elle*,2019 年 3 月 6 日

In real life, saying the right thing at the right moment is beyond crucial. So crucial, in fact, that most of us start to hesitate, for fear of saying the wrong thing at the wrong time. But lately what I've begun to fear more than that is letting the moment pass without saying anything.

现实生活中,在恰当的时机说恰当的话至关重要。也正因为太过重要,因为害怕在错误的时机说了不该说的话,实际上大多数人都会犹豫要不要开口。但近来更让我害怕的,恰恰就是不仅什么都没说,还白白错失了时机。

——专辑《爱的告白》歌词本内页,2010 年 10 月 25 日

Words can break someone into a million pieces, but they can also put them back together. I hope you use yours for good, because the only words you'll regret more than the ones left unsaid are the ones you use to intentionally hurt someone.

言语可以将人伤得千疮百孔，也能让人复旧如初。我希望你用言语友善待人，因为比起没有说出口的话，唯一让人后悔的是那些刻意说来中伤他人的话。

——专辑《爱的告白》歌词本内页，2010年10月25日

When tragedy strikes someone you know in a way you've never dealt with before, it's okay to say that you don't know what to say. Sometimes just saying you're so sorry is all someone wants to hear. It's okay to not have any helpful advice to give them; you don't have all the answers. However, it's not okay to disappear from their life in their darkest hour.

身边某人遭受了你从未经历过的悲剧，你却不知道该说什么。这没关系。有时他需要的就是一句"我很遗憾"。无法给他们提供切实可行的建议也没关系，毕竟你也无法应对所有问题。然而，在他们经历至暗时刻时消失则是不可取的做法。

——*Elle*，2019年3月6日

Apologizing when you have hurt someone who really matters to you takes nothing away from you. Even if it was unintentional, it's so easy to just apologize and move on. Try not to say "I'm sorry, but..." and make excuses for yourself. Learn how to make a sincere apology, and you can avoid breaking down the trust in your friendships and relationships.

当你伤害了对自己至关重要的人,道个歉不会损伤你分毫。即使是无心之过,道歉了就很容易翻篇。尽量不要说"对不起,但是……",不要为自己找借口。学会如何真诚地道歉,就能避免危及友情或恋情中的信任。

——*Elle*,2019年3月6日

"Bad Blood" is a song that I wrote about a new kind of heartbreak that I experienced recently, which was when someone that I desperately wanted to be my friend and thought was my friend ended up really making it very obvious that she wasn't...
This song was kind of the first time I ever really stood up for myself in that relationship because she was always the bolder one and the louder one. And, like, I think it's important to stand up for yourself, and if you can only really come up with the courage to do it in song form, then that's how you should do it.

歌曲《敌对》描述的是我最近体会到的一种伤心,你极力想和某人成为朋友,你以为自己已经和她成了朋友,到头来一切都表明她从没把你当过朋友……
这首歌是我在这段关系里第一次为自己发声,因为她向来是那个更强势、更大声的那一方。我觉得为自己挺身而出很重要,而且,如果你的勇气只够支撑你通过写歌为自己发声,那么就这样做吧。

——歌曲《敌对》解说,出自专辑《1989》
(大机器电台发布特辑版),2018年12月13日

Being sweet to everyone all the time can get you into a lot of trouble. While it may be born from having been raised to be a polite young lady, this can contribute to some of your life's worst regrets if someone takes advantage of this trait in you. Grow a backbone, trust your gut, and know when to strike back. Be like a snake—only bite if someone steps on you.

总是温柔善良地对待他人会给你带来许多麻烦。虽然你可能从小就被教育要做一位彬彬有礼的年轻淑女,但如果有人利用了这一点,就可能发生一些让你一辈子都追悔莫及的事情。要有骨气、相信自己的直觉、知道什么时候该反击。要像蛇一样行事——一旦别人踩你,你就以牙还牙。

——*Elle*,2019年3月6日

There is a tendency to block out negative things because they really hurt. But if I stop feeling pain, then I'm afraid that I'll stop feeling immense excitement and epic celebration and happiness, which, I can't stop feeling those things. So, I feel everything. And I think that keeps me who I am.

人们倾向于屏蔽负面事物,因为它们让人痛苦万分。但如果我感受不到痛苦,恐怕就再也不会激动万分、不会欢呼雀跃、不会感到幸福,这些都是我不能割舍的情感。所以,我拥抱所有情感。这让我得以保持自我。

——《今日美国》(*USA Today*)音频采访,2010年10月27日

If you're an enthusiastic person, you can kind of come back from anything. Even if you have a failure or you're rejected or criticized for something, you can become enthusiastic about the next thing.

满腔热情的人基本能从任何事中走出来。即使经受失败,即使遭人拒绝或被人批评,他们也能热情满满地投入到下一件事中。

——英国广播电台 BBC Radio 1,2014年10月9日

I just really try to, I don't know, live in the moment and be really stoked about everything that happens but never feel entitled for it to keep happening. So when it does keep happening, I'm just really excited about it.

可以说,我努力活在当下,为发生的一切好事激动万分,却也并不奢求这些事再度降临。所以当好事发生时,我只管兴奋就是。

——美国杂志《娱乐之都》(Entertainment City),
2012年10月22日

It's all about walking a tightrope between not being so fragile and breakable that they can level you with one blow and being raw enough to feel it and write about it when you feel it.

写歌就像在钢丝绳上行走,一面不要脆弱易伤、不堪一击,让人一击即倒;另一面还得足够强大,去捕捉你的所感所想,并将其诉诸笔端。

——《时尚先生》杂志,2014年10月20日

If I could go back and tell myself one thing as a 13-year-old, I think I would go back and tell myself that everything that's going to happen to me, even the bad things, are happening for a reason, and that I will actually learn more from the bad things that happened to me than I will the good things.

如果我能回到过去，告诉13岁的自己一件事，我会告诉那时候的自己：将来发生的一切，包括那些不好的事，都自有其道理。比起好事，你会从那些坏事中学到更多。

——*Elle* 封面拍摄幕后，2015年5月8日

The thing about life is that, every time you learn a new lesson, there's just another one right around the corner, you know? You never know everything. I think, you know, for me, I've just kind of given up, and I'm like, you know, I know *nothing* compared to what I'm going to know someday.

生活就是这样，每当你得到了什么教训，下一个教训就在拐角处等着你呢。你不可能知晓一切。我想，对我来说，我基本放弃了（弄清一切）。因为和未来某天我会知道的一切相比，我现在一无所知。

——巡演纪录片《泰勒·斯威夫特：爱的告白世界巡回演唱会》，
2011年11月21日

When I think I haven't done the right thing, haven't done a good enough job, I will punish myself emotionally for it over and over again, going over it in my head. I always have to work on being easier on myself, because overthinking is my greatest adversary when it comes to life, work, love, friendship, career.

每当觉得自己什么事没做对，每当觉得自己某项工作没做好，我就会在情绪上反反复复地惩罚自己，在脑海中一遍一遍琢磨那件事。在生活、工作、爱情、友情和事业方面，我一直都努力不那么苛求

自己，因为思虑过多就是我要对抗的最大敌人。

——*Vogue*（澳大利亚版），2015年11月14日

I heard a quote from Dolly Parton one time and she said that regrets aren't fair to you because you couldn't possibly have known then what you know now. And a lot of times I wish I could live life more like her. Just this clarity about how to process regret. But on this particular subject about the path that I chose in life I do not regret anything. I'm very aware and very conscious of the path I chose in life, and very aware of the path I didn't choose.

有一次，我听多莉·帕顿[1]说过一句话，她说："感到后悔是对自己的不公平，因为你当时不可能知晓现在知晓的一切。"很多时候，我都希望自己能像她一样生活，像她一样清楚地知道自己该如何应对后悔。但在我选择的这条特殊人生道路上，我没什么可后悔的。我非常清楚、非常清醒地知道自己选择了什么样的人生道路，也很清楚我放弃了什么样的人生道路。

——《华尔街日报》，2010年10月22日

If you aren't comfortable in a social situation, the only one who will be able to tell is you—if you carry yourself right, if you walk in with your shoulders back and you make a friend and you say hi to people and you smile. And that's not to say, like, "Oh, put on a mask and fake

---

[1] 多莉·帕顿（Dolly Parton）：美国乡村音乐女歌手，入选美国乡村音乐名人堂和摇滚名人堂。

how... you feel." But, you know, I think that a great deal to do with confidence is acting confident—and then you might end up actually being confident.

如果你在某个社交场合感到不自在,这种感受旁人无法体会——担心自己举止是否得体,走路时有没有挺胸直背,交了什么朋友,有没有跟人们打招呼并微笑……不是说你得"哦,戴上社交面具,现在开始掩饰自己的感受"。其实自信很大程度上源自举手投足间的自我肯定——也许你真的会因此自信起来。
——与科迪斯品牌的联名合作视频,2013年5月15日

I feel like we're sent so many messages every day that there's, like, a better version of us on a social media app with, like, better apps and a better vacation spot. But, like, you're the only one of you. **That's it. There's just you.**

我觉得我们每天都在被迫接收太多信息,好像社交媒体上的我们才是更好的自己,用着更好的应用软件,享受更棒的度假地。但是,事实是,你是独一无二的。**就这样。你就是你。**
——苹果音乐视频,2019年4月26日

Hold on to childlike whims and moonlight / swims and your blazing self-respect.

留下那些,
奇思妙想,月夜畅游。

满腔自尊,永远炽烈。

——Vogue(英国版),2017年12月6日

I try to encourage my fans that they don't have to feel confident every day, they don't have to feel happy every day, they don't have to feel pretty every day, they don't have to feel wanted every day, that they shouldn't put added extra pressure on themselves to feel happy when they're not, you know? I think being honest with yourself emotionally is really important.

我试着鼓励粉丝们,不必每天都得自信满满、开开心心,漂亮和被需要不是每日必需品,不开心时也不必顶着压力强颜欢笑。诚实地面对自己的情绪至关重要。

——"泰勒·斯威夫特1989",2014年10月27日

Life can be beautiful and spontaneous and surprising and romantic and magical without you having some love affair happening. And you can replace all of those feelings you used to have when you were enamored with someone with being enamored with your friends and enamored with learning new things and challenging yourself and living your life on your own terms.

无关风月的生活照样可以美好恣意、充满惊喜又浪漫奇妙。这些爱情能带来的生活体验照样可以从友情中获得,从热衷于学习新事物、挑战自我中获得,从热爱随心所欲的生活中获得。

——英国杂志《Q娱乐世界》(Q),2014年10月28日

It's so much easier to like people, and to let people in, to trust them until they prove that you should do otherwise. **The alternative is being an iceberg.**

喜欢他人、接纳他人、信任他人，原本是再容易不过的事，直到他人的辜负教会你不该如此行事。**另一种选择，就是待人有所保留，只显露自己的冰山一角。**

——《澳大利亚人报》(*The Australian*)，2009年3月5日

When your number-one priority is getting a boyfriend, you're more inclined to see a beautiful girl and think, "Oh, she's gonna get that hot guy I wish I was dating." But when you're not boyfriend-shopping, you're able to step back and see other girls who are killing it and think, "God, I want to be around her."

如果你的头等大事是找个男朋友，那么看到漂亮女孩时，你可能更容易想："哦，她会跟那个我想约会的帅哥在一起。"但要是你不再时时物色男友，就能退一步看到其他出类拔萃的女孩，你会想："天啊，我想和她做朋友。"

——《滚石》杂志，2014年9月8日

I've got friends that I trust and friends I love and, you know, in our 20s, like, everything else is up in the air. We don't know where we're going. We don't know if we're ever gonna fall in love. We don't know what's gonna happen. Like, it's just sort of fun to embrace the unpredictability of life.

我有自己信任、喜爱的朋友们，对20多岁的我们来说，除了有彼此相伴，一切都尚未尘埃落定。我们不知道未来在何方，不知道是否还会爱上别人，也不知道有什么在等着自己。但是，拥抱生活的这种不确定性恰恰也是一种乐趣。

——澳大利亚电台Nova FM 96.9，2013年2月22日

There's an Ernest Hemingway quote that says, "The best way to find out if you can trust somebody is to trust them." That's how I live my life, but at the same time, it's important to surround yourself with people who have proven that trust over and over again.

欧内斯特·海明威有句名言："要检验某人是否值得信任，先给予他信任。"我在生活中践行这句名言，与此同时，把那些久经考验、值得信任的人留在身边也很重要。

——美国杂志《南方生活》(*Southern Living*)，
2014年11月24日

"Look What You Made Me Do," it actually started with just, like, a poem that I wrote about my feelings. And it's basically about, like, realizing that you couldn't trust certain people but realizing you appreciate the people you can trust, realizing that you can't just let everyone in, but the ones you can let in you need to cherish.

歌曲《瞧你们让我做了什么》始于一首我记录自己感受的诗。这首诗的基本内容是意识到某些人不可信任，意识到要对那些可以信任的人心怀感激；明白不能对所有人毫无保留，但要珍视那些可以推

心置腹之人。

——《名誉》专辑秘密试听会，2017年10月

If I had to take a guess and say the one thing that probably everybody in this stadium has in common, I think I would say that one thing would be that we all like the feeling of finding something real, like, you know, finding real friendship, finding real love, somebody who really gets you or someone who's really honest with you. I think that's what we're really all looking for in life, and I think that the things that can scare us the most in life are the things that we think will threaten the prospect of us finding something real.

如果要我猜猜这个体育场里的各位可能有什么共同点，我会猜，我们都喜欢找到真实之物的感觉，比如找到真正的友谊，找到真爱，找到那个真正了解你或真正对你坦诚相待的人。我觉得这是我们在生活中的共同追求，而会对这种找到真实之物的希望造成威胁的事物，就是生活中最可怖的存在。

——巡演纪录片《泰勒·斯威夫特：名誉巡回演唱会》，
2018年12月31日

I want to leave a trail of people behind me who had gotten better opportunities or felt better about themselves because of me or smiled because of me.

我希望能为一些后人造福，希望他们或因我而获得更好的机会，或因我而自我感觉更好，或因我而微笑。

——美国杂志《名利场》，2015年8月11日

A general rule is that if you do the right thing, a lot of times that pans out in a business sense. If you start out trying to do things in a business sense, a lot of times it falls flat on its face.

有一条普遍规律是,做正确的事往往能带来商业意义上的成功。但要是一开始就从商业角度出发做事,结局往往会一败涂地。
　　——美国杂志《60分钟时事》(*60 Minutes*),2011年11月20日

I judge people based on their moral code; I think someone is nothing without a moral code. I don't care if you're talented or celebrated or successful or rich or popular, if you have no moral code. If you will betray your friend, if you will talk about them badly behind their back, if you will try to humiliate them or talk down to them, I have no interest in having a person like that in my life.

道德准则是我评判人们的标准;我认为没有道德准则的人一无是处。如果一个人没有道德准则,哪怕他才华横溢、声名显赫,哪怕他成就非凡、腰缠万贯或广受欢迎,我也不会在乎。我希望自己的生活里不会出现那些背叛朋友、背后中伤朋友、想方设法羞辱或贬低朋友的人。
　　——美国杂志《名利场》,2015年8月11日

I still have recurring flashbacks of sitting at lunch tables alone or hiding in a bathroom stall, or trying to make a new friend and being laughed at. In my twenties I found myself surrounded by girls who wanted to be my friend. So I shouted it from the rooftops, posted pictures, and celebrated my newfound acceptance into a sisterhood, without realizing that other people might still feel the way I did when I felt so alone. It's important to address our long-standing issues before we turn into the living embodiment of them.

我仍然会反复想起一些往事，或是自己孤零零坐在午餐桌前，或是躲在洗手间隔间里，或是试着交朋友却遭人嘲笑。20多岁的时候，我发现身边有很多想和我做朋友的女孩。于是我在屋顶上大喊大叫，发布很多照片，庆祝自己结交了新的女性朋友，却没意识到可能有人正在经历我曾经历的那种孤独。要先解决那些遗留已久的创伤问题，以防自己成为此类问题的鲜活化身，这一点很重要。

——*Elle*，2019年3月6日

Something about "we're in our young twenties!" hurls people together into groups that can feel like your chosen family. And maybe they will be for the rest of your life. Or maybe they'll just be your comrades for an important phase, but not forever. It's sad but sometimes when you grow, you outgrow relationships. You may leave behind friendships along the way, but you'll always keep the memories.

"我们正值20多岁的青春岁月！"这话将人们聚在一起，好像彼此就是互相选择的家人。也许这些人会伴你度过余生。也许他们是你某个重要阶段的战友，但你们终将彼此走散。有时伤感的是你成长了，有些关系却止步不前。成长路上，你可能会与某些友谊渐行渐远，但会永远珍藏那些回忆。

——*Elle*，2019年3月6日

For me, my heroes now are great people first and great artists second. People on that list are Garth Brooks, Reba McEntire and Faith Hill—people that I just feel strive to be great people and kind people first before anything else gets factored in.

对我来说，我现在崇拜的人首先是优秀的人，其次才是出色的艺术家。我的偶像名单上有：加斯·布鲁克斯[1]、瑞芭·麦肯泰尔[2]和菲丝·希尔——我觉得，他们的初心都是竭力变得优秀、变得善良，其次才会考虑其他。

——时尚杂志《嘉人》，2009年6月22日

I try to be really aware of the fact that, like, something is golden and magical and special—for a time. And if you drag it out, I never want people to be like, "Will she just go away now?" Because it happens!

我试着让自己清醒地认识到，那些耀眼、奇妙而特别的事物——只能存在于一时。如果硬要延长它的期限，恐怕人们会疑问道："她能不能现在就消失？"的确存在这种情况！

——美国广播电台Beats 1，2015年12月13日

We live for these fleeting moments of happiness. Happiness is not a constant. It's something that we only experience a glimpse of every once in a while, but it's worth it.

1　加斯·布鲁克斯（Garth Brooks）：美国乡村音乐男歌手，2012年入选乡村音乐名人堂。
2　瑞芭·麦肯泰尔（Reba McEntire）：美国乡村音乐女歌手，在美国唱片业协会评选的"美国乐坛史上最成功女歌手排行榜"上位列第七名。

我们活着就是为了体验那些稍纵即逝的幸福时刻。幸福并非恒久不变。幸福只是我们偶尔经历的一瞬,但一瞬便足以值得。

——电影《赐予者》(*The Giver*)新闻发布会,2014年8月12日

When other kids were watching normal shows, I'd watch *Behind the Music*. And I would see these bands that were doing so well, and I'd wonder what went wrong. I thought about this a lot. And what I established in my brain was that a lack of self-awareness was always the downfall. That was always the catalyst for the loss of relevance and the loss of ambition and the loss of great art. So self-awareness has been such a huge part of what I try to achieve on a daily basis.

其他孩子还在看普通节目时,我在看《音乐背后》[1]。看到那些原本发展顺利的乐队,我会思考他们到底哪里出了问题。我想了很多。最后得出的结论是,缺乏自我意识是他们走下坡路的起点,是他们与听众失去联结、不再雄心勃勃、无法创作出杰出艺术的催化剂。因此,提高自我意识一直是我每天努力实现的重要目标。

——*GQ*,2015年10月15日

Sometimes you see these people who are just so—*God*—so affected by all of it, where ambition has taken precedence over happiness. But when I meet people who really embody this serenity of knowing that they

---

[1] 《音乐背后》(*Behind the Music*):美国电视纪录片节目,每期节目聚焦一个音乐团体或一位音乐家,介绍其成功之道、经验教训等。

have had an amazing life—James Taylor, Kris Kristofferson, and Ethel Kennedy... they just seem to be effervescent.

有时候你会看到那些被事业的方方面面完全影响了的人，他们的抱负凌驾于幸福之上。然而遇到那些知道自己过着令人惊叹的生活，但内心依旧保有宁静平和的人——詹姆斯·泰勒[1]、克里斯·克里斯托佛森[2]、埃塞尔·肯尼迪[3]……他们似乎充满了活力。

——*Vogue*，2012年1月16日

The stakes are really high if you mess up, if you slack off and don't make a good record, if you make mistakes based on the idea that you are larger than life and you can just coast... If you start thinking you've got it down, that's when you run into trouble—either by getting complacent or becoming mouthy.

无论是你搞砸了某事，还是因为懈怠而没做出好唱片，又或是因为自命不凡，因为觉得成功唾手可得而犯了错，凡此种种，代价都很高……一旦开始自以为是，你就会惹上麻烦——因为你要么会变得沾沾自喜，要么会变得口无遮拦。

——*Vogue*，2012年1月16日

---

1 詹姆斯·泰勒（James Taylor）：美国民谣男歌手，2000年入选美国摇滚名人堂和创作人名人堂。
2 克里斯·克里斯托佛森（Kris Kristofferson）：美国乡村音乐男歌手，2004年入选美国乡村音乐名人堂。
3 埃塞尔·肯尼迪（Ethel Kennedy）：美国人权活动家，被媒体称为"肯尼迪家族的女族长"，亡夫为美国前司法部长、参议员罗伯特·肯尼迪。

You feel kind of this wave of wistful romance when you get a letter and you see someone's handwriting, the same way when you take a picture and someone hands you the Polaroid and you put it in your pocket and you find it later. It's like it's something you truly have, and if you lose it, it's truly lost. And I think there's something kind of poetic about the idea of your memories being something you want to hold on to, preserve, and not misplace.

当你收到一封信,看到那人的笔迹时,你会被那股裹挟着思念的浪漫浪潮席卷。拍照时,某人递给你一张宝丽来相片,你把它装进口袋,过后再发现那相片时也会被那股同样的浪潮席卷。此类事物都是你真正拥有的实物,弄丢了就再也无法寻得。将记忆外化成可以留下、保存却不可随意搁置之物,是略带诗意的想法。
　　——美国电视节目 *Big Morning Buzz Live*,2014年10月27日

During the first few years of your career, the only thing anyone says to you is "Enjoy this. Just enjoy this." That's all they ever tell you. **And I finally know how to do that.**

职业生涯初期,人们都跟我说要"享受这一切。好好享受这一切"。大家告诉我的只有这句话。**现在我终于知道该怎么享受了。**
　　——*GQ*,2015年10月15日

I'm also thankful that when I go to sleep at night I get to know that I've been myself that day. **And I've been myself all the days before that.**

晚上睡觉前,想到当天我在做自己,我就会感到非常庆幸。**不仅如**

此，在那之前的每一天，我都在做自己。

——美国"NBC年度人物"系列节目，2009年11月26日

I get really, really excited and happy about the same things that I used to get excited and happy about, like the small things like going to the grocery store and like hanging out with friends and all that. I think if you stay on a level where you can be happy about little things as well as the crazy, big things that are going on in your life, it keeps it balanced.

从前那些让我兴奋快乐的事，像是去杂货商店、和朋友们外出游乐之类的小事，现在依然让我感到非常兴奋、非常快乐。我觉得，如果你既能为生活中那些疯狂的大事感到快乐，也能从生活中的小事中获得乐趣，保持住，你的生活会因此得到平衡。

——第52届格莱美奖颁奖典礼排练现场，2010年1月31日

Both of my parents have had cancer, and my mom is now fighting her battle with it again. It's taught me that there are real problems and then there's everything else. My mom's cancer is a real problem. I used to be so anxious about daily ups and downs. I give all of my worry, stress, and prayers to real problems now.

我父母都曾患癌，而我母亲现在又在与癌症抗争。这让我明白，重大问题面前，其他什么都不重要。我母亲的癌症就是重大问题。从前我总是为每日的起起落落焦虑。现在，我只为重大问题担忧、焦虑和祈祷。

——*Elle*，2019年3月6日

The thing about doing what you love is you never know if it's gonna happen, and you never know if you're gonna get to do it one more day. But the fact that you're doing it right now, or trying to do it, or working towards it, it's like stepping stones… If you really love it, the stepping stones working towards it are just as rewarding as getting to do it and ending up with that as your job.

做自己热爱的事，你不知道自己能不能成功，也不知道明天是否还能继续做下去。但是，不论当下你正在做自己热爱的事，或者正在尝试做自己热爱的事，又或者正在为之奋斗，此刻你所做的一切都是你的垫脚石……如果你真的热爱，那么这些奋斗路上的垫脚石，便与将你的热爱变成工作一样，是值得去做、会让你大受裨益的事。

——美国VH1频道音乐节目 *Storytellers*，2012年11月11日

One thing i've learned, and possibly the only advice I have to give, is to not be that person giving out unsolicited advice based on your own personal experience. I've always had a lot of older people giving me advice because I'm young, and in the end, it all comes down to who you want to be remembered as. Just be that.

我学到的一个教训，也可能是我唯一能给别人的建议，就是不要基于自己的个人经验，不请自来地给别人提建议。因为年轻，所以总是有很多前辈给我提建议，但最终我发觉，一切都取决于自己想被他人以何种模样记住。朝着那个方向努力就好。

——美国杂志《公告牌》，2013年3月25日

Every part of you that you've ever been, every phase you've ever gone through, was you working it out in that moment with the information you had available to you at the time. There's a lot that I look back at like, "Wow, a couple years ago I might have cringed at this." You should celebrate who you are now, where you're going, and where you've been.

每个曾经的自我,每个成长的阶段,在那个当下,都是你用自己所知范围内的信息铸就的。很多时候我回首往事,会想:"哇,几年前我可能还为这事难为情过。"你应该赞颂如今的自己,赞颂未来的目的地和你曾经的来路。

——《时代周刊》,2023年12月6日

There's something about the complete and total uncertainty about life that causes endless anxiety, but there's another part that causes sort of a release of the pressures that you used to feel. Because if we're going to have to recalibrate everything, we should start with what we love the most first.

生活中的一部分充满了极度的不确定性,让人产生无穷无尽的焦虑,而另一部分则会减缓你感受到的压力。如果我们想将一切拨回正轨,就该从自己最热爱的事物入手。

——谈及如何在混乱的新冠疫情期间开辟音乐上和生活上的新出路,
纪录片《民间故事:长池录音室》,2020年11月25日

It turned out that everyone needed a good cry, as well as us.

后来发现大家都需要好好哭一场，和我们一样。
　　　　——谈及新冠疫情期间专辑《民间故事》的影响，
　　纪录片《民间故事：长池录音室》，2020年11月25日

[folklore] was the first album that I've ever let go of that need to be 100% autobiographical... I think that's been my favorite thing about this album is that it's allowed to exist on its own merit without it being "Oh, people are listening to this because it tells them something that they could read in a tabloid."... It, to me, feels like a completely different experience.

《民间故事》是我第一张没有完全依据亲身经历创作的专辑……我最喜欢这张专辑的地方，就在于它完全以自身的价值独立存在，丝毫不迎合"哦，人们听这张专辑，是因为它讲述了能在小报上看到的八卦"……于我而言，这是一次非常独一无二的经历。
　　　　——纪录片《民间故事：长池录音室》，2020年11月25日

There's always some standard of beauty that you're not meeting. 'Cause if you're thin enough, then you don't have that ass that everybody wants. But if you have enough weight on you to have an ass, then your stomach isn't flat enough. It's all just fucking impossible.

总有些美丽的标准你无法企及。如果足够苗条，就没法拥有人们渴望的那种丰满臀部。但要是有足够的体重让臀部丰满起来，腹部又不够平坦了。这一切简直是天方夜谭。
　　　　——纪录片《美利坚女士》，2020年1月23日

No matter how hard you try to avoid being cringe, you will look back on your life and cringe retrospectively... You can't avoid it, so don't try to... Trends and phases are fun, looking back and laughing is fun.

无论你多么努力避免"社死"，回顾过往人生时还是会陷入过往的尴尬中……既然无法避免，索性坦然接受……追逐潮流和凸显个性很有趣，回顾过往并开怀大笑也很有趣。

——纽约大学毕业演讲，2022年5月18日

I'm a big advocate for not hiding your enthusiasm for things. It seems to me that there is a false stigma around eagerness in our culture of unbothered ambivalence. This outlook perpetuates the idea that it's not cool to want it. That people who don't try are fundamentally more chic than people who do... Never be ashamed of trying. Effortlessness is a myth... The people who wanted it the most are the people I now hire to work for my company.

我极力倡导大家不要刻意隐藏你对某个事物的热情。我们的文化中那种不以为然的矛盾心理，让我们错误地以热情为耻。这长久以来助长了"有所渴求就不够酷"的观念，滋长了"不汲汲以求些什么的人要比有所求的人更时髦优雅"的观念……永远都别以努力为耻。没人能不费吹灰之力做成事……那些充满渴求的人，才是现在公司里与我共事之人。

——纽约大学毕业演讲，2022年5月18日

But, like, do you really care if the Internet doesn't like you today if your mom's sick from her chemo?... You gotta be able to really prioritize what matters to you. For me, it's my family and my friends.

但扪心自问，如果你妈妈今天因为化疗而身体不适，你真的还会在乎网上的人不喜欢你吗？……你必须得优先考虑对自己来说重要的事物。于我而言，我的家庭和朋友最重要。

——纪录片《美利坚女士》，2020年1月23日

大事记

1989

- 泰勒·艾莉森·斯威夫特（Taylor Alison Swift），1989年12月13日生于宾夕法尼亚州雷丁。父亲斯科特·斯威夫特（Scott Swift）曾在美林证券公司担任股票经纪人，母亲为安德莉亚·斯威夫特。泰勒的童年时代在父母位于宾夕法尼亚州怀奥米辛的圣诞树农场度过。

2002

- 泰勒在费城76人队的一场比赛上演唱国歌。

2003

- 泰勒与美国广播唱片公司签订发展合约。2003年底，该公司决定在泰勒年满18岁前暂不考虑为其发行专辑。泰勒决定放弃等待，离开该公司。
- 泰勒为阿贝克隆比＆费奇（Abercrombie & Fitch）品牌的明日之星项目担任广告模特。

2004

- 泰勒与音乐表演权利组织美国广播音乐协会（Broadcast Music, Inc., BMI）签约。

- 泰勒的歌曲《局外人》被收录于合集专辑《美宝莲纽约呈现个性少女》（*Maybelline New York Presents Chicks with Attitude*）。
- 为了让女儿更接近纳什维尔的音乐街，斯科特·斯威夫特转调美林证券公司纳什维尔办公室。斯威夫特全家居住在田纳西州纳什维尔郊区的亨德森维尔。
- 泰勒在亨德森维尔高中就读高一，并在那里结识了挚友阿比盖尔·安德森（Abigail Anderson），阿比盖尔是歌曲《15岁》的主要记述对象。
- 泰勒在纳什维尔的蓝鸟咖啡馆演出。斯科特·波切塔当时在台下的观众中，他熟悉乡村音乐，曾就职于环球音乐集团纳什维尔分部。波切塔认为泰勒的原创歌曲极具潜力，因此向她发出签约邀请，随后开始筹备成立大机器唱片公司。

2005

- 泰勒与索尼／联合电视音乐出版公司签订出版合约，成为该公司旗下最年轻的词曲作者。
- 波切塔成立大机器唱片公司，泰勒与大机器唱片公司签约。

2006

- 泰勒在亨德森维尔高中读完高中二年级，随后离校，选择在家自主学习，以便有更多时间投身于自己的音乐创作和音乐事业。

- 泰勒的第一首单曲《蒂姆·麦格劳》发行。念及秋季即将搬去大学的男友,她在高中课堂上写下了这首歌。老搭档利兹·罗斯参与该曲制作,罗斯经常自称泰勒的"编辑"。该单曲在公告牌热门乡村单曲榜上最高位列第六名——其成功可能也与该曲以著名乡村音乐歌手蒂姆·麦格劳的名字命名有关。
- 首张专辑《泰勒·斯威夫特》发行。专辑中许多歌曲都创作于泰勒的高中时期,由她与利兹·罗斯共同创作。与多位经验丰富的制作人试合作后,泰勒请来了自己的长期样带合作伙伴内森·查普曼(Nathan Chapman),除一首歌外,这位初出茅庐的制作人参与制作了专辑中的全部曲目。历时数月,泰勒在全国范围内的电台巡回宣传这张专辑,使该专辑最终拿下公告牌200强专辑榜第五位的好成绩,并被美国唱片业协会[1]认证为"七倍白金唱片[2]"。除了首单《蒂姆·麦格劳》,《泪洒吉他》、《我们的歌》、《烧掉的回忆》("Picture To Burn")也是该专辑中的重要单曲。
- 泰勒担任流氓弗拉德乐队(Rascal Flatts)《我和我的死党》巡回演唱会(Me and My Gang Tour)的开场嘉宾。

2007
- 泰勒与凯丽·皮克勒(Kellie Pickler)、杰克·英格拉姆

---

[1] 美国唱片业协会(Recording Industry Association of America,RIAA):代表美国唱片业的贸易团体,负责为美国专辑、单曲等进行认证。

[2] 白金唱片:在美国,专辑销量达到100万张即可认证为白金唱片。

- （Jack Ingram）一同担任布拉德·派斯里（Brad Paisley）《篝火与音响》巡回演唱会（Bonfires & Amplifiers Tour）的开场嘉宾。
- 泰勒获第42届美国乡村音乐学院奖最佳新人女歌手奖项提名。虽未获奖，但她在颁奖现场表演歌曲《蒂姆·麦格劳》时第一次见到了蒂姆·麦格劳。
- 泰勒担任蒂姆·麦格劳和菲丝·希尔Soul2Soul II联合巡回演唱会（Soul2Soul II Tour）部分场次的开场嘉宾。
- 《我们的歌》作为单曲发行，成为泰勒在公告牌热门乡村单曲榜上的第一首冠军单曲。
- 泰勒发行迷你专辑《季节之声：泰勒·斯威夫特假日精选集》（Sounds of the Season: The Taylor Swift Holiday Collection），致意她最喜爱的假日圣诞节。
- 泰勒赢得2007年美国乡村音乐协会奖[1]的地平线奖项，该奖颁专门为前途无量的新人艺人设置。

2008

- 泰勒赢得美国乡村音乐学院奖的最佳新人女歌手奖项。
- 泰勒与乔·乔纳斯恋爱，她在脱口秀节目《艾伦秀》上提到，乔纳斯在一通仅有25秒的电话中甩了自己。乔纳斯是泰勒为数不多公开承认的男友之一，她随后不再轻易谈论

---

[1] 美国乡村音乐协会奖（Country Music Association Awards，CMA Awards）：美国乡村音乐协会主办的音乐类奖项，为美国三大乡村音乐奖之一。

自己的恋爱状况。

- 与乔纳斯恋爱期间，泰勒与赛琳娜·戈麦斯（Selena Gomez）成为朋友，后者当时正与乔的弟弟尼克·乔纳斯恋爱。两人的恋情均已分手告终后，泰勒与戈麦斯的友情（以及事业）迅速升温。
- 泰勒高中毕业。
- 泰勒的迷你专辑《美丽双眸》(Beautiful Eyes)由沃尔玛独家发行。
- 专辑《放手去爱》的首张单曲《爱情故事》发行，泰勒在歌里讲述了一段遭到父母反对的爱情故事。《爱情故事》成为泰勒早期热门跨界单曲之一，在流行音乐和乡村音乐榜单上均表现不俗。该歌曲还在国际上取得了多项成就，在加拿大和澳大利亚的音乐榜单上都位居首位。
- 泰勒的第二张专辑《放手去爱》发行。这张专辑的合作者不仅包括之前的罗斯和查普曼，还有新合作者蔻比·凯蕾（Colbie Caillat）和约翰·里奇（John Rich）。这也是泰勒首次参与专辑中所有曲目的联合制作。泰勒许多颇具代表性的歌曲，如《爱情故事》《你应该和我在一起》《15岁》，均出自这张专辑并作为单曲发行。与单曲《爱情故事》一样，专辑《放手去爱》也取得了巨大成功，该专辑登上了公告牌200强专辑榜首位，并成为2009年最畅销的专辑。在公告牌200强专辑总榜上，《放手去爱》名列第四。
- 泰勒获得全美音乐奖最受喜爱的乡村女歌手奖项。

2009

- 泰勒圆梦参演其最喜爱的电视连续剧之一《犯罪现场调查》（Crimes Scene Investigation），在剧中饰演一位谋杀事件的受害人。
- 泰勒举办首场个人巡回演唱会，为专辑《放手去爱》助阵。演出门票一售而空，巡演从印第安纳州的埃文斯维尔启程，途经亚洲、澳洲和欧洲。
- 泰勒在电影《乖乖女是大明星》（Hannah Montana: The Movie）中饰演一个小角色，并为该电影献唱原创歌曲《更疯狂》（"Crazier"）。
- 为表彰其为乡村音乐吸纳年轻群体和国际听众的成就，泰勒获颁第44届美国乡村音乐学院奖的特别贡献奖。她还凭专辑《放手去爱》拿下年度专辑奖项。
- 泰勒担任凯斯·厄本（Keith Urban）《一起逃离世界》巡回演唱会（Escape Together World Tour）部分场次的开场嘉宾。
- 泰勒凭借歌曲《你应该和我在一起》赢得2009年度MTV音乐录影带大奖的最佳女艺人音乐录影带奖。但其获奖感言被歌手坎耶·韦斯特上台打断，后者坚称该奖得主应为碧昂斯，这一行为使韦斯特瞬间臭名昭著。泰勒获得了包括碧昂斯、时任美国总统布莱克·奥巴马等人的广泛支持，但该事件也成为泰勒和韦斯特长期不和局面的导火索。
- 《放手去爱》达成白金唱片成就后，《放手去爱（白金版）》（Fearless Platinum Edition）发行。白金版专辑收录了几首新歌,并包含一张刻录了音乐录影带和幕后花絮的光碟。
- 泰勒在喜剧综艺节目《周六夜现场》(Saturday Night Live)上担任主持和表演嘉宾,并在其个人音乐独白中极尽调侃自己总是写为爱疯狂的歌词。
- 歌曲《爱情故事》获提第57届BMI乡村音乐奖[1]年度歌曲奖项。
- 泰勒凭借专辑《放手去爱》赢得包括年度艺人、年度专辑在内的5项美国乡村音乐协会奖奖项。
- 泰勒获全美音乐奖6项提名,最终凭专辑《放手去爱》拿下年度艺人和年度乡村专辑在内的5个奖项。
- 泰勒与约翰·梅尔短暂相恋。
- 泰勒购入自己的首套房产,从父母家搬出后搬进了纳什维尔一座市值199万美元的公寓。

2010

- 泰勒凭歌曲《白马》获得格莱美奖[2]最佳乡村女歌手奖项,这是其职业生涯的首座格莱美奖,她还凭专辑《放手去爱》获得了年度专辑奖项,成为获得该奖项的最年轻艺人[3]。专辑《放手去爱》同时拿下了最佳乡村专辑奖,歌曲《白马》还

---

1 BMI乡村音乐奖(BMI Country Awards):BMI音乐奖分支。
2 格莱美奖(Grammy Awards):与电影类的奥斯卡金像奖(Oscars Awards)、电视类的艾美奖(Emmy Awards)及戏剧类的托尼奖(Tony Awards)共称为美国年度四大娱乐奖项。
3 该纪录于2020年被美国女歌手比莉·艾利什(Billie Eilish)打破。

赢得了最佳乡村歌曲奖。
- 泰勒在群像浪漫喜剧电影《情人节》(Valentine's Day)中出演一个小角色。在电影拍摄现场,泰勒结识了饰演其男友的泰勒·洛特纳,并与其短暂相恋。
- 歌曲《我的》在互联网泄露,随后作为泰勒待发行专辑《爱的告白》的首张单曲发行。该单曲在公告牌热门乡村单曲榜上位列第二。
- 泰勒在MTV音乐录影带大奖颁奖现场表演歌曲《无辜者》。这首歌被公认为向坎耶·韦斯特伸出的橄榄枝,韦斯特曾在前一年的颁奖典礼现场打断泰勒的获奖感言。
- 专辑《爱的告白》发行。该专辑没有任何合作者,是泰勒截至当时唯一独立创作的专辑。这张专辑原定名为《着迷》,但在大机器唱片公司的说服下,泰勒更改了专辑名称,以摆脱其极具青春童话色彩的风格。除歌曲《我的》,《回到十二月》("Back To December")和《卑鄙》也是该专辑中的成功单曲。专辑《爱的告白》发行首周即登顶公告牌200强专辑榜,首周销量达到100万张。
- 泰勒与演员杰克·吉伦哈尔恋爱。据报道,他们的恋情和分手为专辑《红》提供了许多灵感(尽管泰勒从未在任何场合指名道姓)。
- 在第58届BMI乡村音乐奖颁奖典礼上,泰勒成为最年轻的年度词曲作者奖获得者。她还凭借歌曲《你应该和我在一起》获得年度歌曲奖项。
- 泰勒获得全美音乐奖最受喜爱的乡村女歌手奖。

2011

- 泰勒拿下第46届美国乡村音乐学院奖的最高奖项年度艺人奖。
- 《爱的告白》巡回演唱会首场在新加坡开唱,并成为2011年度最卖座的个人巡回演唱会。
- 泰勒购入位于加利福尼亚州比弗利山庄的首套住宅。
- 《爱的告白》巡回演唱会北美场次开始前,泰勒在纳什维尔为粉丝们举办了一场预演,演出所得均用于资助美国东南部遭受飓风袭击的人员。
- 凭借专辑《爱的告白》,泰勒赢得公告牌音乐奖[1]的最佳公告牌200强艺人奖、最佳乡村歌手奖及最佳乡村专辑奖。
- 泰勒在美国乡村音乐学院奖荣誉现场[2]赢得吉姆·里夫斯国际大奖(Jim Reeves International Award)。该奖项用以表彰为乡村音乐吸引世界目光的音乐家。
- 泰勒提名公告牌2011年度女性奖。
- 一只苏格兰折耳猫进入泰勒的生活,泰勒以美剧《实习医生格蕾》的主角梅雷迪斯·格蕾为其命名。
- 泰勒第二次获得美国乡村音乐协会奖的年度艺人奖。
- 泰勒在全美音乐奖赢得最受喜爱的乡村女歌手奖和年度艺

---

1 公告牌音乐奖(Billboard Music Awards,BBMAs):美国音乐杂志《公告牌》主办的音乐奖,奖项颁发以其榜单数据为依据。
2 美国乡村音乐学院奖荣誉现场(ACM Honors):美国乡村音乐学院奖颁奖典礼后举行的现场活动,为特殊奖项获得者、幕后得奖者、美国乡村音乐学院奖业内人员等举行庆祝活动。

人奖,并凭借专辑《爱的告白》赢得最受喜爱的乡村专辑奖。

2012

- 泰勒凭借歌曲《卑鄙》获得两项格莱美奖。
- 泰勒首次参与电影配音,为改编自苏斯博士(Dr. Seuss)同名原著的电影《老雷斯的故事》(*The Lorax*)中的奥黛丽配音。
- 时任美国第一夫人米歇尔·奥巴马(Michelle Obama)在第25届儿童选择奖[1]上为泰勒颁发杰出贡献奖项(the Big Help Award),以表彰其在慈善领域做出的贡献。
- 泰勒连续第二年在美国乡村音乐学院奖上赢得年度艺人奖项。
- 泰勒与肯尼迪家族的康纳·肯尼迪(Conor Kennedy)恋爱。
- 泰勒与艾德·希兰成为好友,两人都表示希望与对方合作。据报道两人共同创作的第一首歌《一切皆变》是在蹦床上写下的。
- 专辑《红》的首张单曲《我们再也回不去了》发行,成为泰勒在公告牌热门单曲100强榜上的第一首冠军单曲。
- 鞋类品牌科迪斯与泰勒合作,发行系列联名产品并拍摄系

---

1 儿童选择奖(Nickelodeon Kids' Choice Awards):1988年起由美国儿童电视频道尼克罗迪恩频道举办并播出。

列广告,其联名旨在鼓励年轻女孩勇敢起来。
- 专辑《红》发行。尽管泰勒之前的几张专辑都融合了流行音乐和乡村音乐元素,但专辑《红》包含的乡村音乐元素更少,体现出向流行音乐的明显靠拢。泰勒首次与著名流行音乐制作人马克斯·马丁及希尔贝克合作,两人参与制作了歌曲《22》《我知道你是大麻烦》和《我们再也回不去了》。在公告牌200强专辑榜上,该专辑进榜即登顶首位,首周销量达到120.8万张。
- 泰勒在全美音乐奖赢得最受喜爱的女艺人奖项,并在颁奖典礼上表演歌曲《我知道你是大麻烦》。
- 泰勒与单向组合(One Direction)成员哈里·斯泰尔斯(Harry Styles)恋爱数月。粉丝推测,泰勒第五张专辑《1989》中的多首歌曲均与斯泰尔斯有关。

2013

- 泰勒担任健怡可乐的品牌代言人。
- 泰勒在美国内布拉斯加州的奥马哈开启《红》巡回演唱会(The *Red* Tour)。巡演途经欧洲和澳洲,最后在亚洲结束,成为当年票房最高的巡回演唱会。
- 泰勒以1 775万美元的售价购入位于罗德岛守望山(Watch Hill)的一座海边豪宅。
- 泰勒拿下包括最佳艺人在内的8项公告牌音乐奖奖项。
- 据称,丹佛当地DJ大卫·穆勒在演唱会前与泰勒的见面会上摸了她的臀部。穆勒和粉丝离场后,泰勒向其团队讲述了穆勒的所作所为，保镖随后将穆勒从演唱会现场带离。穆勒所属的KYGO电台对该事件进行调查后解雇了穆勒。

- 泰勒凭借歌曲《我知道你是大麻烦》获音乐录影带大奖的最佳女艺人音乐录影带奖。

- 泰勒向乡村音乐名人堂与博物馆[1]捐赠400万美元，该机构随后在纳什维尔成立了泰勒·斯威夫特教育中心，旨在为年轻群体举办相关展览，提供亲身接受音乐培训的机会。

- 泰勒成为继加斯·布鲁克斯后第二位获得美国乡村音乐协会奖巅峰奖（the Pinnacle Award）的歌手。巅峰奖用以表彰在乡村音乐领域取得独一无二成就的艺人，该奖并非每年颁出。

- 泰勒在全美音乐奖上获得最受喜爱的流行/摇滚女歌手、最受喜爱的乡村女歌手、最受喜爱的乡村专辑（《红》）和年度艺人奖项。

2014

- 泰勒搬到纽约，买下了原属彼得·杰克逊（Peter Jackson）的一处公寓。

- 泰勒的第二只苏格兰折耳猫以电视剧集《法律与秩序：特殊受害者》中的奥利维亚·本森探长命名。

---

1 乡村音乐名人堂与博物馆（The Country Music Hall of Fame and Museum）：位于美国纳什维尔。

- 泰勒在电影《赐予者》中饰演一个小角色,该电影由杰夫·布里吉斯(Jeff Bridges)、梅丽尔·斯特里普(Meryl Streep)主演。
- 泰勒发行单曲《统统甩掉》,该曲是其在公告牌热门单曲100强榜上的第二首冠军单曲。《统统甩掉》也是专辑《1989》的首发单曲。
- 泰勒获提公告牌年度女性奖,成为首位两次获此殊荣的艺人。
- 泰勒的首张纯流行乐专辑《1989》发行。专辑以泰勒的出生年份命名,代表她作为歌手及其音乐的重生。这张专辑从20世纪80年代的合成器流行乐、明亮恣意的声音色彩以及独立意识中汲取灵感。马克斯·马丁及希尔贝克再度参与专辑制作,泰勒还与新制作人杰克·安东诺夫(Jack Antonoff)及瑞恩·泰德展开合作。泰勒制作流行专辑的决定遭到了大机器唱片公司的反对,公司担心她会因此丢掉在乡村音乐界的根基,但她还是坚持将这张专辑制作了出来。《欢迎来纽约》《敌对》《空白格》皆是出自这张专辑的流行乐曲。《1989》在公告牌200强专辑榜上入榜即登上首位,首周销量达到128.7万张,远远超过大多数媒体的预测数据。
- 专辑《1989》发行当日,纽约市委任泰勒为纽约城市宣传大使。
- 泰勒宣布将歌曲《欢迎来纽约》的全部所得捐给纽约市的公立学校。

- 泰勒在《华尔街日报》的特约专栏中提到，流媒体服务平台不应该免费为用户提供音乐作品。数月后，她将自己在声破天音乐平台上的过往作品全部下架。专辑《1989》也未在该平台上首发。
- 泰勒在全美音乐奖颁奖典礼上成为首位获得迪克·克拉克终身成就奖的艺人，以表彰其取得前无来者的连续三张专辑首周销量均突破百万的成就。
- 格莱美博物馆推出展览《走近泰勒·斯威夫特》(*The Taylor Swift Experience*)，展出泰勒职业生涯中的手写歌词、相关照片、巡演物品和早期用品。
- 泰勒入选电视特辑节目《芭芭拉·沃尔特斯：2014年十大魅力人物》。

2015

- 泰勒在全英音乐奖[1]颁奖典礼上获得最佳国际女歌手奖。
- 泰勒与DJ、制作人加尔文·哈里斯恋爱。
- 泰勒在轻博客网站汤博乐上透露自己的母亲安德莉亚确诊患癌。她鼓励粉丝们接受癌症筛查并督促自己的亲人尽早接受筛查。
- 泰勒在第50届美国乡村音乐学院奖颁奖典礼上获得"50周年里程碑奖"（the 50th Anniversary Milestone Award），母

---

1 全英音乐奖（The Brit Awards）：英国唱片业协会举办的英国最有影响力的音乐奖项。

亲安德莉亚·斯威夫特为其颁奖。
- 《1989》巡回演唱会在日本东京拉开帷幕。每场演唱会上泰勒都会邀请一位惊喜嘉宾上台，如米克·贾格尔（Mick Jagger）、艾伦·德詹尼丝（Ellen DeGeneres）等。巡演总票房超过2.5亿美元，超过此前《放手去爱》《爱的告白》《红》3张专辑的巡演总票房。
- 泰勒赢得包括最佳艺人奖、最佳女歌手奖在内的8项公告牌音乐奖奖项，成为公告牌音乐奖历史上获奖最多的艺人。该记录后被歌手德雷克（Drake）打破，他共计获得了27项公告牌音乐奖，超越了泰勒23项公告牌音乐奖的纪录。泰勒还在颁奖典礼上首映了歌曲《敌对》的音乐录影带。
- 《福布斯》杂志的全球100位最具影响力的女性榜单上，泰勒位居第64位。
- 泰勒向苹果音乐写了一封公开信，指责其流媒体服务在用户3个月的试用期期间，拒绝向艺人支付版权费。不到一周后，苹果音乐更改平台条款，宣布在3个月试用期内同样会向艺人支付报酬。作为回应，泰勒宣布将在苹果音乐上架包括《1989》在内的所有专辑。
- 泰勒凭借《敌对》获得音乐录影带大奖的年度音乐录影带奖项。颁奖典礼上，她还向坎耶·韦斯特颁发了迈克尔·杰克逊先锋终身成就奖。
- 泰勒购入其在比弗利山庄的第二处居所。这座原属塞缪尔·戈尔德温（Samuel Goldwyn）的房产售价2 500万美元。

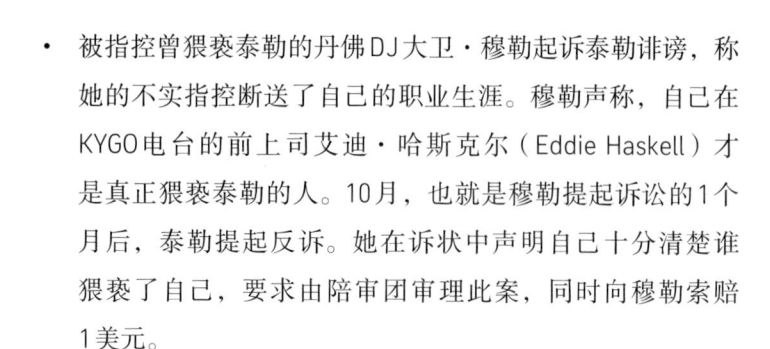

- 被指控曾猥亵泰勒的丹佛DJ大卫·穆勒起诉泰勒诽谤，称她的不实指控断送了自己的职业生涯。穆勒声称，自己在KYGO电台的前上司艾迪·哈斯克尔（Eddie Haskell）才是真正猥亵泰勒的人。10月，也就是穆勒提起诉讼的1个月后，泰勒提起反诉。她在诉状中声明自己十分清楚谁猥亵了自己，要求由陪审团审理此案，同时向穆勒索赔1美元。
- 泰勒凭借交互视频应用"美国运通独家呈现：沉浸式体验泰勒·斯威夫特《空白格》MV场地"（"AMEX Unstaged: The Taylor Swift Experience"）获得艾美奖[1]的交互媒体杰出创意成就奖——原创互动节目类。粉丝可以在该视频应用中尽情探索歌曲《空白格》音乐录影带中的场景。
- 词曲创作者杰西·布拉汉姆（Jessie Braham）起诉泰勒的歌曲《统统甩掉》抄袭其歌曲《憎恨者只会憎恨》（"Haters Gone Hate"）。值得一提的是，法官在驳回其诉讼时引用了几首泰勒的歌。
- 泰勒在全美音乐奖上凭借专辑《1989》获得最受欢迎的当代成人歌手奖和最受喜爱的专辑奖，并凭歌曲《敌对》获得年度歌曲奖项。
- 泰勒在苹果音乐上发行巡演特辑《泰勒·斯威夫特：1989世界巡回演唱会》，这也是该平台首次发行的大型视频作品之一。

---

1 艾美奖：美国电视界最高奖项。

2016

- 坎耶·韦斯特发行歌曲《颇负盛名》，其中一句歌词为"我感觉自己和泰勒可能还会做爱／为什么？我让那个贱人出名了。"泰勒的团队声明，她本人并不赞成使用"贱人"（bitch）一词，但韦斯特声称使用该词已征得泰勒同意。
- 第58届格莱美颁奖典礼上，泰勒凭歌曲《敌对》赢得最佳音乐录影带奖，凭专辑《1989》拿下最佳流行演唱专辑和年度专辑奖项。这也让泰勒成为史上第一位两度获得格莱美年度专辑奖项的女性（泰勒曾凭《放手去爱》首度赢得该奖项）。她在获奖感言中鼓励女性无视那些贬低自己成就的声音，一些人将此解读为对韦斯特《颇负盛名》歌词的反击。
- 泰勒向美国歌手凯莎（Kesha）捐赠25万美元，用于支付其司法开销。此前，凯莎向法庭要求强制解除其与制作人戈特瓦尔德（Dr. Luke）所在的索尼旗下唱片公司的合约，但该诉求被法庭驳回。
- 泰勒在第64届BMI流行音乐奖[1]典礼上首次获得由自己名字命名的泰勒·斯威夫特奖（Taylor Swift Award）。
- 泰勒赢得公告牌音乐奖的最佳巡演艺人奖项。
- 泰勒创下"年度最高收入的流行女星"吉尼斯世界纪录。
- 泰勒与演员汤姆·希德勒斯顿（Tom Hiddleston）约会。
- 泰勒的前男友加尔文·哈里斯，对传言泰勒化名为尼尔

1　BMI流行音乐奖（BMI Pop Awards）：1952年创办，BMI音乐奖的最重要分支。

斯·斯约堡（Nils Sjoberg）参与制作其歌曲《你为此而来》（"This Is What You Came For"）做出回应。哈里斯证实了该说法，向泰勒表示了对其写歌水平的赞赏，但同时指责她试图像"打击"凯蒂·佩里一样"打击"自己（据报道，泰勒当时与佩里不和）。两人曾就不对外公开泰勒为该歌创作者的身份达成共识，以免使该曲蒙上两人过往恋情的阴影。

- 泰勒被《福布斯》杂志评选为当年收入最高的名人。2016年，泰勒入账1.7亿美元。
- 金·卡戴珊发布录像视频，视频中泰勒对韦斯特的歌曲《颇负盛名》表示支持[1]。卡戴珊用表情符号蛇代指泰勒，卡戴珊的粉丝纷纷效仿，泰勒的社交媒体页面随后被该表情符号席卷。泰勒再次发表声明，称她虽然曾想支持该歌曲，但从未支持韦斯特使用"贱人"一词。
- 大卫·穆勒试图让法院撤销泰勒控告其猥亵的反诉，但该请求被法院驳回。
- 泰勒为乡村音乐组合小大城镇（Little Big Town）创作歌曲《更好的人》（"Better Man"）。该组合最初对泰勒的参与持保密态度，表示不想让人们因为她的盛名而忽略了歌曲本身。

---

[1] 2020年3月，泰勒与韦斯特通话的原始视频泄出，证明卡戴珊发布的视频为刻意歪曲事实的蓄意剪辑版本。

2017

- 泰勒与演员乔·阿尔文（Joe Alwyn）恋爱，并成功将两人的恋情保密数月。为了保护隐私，两人既不一同亮相红毯，也不在采访中谈论这段感情。
- 泰勒的过往曲目上架声破天音乐平台。《1989》此前从未在此流媒体服务平台上架过。大机器唱片集团表示，此次上架过往曲目是为了庆祝专辑《1989》销量达到1 000万张。有人猜测，选择6月9日重新上架其过往曲目是另有所图，据称当天也是凯蒂·佩里新专辑《见证》（*Witness*）发行的日子。
- 泰勒与穆勒在科罗拉多州丹佛市民事法庭出庭。泰勒与她的团队（包括其母亲安德莉亚在内）度过了4天的艰难作证，最终8人陪审团作出了有利于泰勒的判决，认定穆勒对泰勒构成猥亵事实，且泰勒团队并未非法要求解雇穆勒。泰勒获赔1美元，但据称穆勒尚未支付该赔偿。
- 泰勒向快乐的心基金组织（Joyful Heart Foundation）捐款，该组织致力于帮助性侵事件的受害人。
- 泰勒清空了自己的社交媒体账号内容，外界纷纷猜测这意味着她即将发行新专辑。清空账号内容后，泰勒发布了几则以蛇为内容的视频，预告了其专辑《名誉》的主题和意象。
- 歌曲《瞧你们让我做了什么》发行。该歌曲发行当日即在流媒体上取得了800万次播放量成就，打破了此前的首日播放纪录。《瞧你们让我做了什么》及其音乐录影带着眼过去数年间纠缠泰勒的争议和媒体猜测,提到了她和坎耶·韦斯特、凯蒂·佩里及加尔文·哈里斯之间的不和,并讽刺了媒体对泰勒本人的过度解读。

- 专辑《名誉》发行。该专辑将蛇打造为泰勒的新人设,但也包含了几首情感脆弱的情歌,据报道这些歌曲的创作灵感均来自其男友乔·阿尔文。泰勒只邀请了马克斯·马丁、希尔贝克和杰克·安东诺夫担任该专辑的制作人,他们当时都是泰勒信赖的合作伙伴。除了单曲《瞧你们让我做了什么》,《准备好了吗?》、《如此动人》("Gorgeous")及《易碎》也先后作为专辑中的单曲发行。专辑发行期间,泰勒并未接受任何采访,也未曾在任何媒体上露面,她仅与美国联合包裹运送服务公司(United Parcel Service)、零售商超塔吉特及美国电话电报公司(International Telephone and Telegraph Corporation)达成相关合作以提升其专辑销量。专辑《名誉》登上公告牌200强专辑榜首位,首周销量超过120万张。
- 泰勒被《时代周刊》评选为"打破沉默"的"我也是"反性骚扰运动(#MeToo movement)年度人物之一。泰勒在采访文章中讲述了自己遭遇性骚扰的经历和随后展开的民事法庭案件,她鼓励相关受害者不要为自己的遭遇自责。

2018

- 泰勒在社交媒体照片墙上宣布向为我们的生命游行(March

for Our Lives）运动捐款，该运动旨在呼吁枪械改革。
- 泰勒重返蓝鸟咖啡馆，与词曲作者克雷格·怀斯曼（Craig Wiseman）一同带来惊喜演出。泰勒在现场表演了歌曲《统统甩掉》《爱情故事》，以及为小大城镇写的原创歌曲《更好的人》。
- 《名誉》巡回演唱会在亚利桑那州的格伦代尔市举行首场演出，随后开往北美洲、欧洲、大洋洲及亚洲各地。这场巡演打破了此前纪录，成为北美收入最高的女艺人巡回演唱会。
- 时隔许久，泰勒首次参加颁奖典礼，并赢得公告牌音乐奖的最佳女歌手奖和最畅销专辑奖。
- 泰勒首度表明其政治立场，为公职竞选人拉票。她在照片墙上发帖支持民主党人菲尔·布莱德森和吉姆·库珀（Jim Cooper），当时两人正在参加田纳西州的中期选举。在帖子中，她还表达了对维护妇女群体、性少数群体及"有色人种"群体权利的支持。美国投票网站Vote.org称，泰勒发表政治观点后的24小时内，大约16.6万新选民在该网站注册并参与投票，将近半数新选民的年龄在18至29岁。
- 泰勒赢得全美音乐奖年度艺人、最受喜爱的流行/摇滚音乐女歌手、最受喜爱的流行/摇滚专辑及年度巡演奖项，成为全美音乐奖历史上获奖数量最多的女性艺人。
- 泰勒与环球音乐集团签订多张专辑合约。根据该合约，泰勒未来的母带唱片版权皆归她本人所有。环球唱片还同意以"不可扣除"的方式,将出售声破天股份所得的资金返还给旗下艺人。这意味着即使艺人尚未赚回环球音乐预付给他们的所有款项,也能从集团出售声破天股份中获利。

2019

- 泰勒在美国iHeartRadio音乐奖颁奖现场赢得年度巡演和最佳音乐录影带(得奖作品为歌曲《易碎》)两大奖项。泰勒在获奖感言中提到,此前许多人都不看好《名誉》巡回演唱会,是粉丝们让这场巡演大获成功。她还告诉粉丝们,一旦有新音乐,他们会第一时间知道。
- 泰勒向田纳西平等项目组织(Tennessee Equality Project)捐款11.3万美元,该组织致力于为维护田纳西州性少数群体的权利发声和宣传。
- 泰勒入选《时代周刊》100位最具影响力人物名单。流行歌手肖恩·蒙德兹(Shawn Mendes)为泰勒撰文。
- 泰勒委托艺术家凯尔西·蒙塔古(Kelsey Montague)在纳什维尔创作了一幅蝴蝶壁画。蝴蝶翅膀上画满爱心、小猫、彩虹和花朵——这些图案都是泰勒待发行专辑的线索。
- 在社交媒体上预告数周后,泰勒发行单曲《我!》。这首欢快的流行歌曲赞颂自爱,充满糖果色彩的音乐录影带细节满满——像是包括南方小鸡乐队成员在内的"酷女孩"照片,一条爆炸后化身万千粉色蝴蝶的蛇,以及泰勒的新猫咪本杰明·巴顿。该单曲发行几周后，泰勒确认即将发行更多新歌。

- 循着《我！》音乐录影带中的线索，泰勒在社交媒体照片墙上直播宣布新专辑《恋人》即将发行。当日晚，她发行了该专辑的第二首单曲《你需要冷静》。

- 泰勒前唱片公司大机器唱片公司的创始人斯科特·波切塔，将泰勒前6张专辑的母带卖给了斯库特·布劳恩。泰勒曾试图自己买下这些母带，但合同条款规定，要想"赚回"自己的旧专辑，她必须为大机器唱片公司录制6张新专辑，泰勒因此选择了放弃。她认为布劳恩是一位"善于操纵"的霸凌者，因此并不想让其从自己的音乐中获益。泰勒拒绝了从布劳恩手中买回自己专辑母带的机会，因为合约中要求她签署一份只允许正面评价布劳恩的保密协议。在美国哥伦比亚广播公司（Columbia Broadcasting System, CBS）的周日午间新闻栏目中，泰勒接受了采访，宣布为了重新获得旧专辑的母带，降低布劳恩手中旧专辑的价值，她将重录自己过往的所有专辑。

- 泰勒向田纳西州参议员拉马尔·亚历山大（Lamar Alexander）写信，催促他支持《平等法案》，该法案致力于保护性少数群体的权利，禁止基于性、性取向和性别认同的歧视。在信中，泰勒批评了时任美国总统唐纳德·特朗普对该法案的所持立场以及他对待性少数群体的方式。她还发起了一份请愿书，民众可以在上面签字以表达对《平等法案》的拥护。

- 泰勒的第七张录音室专辑《恋人》发行。《恋人》是泰勒与环球音乐集团旗下音乐厂牌共和唱片（Republic Records）签订新合约后发行的第一张专辑，专辑母带由泰勒本人持有。该专辑明媚欢快，大部分歌曲是泰勒与乔·阿尔文恋爱期间所写的情歌。泰勒还借由这张专辑表达了她对性少数群体权利的支持，在其歌曲《你需要冷静》及其音乐录影带中大张旗鼓地表明了自己的支持态度。与专辑《名誉》的宣传方式不同，泰勒借由社交媒体、访谈节目、脱口秀节目以及多种电视活动宣传这张专辑。该专辑发行的单曲包括《我！》《你需要冷静》《弓箭手》（"The Archer"）、《人中翘楚》（"The Man"）。
- 泰勒公布其2020年《恋人》巡回演唱会（*Lover* Fest）的巡演日期，该巡演原本定位为音乐节性质的小型巡演，巡演地点包括欧洲和南美洲的部分城市，以及美国的洛杉矶和波士顿。
- 泰勒在全美音乐奖上赢得十年艺人、年度艺人、最受喜爱的流行/摇滚女歌手、最受喜爱的当代成人歌手奖项，并凭借歌曲《你需要冷静》获得最受喜爱的音乐录影带奖项。
- 泰勒在音乐剧改编电影《猫》（*Cats*）中饰演邦贝鲁琳娜（Bombalurina）一角。
- 专辑《恋人》打破吉尼斯世界纪录，成为全球最畅销的个人专辑。

2020

- 纪录片《美利坚女士》在流媒体平台网飞（Netflix）发行。影片记录了专辑《恋人》的制作经过和泰勒创作歌曲的过程，呈现了名气为她带来的诸多挑战和她尝试在私人生活中保持平和心态的努力。这部纪录片以更加开诚布公的态度讨论了泰勒的政治立场，提到2018年美国中期选举期间，泰勒决定发声支持民主党候选人时，与其团队之间产生的分歧。
- 泰勒、韦斯特及卡戴珊之间的完整争议对话视频泄露。该视频证明，卡戴珊早先发布的视频为剪辑版本，泰勒自始至终从未说谎，即她从未听过、更未认可韦斯特在歌曲《颇负盛名》中使用的最终版歌词。泰勒在此事的回应中请求粉丝们对更重要的事给予关注，并附上了一家新冠疫情救援慈善组织的链接。
- 因新冠疫情，泰勒推迟《恋人》巡回演唱会。
- 泰勒更新其社交媒体照片墙的主页照片，黑白照片里，她身处一片丛林中，风格与其上一张专辑的整体风格截然不同。当日晚些时候，泰勒宣布这张照片就是她第八张录音室专辑《民间故事》的封面，该专辑于当日午夜发行。
- 专辑《民间故事》成为一种流行文化现象，也是2020年最畅销的专辑。在这张专辑中，泰勒的词曲创作技巧展现得淋漓尽致，其歌曲创作基于虚构人物、历史人物及泰勒的个人生活。与其以往的流行曲风不同，《民间故事》听起来更像独立民谣。成熟的歌词和全新的听感为泰勒的这张专辑赢得了普遍好评和更多听众。由于专辑制作期间新冠疫情尚未结束，泰勒大多数时候只得与制作人杰克·安东诺夫及艾伦·德斯纳进行远程工作。专辑内容的灵感最初来自新冠疫情早期泰勒在隔离期间的想象。

- 泰勒宣布纪录片《民间故事：长池录音室》及其配套现场专辑将在（2020年11月25日）午夜于在线流媒体平台迪士尼+（Disney+）上发行。泰勒在片中表演了专辑《民间故事》中的所有曲目，并与杰克·安东诺夫及艾伦·德斯纳讨论该专辑的创作。这部纪录片是泰勒首度独立导演并独立制作的影片。《民间故事：长池录音室》及其现场专辑赢得了广泛欢迎。

- 12月，泰勒再次发布一组照片，9张照片组合起来是她身处森林中的景象。当晚，泰勒发行专辑《永恒故事》，并称这张专辑为《民间故事》的姊妹专辑。与专辑《民间故事》一样，《永恒故事》中的一些歌曲也写于新冠疫情隔离期间，泰勒与杰克·安东诺夫及艾伦·德斯纳拍摄完《民间故事：长池录音室》纪录片后，在长池录音室录制了《永恒故事》中的数首歌曲。专辑《永恒故事》与《民间故事》的风格相似，歌曲所述故事均取材于泰勒的想象和真实生活。《永恒故事》延续了《民间故事》的独立民谣风格，但在音乐上更具试验性。

- 泰勒赢得全美音乐奖的年度艺人和最受喜爱的流行/摇滚女歌手奖项，并凭借歌曲《羊毛衫》（"cardigan"）赢得最受喜爱的音乐录影带奖项。

2021

- 泰勒正式取消《恋人》巡回演唱会，并向已经购票的粉丝退回票款。
- 泰勒凭借专辑《民间故事》赢得格莱美年度专辑奖项。
- 泰勒的首张重录专辑《放手去爱（重制版）》发行。首张重录单曲《爱情故事（重制版）》["Love Story" (Taylor's Version)]登顶公告牌热门乡村歌曲榜首位，这使泰勒成为继多莉·帕顿之后第一位同一首单曲的原版和重录版本均登顶该榜的歌手。该专辑拿下多个排行榜榜首，粉丝和乐评人对该专辑的评价普遍积极，认为泰勒的唱功和配乐水平都有所提高。
- 泰勒的第二张重录专辑《红（重制版）》发行。为宣传该专辑，泰勒出席了数场脱口秀节目，与星巴克达成相关合作，并在电视节目《周六夜现场》上带来现场演出。这张重录专辑既包括20首原《红》豪华版专辑中的歌曲，还有6首新歌、3首已独立发行的歌曲，以及原专辑中备受歌迷喜爱的《回忆太清晰》的10分钟版本。泰勒还为歌曲《回忆太清晰》创作并导演了一部微电影作为该歌曲的音乐录影带，其内容为歌曲所述的秋日浪漫恋情和心碎结局。
- 泰勒再次在全美音乐奖上赢得最受喜爱的流行/摇滚女歌手奖项，并凭借专辑《永恒故事》拿下最受喜爱的流行/摇滚专辑奖项。
- 泰勒在公告牌音乐奖上赢得最佳公告牌200强艺人奖和最佳

女歌手奖。
- 泰勒在全英音乐奖上获颁全球偶像大奖[1]。
- 专辑《民间故事》赢得格莱美年度专辑奖项。

2022

- 泰勒获纽约大学荣誉艺术博士学位，并在该校毕业典礼上发表致辞。
- 泰勒的第十张录音室专辑《午夜》发行。《午夜》标志着她从《民间故事》和《永恒故事》代表的田园民谣风格重回流行曲风。泰勒将《午夜》形容为一张概念专辑，是对她生活中诸多无眠之夜的探索。专辑发行当日的凌晨三点，泰勒发行《午夜（凌晨三点版）》[*Midnights (3am Edition)*]，该版本中包含数首从标准版专辑中删掉的歌曲。专辑《午夜》共有3首歌曲打单：《反英雄》("Anti-Hero")、《薰衣草迷雾》("Lavender Haze")及《因果报应》("Karma")。尽管许多从专辑《民间故事》时期成为泰勒歌迷的粉丝对新专辑略有失望，但《午夜》取得了压倒性的好评。
- 泰勒成为有史以来首位一周内占据公告牌热门单曲100强榜前十位的歌手。
- 泰勒宣布举行时代巡回演唱会，这场巡演囊括了泰勒的整个职业生涯。仅在预售期间，200万张巡演门票就已经售

1　全球偶像大奖（The Global Icon Award）：全英音乐奖的最高荣誉。

馨，这一数量相当于其北美全部演出席位的90%。由于库存不足，后续公开售卖被取消。时代巡演取得了前所未有的成功，许多城市称这场巡演为演出当地带来了良好的经济效应。
- 泰勒宣布自己将为（福克斯）探照灯影业（Searchlight Pictures）指导一部故事片。一周后，她现身《综艺》杂志的"导演面对面"访谈节目，与马丁·麦克唐纳（Martin McDonagh）对谈，谈到了自己一路从创作音乐到指导制作音乐录影带的历程和转变，并表示未来想要拍摄电影。
- 泰勒在音乐录影带大奖上凭借《回忆太清晰：微电影》（*All Too Well: The Short Film*）赢得最佳长篇音乐录影带奖和年度音乐录影带奖。
- 泰勒在全美音乐奖上获得年度艺人、最受喜爱的乡村女歌手、最受喜爱的流行/摇滚女歌手奖项。她还凭《回忆太清晰：微电影》赢得了最受喜爱的音乐录影带奖，凭专辑《红（重制版）》拿下最受喜爱的乡村专辑和最受喜爱的流行专辑奖项。
- 泰勒在公告牌音乐奖上赢得最佳公告牌200强艺人奖、最佳乡村歌手及最佳乡村女歌手奖。专辑《放手去爱（重制版）》提名最佳乡村专辑奖项，但《红（重制版）》最终拿下了该奖项。

2023

- 泰勒凭借《回忆太清晰：微电影》获得格莱美最佳音乐录

影带奖项。该影片还在好莱坞影评人协会奖[1]上赢得最佳微电影奖。

- 泰勒在儿童选择奖上获得最受喜爱的女歌手奖项,并凭借专辑《午夜》赢得最受喜爱的专辑奖。其爱猫奥利维亚·本森获得最受喜爱的宠物奖项。
- 时代巡回演唱会在亚利桑那州的格伦代尔市拉开帷幕,巡演为当地创收的总值超过此前在该场馆举办的超级碗[2]比赛。
- 泰勒赢得美国iHeartRadio音乐奖的创新奖(the Innovator Award),专辑《午夜》获得年度专辑和年度歌曲奖项,歌曲《反英雄》赢得最佳作词奖,歌曲《珠光宝气》("Bejeweled")赢得TikTok年度热曲奖,歌曲《问题……?》("Question…?")赢得最受喜爱的配乐奖。
- 泰勒结束与乔·阿尔文的爱情长跑。二人分手的消息传出前后,泰勒发行歌曲《与众不同》("Hits Different")和《你正失去我》("You're Losing Me"),歌迷们猜测这两首歌记述的就是这段恋情的终结。
- 泰勒凭歌曲《卡罗来纳州》[3]赢得美国MTV电影电视奖的最

---

1 好莱坞影评人协会奖(Hollywood Critics Association Film Awards):由好莱坞影评人协会主办的电影类奖项。

2 超级碗(The Super Bowl):美国国家橄榄球联盟(National Football League, NFL)职业橄榄球大联盟的年度冠军赛。

3 歌曲《卡罗来纳州》("Carolina")为电影《沼泽深处的女孩》(Where the Crawdads Sing)的配曲之一。电影于2022年上映,改编自美国作家迪莉娅·欧文斯(Delia Owens)的同名小说《蝲蛄吟唱的地方》(Where the Crawdads Sing)。

佳歌曲奖项。

- 泰勒的专辑《恋人》发行大约4年后，其中歌曲《残酷夏季》（"Cruel Summer"）作为单曲发行。时代巡回演唱会中，这首广受歌迷喜爱的歌曲在排行榜上一路高升，促使泰勒的唱片公司采取非常举措为这首老歌宣传。
- 泰勒与1975乐队主唱马蒂·希利（Matty Healy）短暂约会并引发外界争议[1]，这段经历最终成为专辑《苦难诗社》中数首歌曲的灵感来源。
- 《爱的告白（重制版）》发行。这张重录专辑包含6首私藏版曲目，与原版一样，歌曲均由泰勒独立写成。尽管一些乐评者和歌迷认为泰勒如今成熟的嗓音令这张专辑略有失色，但《爱的告白（重制版）》仍然收获了如潮好评。
- 泰勒在音乐录影带大奖上凭歌曲《反英雄》赢得年度音乐录影带、年度歌曲、最佳流行音乐录影带、最佳导演、最佳摄影和最佳视觉效果奖项。专辑《午夜》拿下年度专辑奖。泰勒还获得了年度艺人和最佳夏日演出奖。
- 泰勒与堪萨斯城酋长队[2]近端锋特拉维斯·凯尔斯相恋。泰勒首次到场观看凯尔斯比赛时，凯尔斯的球衣销量当天就增加了400%，而在她观看第二场比赛时，女性观众人数增加了200多万。

---

1 马蒂本人行为放荡，常有过激言论和出格举动，曾多次身陷种族歧视乃至毒品风波，泰勒与马蒂的恋情因而在网络上遭到了许多粉丝与外界人士的抵制。
2 堪萨斯城酋长队（Kansas City Chiefs）：位于密苏里州堪萨斯城的职业美式橄榄球队。

- 泰勒发行电影《泰勒·斯威夫特：时代巡回演唱会》，这部以时代巡回演唱会为内容的影片成为有史以来票房最高的演唱会电影。
- 彭博社基于对泰勒音乐、房产、流媒体交易、演唱会门票和相关商品的估值，宣称泰勒已跻身亿万富翁行列。
- 10月27日，《1989（重制版）》专辑发行。当日，该专辑为声破天音乐平台创下2023年度当日流媒体最高播放量的记录，为苹果音乐创下史上流媒体播放量最高日的成就。《1989（重制版）》是泰勒第十三张登顶公告牌200强专辑榜的专辑，也成为21世纪黑胶唱片销量最高的专辑。与泰勒之前发行的重录版专辑一样，《1989（重制版）》大获好评，其日益精进的唱功和私藏版新曲目尤为瞩目。
- 12月，泰勒被《时代周刊》提名为年度人物。

2024

- 泰勒在第66届格莱美颁奖典礼上，凭专辑《午夜》赢得年度专辑和最佳流行演唱专辑奖项。泰勒发表获奖感言时，宣布将于4月19日发行新专辑《苦难诗社》。她表示自己刚制作完专辑《午夜》，就开始着手写新专辑的曲目，并在时代巡回演唱会期间秘密推进专辑制作。
- 泰勒的第十一张录音室专辑《苦难诗社》发行。两小时后，泰勒发行数字豪华版专辑《苦难诗社：选集》，《苦难诗社》由此成为双专专辑。泰勒在这张中速节奏专辑中延续了自己的流行风格并注重抒情，歌曲主题探索名誉、与粉丝间的关系以及个人生活。《苦难诗社》收到的乐评褒贬不一，有些人批评这张双专专辑体量过于庞大，有些人则对歌曲的创作大加赞赏，但整体乐评仍属积极。专辑中的歌曲《十四个日夜》（"Fortnight"）和《纵然心碎，也能做到》（"I Can Do It With A Broken Heart"）先后作为单曲发行。

- 时代巡回演唱会维也纳站（共计3场演唱会）因恐怖袭击预告而取消[1]。
- 哈里斯与特朗普的首场竞选辩论[2]结束不久，泰勒在照片墙平台上发帖，正式宣布自己将在2024年的美国总统大选中投票给卡玛拉·哈里斯和蒂姆·沃尔兹。她认为哈里斯是一位颇具才华的领导者，并在帖文中提到了哈里斯对保障性少数群体权利和女性群体权利的主张。她鼓励粉丝登记投票，帖文发布后数小时，超过33万名选民登录vote.gov网站投票。
- 泰勒与波兹·马龙[3]合作单曲《十四个日夜》的音乐录影带

---

1 原定于2024年8月8日至8月10日举行的时代巡回演唱会维也纳站，预计吸引19.5万观众到场。8月7日，奥地利政府拘留了两名涉嫌在演唱会上策划、发动恐怖袭击的嫌疑人。出于安全考虑，泰勒的团队与主办方随后宣布取消时代巡演维也纳站的3场演唱会，并向粉丝开启退票通道。

2 2024年9月11日，美国民主党候选人、副总统卡玛拉·哈里斯与共和党候选人、前总统唐纳德·特朗普在美国广播公司（ABC）于费城举行的总统辩论中对决。随后，社交媒体上流传着由人工智能软件生成的"泰勒站队特朗普"的不实信息。作为回应，泰勒发布了这条帖文。

3 波兹·马龙（Post Malone）：本名奥斯汀·理查德·波兹（Austin Richard Post），美国男歌手、词曲作者，2015年出道即在嘻哈、流行、摇滚等音乐领域引起广泛关注，成绩斐然，2024年发布专辑*F-1 Trillion*，转而深耕乡村音乐领域。

赢得MTV音乐录影带大奖的年度音乐录影带奖项。泰勒还获得了包括年度艺人在内的其他奖项，并与碧昂斯一道成为获得最多MTV音乐录影带大奖的艺人。

粉丝告白[1]

写在2024年结束时

2024年会作为"Taylor's Version"的第二年被永远铭记。我们见证悉尼、新加坡、伦敦、巴黎、多伦多等全球各大城市为她所倾,她作为独立的经济与文化现象在历史上写下了独属于自己的光彩一页。她的"统治"本身丝毫不让人意外,可惊喜依旧是这一年无可争议的关键词:在被《时代周刊》评为2023年度人物后,2024年的她哪怕仅仅是按部就班完成巡演,就已经可以轻松续写一段传奇;但她在常规计划之外从未止息,一刻不停地向前奔跑,在"原本"与"传统"之外,用真诚回馈粉丝一次又一次大礼。

"四封年专""前14占14""首周261万""20亿美元巡演票房"[2]

---

[1] 本部分为中文版特别策划,英文原版未收录。第1篇是国内粉丝为泰勒撰写的生日贺辞,其余2篇出自本书译者、编者。3位作者皆为泰勒粉丝,提及泰勒歌曲惯用其英文名,为体现真挚情感,不作译出,亦不收录于书末"译名对照表"。文中"霉霉""泰勒丝""taytay"等,皆为国内粉丝对泰勒的昵称。"霉粉""小草莓""Swiftie"等,则是对泰勒粉丝的昵称。——编者注

[2] "四封年专"指泰勒成为首位四度斩获格莱美年度专辑大奖的歌手,其获奖专辑分别为《放手去爱》《1989》《民间故事》《午夜》。"前14占14"指专辑《苦难诗社》发行后,其中歌曲在公告牌"本周单曲榜"包揽前14位的成绩。"首周261万"指专辑《苦难诗社》发行首周在美国本土的销量达到惊人的261万张。"20亿美元巡演票房"指时代巡回演唱会票房收入达到20.776亿美元,成为流行音乐史上首个票房收入突破20亿美元的巡演。——编者注

是描绘这一年的突出数字，但在世人瞩目的、反复传颂的成就之外，更为人感动的是她难能可贵的纯粹善良：她为巡演所至的每座城市的食物银行私下捐出大量款项，直到负责人纷纷对媒体发表感谢声明才为人所知；她为巡演团队的每个人分发高额奖金，从卡车司机到伴舞纷纷表示获得了人生中最幸运的一段时光；她在年终华丽的BBMAs颁奖典礼获得10项大奖，却选择在这一天前往儿童慈善医院探访患病孩童；她从不吝于关怀后辈，每一个与其照面的歌手都会讲述她的平和、善意与真诚，我们见证"霉系艺人"在2024年纷纷大放异彩，也见证她对这一切发自内心的支持、欣喜与感动；她既是舞台中央光影闪烁里的表演家，用精美视效与舞美征服舞台下与荧幕前的观众，也在每个晚上坐在钢琴前给上万人诉说跨越国界和语言的动人故事；她是名利场里咖位颇大的女王，是创造全新商业模式的破局人，却也带着一丝"局外人"的纯粹与千帆过尽的善良。

当然，这并不是平坦的一年。这一年她所发布的唯一专辑是THE TORTURED POETS DEPARTMENT，她的34岁也一如这张专辑的标题，tortured与poets构成生活的互文，折磨与苦难同样是解读她的关键词。2024年的世界乐坛百花齐放，Taylor却在喧嚣与公关中显得分外低调踏实；可即便如此，当"世一"的名头被默认及传颂，荣耀之外的恶意依旧如影随形。她的一举一动常被放大和嘲讽，真诚善意被质疑商业考量，提携后辈被质疑刻意打压，恋情选择被粉丝威胁抵制，观看球赛被抱怨曝光太多，性别歧视与身材羞辱也依旧是刁难常态。我们共同见证打卡时代巡演的知名演员数量是当红歌手的10倍不止，也目睹心怀不满的行业人与居心叵测的媒体人接二连三的恶意黑稿与侮辱性言辞；因为太有名、太成功、太完美，所以讨厌她在部分人眼中成了很酷的事情。而在毫无黑料可挖的窘况里，无中生有的造谣污蔑亦步亦趋。她却从不制造争议也鲜少回应恶意，只是用音乐与创作建构自己的时代，在旋涡中心始终如一地顽强矗立。

于是她将经受的无端折磨浴血写成宏大诗篇。怒火与痛楚、困惑与哲思相互交织，或许也是对当下最独到和全面的总结："So tell me everything is not about me, but what if it is?"

让我们重新回顾她光芒夺目又真诚坚韧的34岁：

2月，成为格莱美"四封年专"历史第一人，而在领取最佳流行演唱专辑时官宣TTPD的发行，更是让全球霉粉陷入无限焦灼与猜想；随后重新启程的巡演从日本、澳大利亚到新加坡，惊喜曲目升级到两首mix版本，新专辑的不同封面与加曲也在不同城市次第揭晓。

4月19日，第十一张专辑正式来临，绵密的词汇与情绪让人应接不暇，发行两小时后的双专留给解读者万千可能。"Fortnight"创下歌曲单日播放量纪录，一周后单曲榜前14占14、专辑榜首周261万的惊人战绩亦证明她当之无愧、与日俱增的世一号召力。

春夏之交，时代巡演在巴黎迎来新的篇章。巴黎站演唱会开始前流出的彩排图让2.0版巡演承载无限期待，而全新改版的细节也的确让世界不同时区观看直播的粉丝惊喜万分。与瓜西[1]合作的

---

1 瓜西：格蕾丝·艾布拉姆斯（Gracie Abrams），美国创作型歌手。"瓜西"为国内粉丝对其的昵称。——编者注

"us."惊喜上线，随后在伦敦获得现场首演；随之而来的还有单曲《破碎心》[1]的MV首播，在8年之后重新延续了巡演MV的传统。

2024年的夏天，时代巡演在欧洲继续场场售空，我们既见证了慕尼黑场馆外20万人会集的人山人海，也见证了维也纳的阴云和粉丝走上街头的欢笑与勇气。欧巡以伦敦的二巡落幕，英国王室与首相纷至沓来，白金汉宫为她特别奏乐；机器姐[2]与黄老板[3]惊喜登场，当红新生艺人成为新增开场嘉宾，为这场席卷欧洲的"Cruel Summer"画上完美句点。

秋天的Taylor连续第三年出现在VMA颁奖礼现场，也连续第三年拿下最大奖年度MV；她选择在大选中表明立场，一如首次发声的6年前，继续表达对性少数群体及女性群体的支持。在巡演的空窗期，她突然官宣时代巡演场刊发布，在跨越音乐与电影行业后踏上了新的独特征程，也继续用"全年销量第一"的数字证实自己的影响力能够跨越全新行业。

冬天的她毫无意外地在各大年终盘点中席卷榜单，是所有主流音乐平台全年播放量最高的艺人，TTPD亦成为全年播放量最高的专辑。在"Midnight Rain"的倒计时中，我们迎来时代巡演的落幕，12月的生日像是早早设立的句点，也像是留给全新一年的最好开端。

而在大洋彼岸，我们用特别的方式在这一年与她同频共振。

1　泰勒粉丝对歌曲《纵然心碎，也能做到》的简称。——编者注
2　机器姐：弗洛伦斯·韦尔奇（Florence Welch），英国乐队Florence+The Machine的主唱。"机器姐"为国内粉丝对其的昵称。——编者注
3　黄老板："黄老板"为国内粉丝对英国流行男歌手艾德·希兰的昵称。——编者注

粉丝告白

2024年对于中国霉粉是格外充实的一年：从跨年场惊喜上线的大电影启航，包场观影团让许多分散的粉丝都找到了属于自己的家园，我们在电影院一次次尽兴而归，见证票房破亿的历史纪录；2—3月，不少粉丝前往日本与新加坡实现多年来的梦想，现场打卡的华语明星不计其数。这个春天，在巡演效应下，北大、清华、浙大、武大、南开等多所知名高校举办了多样主题校园活动；夏天的奥运赛场上，以"最会打乒乓球的霉粉"为代表的体坛霉粉们同样牵动人心，不同歌词被赋予新的内涵与时代意义。泰勒·斯威夫特的经济与文化效益正在一步步为人所知所感，多家传统纸媒推出报道特辑，杭州、上海、香港等城市特别公开表达了引进霉霉演唱会的意愿，11月上映的电影《好东西》则成为其影响力的最新例证。

29岁的Taylor在纪录片里说："我担心这是我最后一次机会能被大众接受取得成功，因此我只想加倍努力好好工作。"35岁的Taylor拥有更加广阔的前程与愿景，她拥有尚未开拍的电影项目，拥有两张还未发行的重录专辑，拥有一群满怀期待与包容的粉丝，还拥有一腔似乎从未枯竭的灵感和从未止歇的行动力。作为粉丝，我们当然猜不出她此刻正在计划着什么、创作着什么，但我们相信她新的一岁只会更加精彩——一如过去的每一天。

生日快乐！期待见证你每一个绚烂明天！
We had the time of our lives with you!

Rico

2024年12月13日

译后记 | Dear Reader

亲爱的读者，一切始于一个女孩学会了几个吉他和弦。

第一次听到泰勒的歌，"霉霉"的昵称还未被大众熟识，搜索引擎给出的结果是一位涂着红唇的年轻乡村歌手，以及诸多调侃她约会和唱功的小报文章。当时她还未拉直卷发，酷爱比心手势和幸运数字13，已经有了发专日到当地超市签售的传统，为了给排队的歌迷签名，一站就是13个小时。如她所述，早年温和礼貌的少女形象太过平易近人，尽管是当时最年轻的格莱美年专得主，但似乎对任何榜单和"竞争对手"都"不具威胁"，人们乐于消遣调侃的只剩歌里写了哪位男友的八卦，以及歌曲词库里都是"四六级词汇"。泰勒的童话梦结束于2014年专辑《红》末期，她开始尝试更时髦的装束，对情感的感知和捕捉更为多样、隐蔽及精准，对音乐的追求也不再局限于乡村曲风，而那年格莱美的虚晃一枪，似乎更加坚定了她转型的脚步。毋庸赘述，《1989》时期是泰勒乃至所有粉丝经历的最重要时期之一，她的作品和她本人都是光环簇拥的存在，一如意气风发的她站在帝国大厦顶端的猎猎夏风中，挥别少女时代和纳什维尔，身后纽约城的万花镜折射出危机四伏的名利场。《名誉》前夕是一场灭顶般的生长痛，这场震动延续数年，甚至在《苦难诗社》中仍有余韵。泰勒对忠诚、恋人、伙伴、自我价值的认知悉数坍塌，像一颗破碎的镜面球失去了所有光源。而此后数年间发行的专辑，似乎是一场漫长而反复的疗伤——在《恋人》里庆祝可以信赖的"健康"亲密关系，在《民间故事》和《永恒故事》中驶离创作的边界，在《午夜》中直面那些暗色的自我，在《苦难诗社》中坦白最深的欲望和无法排解的苦痛。

人类渴望情感共鸣，因而借由创作冲动或艺术作品向更深的自我或其他个体寻求联结。而泰勒之所以能成为21世纪难得一见的全球文化现象，则在于无数个我们共享友谊手链、复活节彩蛋、小丑理论家的密语，共享新年日的电影与跨越国境的相见；在于不管15岁、25岁还是35岁，始终有那么一首歌使你感同身受——与你共享暗自发酵的年少心事、第一次离家的不安焦虑、无法直视太阳般的自我审视、天马行空的文学幻想和与世界交手的孤独迷茫。歌曲成为封存光影、气味、感受与记忆的相框，她的日记本成了一代人的日记本，记满年少时的无畏与雀跃、无可避免的稚气与尴尬、寻求改变和成长的勇气、亲密关系中的困境与醒悟……即使于音乐或创作无甚造诣，即使于泰勒本人无甚了解或记忆连接，我们依然共享全人类在生活和情感体验上的共鸣。而这本书存在的意义之一，在于不必转引他人之口（如果翻译不算一种转述的话），直接体会泰勒对音乐创作、爱情友情、性别议题、政治主张、自我认知等话题的态度与成长，直接见证一位聚光灯下成长起来的成熟女性，如何用坦诚至极的音乐笔触坦然接受、勇敢表达自己的所知所感，如何正视自己的情感需求与事业抱负，如何追逐梦想、开拓革新，如何定位自我的性别和社会角色，为行业不公、女性处境和少数群体勇敢发声。

译事难，本书涉及的话语横跨泰勒出道以来的18年时光，虽然我与编辑都是多年歌迷,熟知大部分话语的出处与语境,在翻译过程中也力求多方查证,但限于部分背景信息欠缺,难免有所疏漏。对于需要提供背景或语境的部分话语,笔者或增译相关信息,或提供脚注,以期在力所能及的范围内减少读者的阅读阻碍。此类文本常有话语结构松散、语法不够严谨、代词变换频繁等特点,因而在保证表意无误、行文流畅的同时,笔者省译了许多无意义的口语词,合并或调整了意群表意,以提高文本的可读性。此外,本书的语言风格既有平易近人的闲聊式采访,也不乏大量文学性、哲理性的感悟或幽默之语,因此并未全文采用大白话的翻译方式。翻译是缺憾的艺术,每次审校都常觉还有改进空间,译者、编辑与审校竭尽所能字斟句酌,力图呈现好每一条内容。

收到试译通过的邮件,是在一个晴朗的傍晚,皮肤上黏着六月潮热的水汽,大脑因弹出的邮件惊喜到片刻空白。无论作为年轻译者,还是作为泰勒丝女士十几年的粉丝,这本书对我来说都意义非凡。我很少用"偶像"称呼泰勒,偶像意味着遥不可及的星光和一时而至的狂热,而她是生活中更为鲜活真实的存在,是晚自习的草稿纸上无意写下的名字,是听到校园广播时独自雀跃的秘密,是和异国友人寒暄时的共同好友,是无数女孩男孩成长过程中或浓或淡的注脚。本书的大部分翻译工作完成于我至今浅薄生命体验中的"残酷夏季",江南长久的梅雨后是灼灼烈日,杜厦的冷气很足,冷饮在深褐色的釉质桌面上留下湿漉漉的印痕。与译稿相伴的日子,我经历了身心上的动荡与迷茫,而那些十几年间烂熟于心的歌词与旋律,在自我深处生长拔节的痛楚与欢悦中,与这段绝无仅有的体验重合，才听懂曲中之意，成为曲中之人。在这期间，非常感谢编辑的信任与陪伴，她的热忱细心和在有限出版条件下的努力，是本书得以面世的重要推力。

亲爱的读者，愿你在这数条话语中找到能够慰藉自己来路或前路的那一条，愿你仍能在戾气与冷气中感受到生命的丰盈与联结、无畏与自由。

2025年1月19日
于仙林

编后记:"热爱与工作同轨"的 Swiftie

"人们不会一直陪着我,但音乐一直都在",taytay 如是说。我们这一生,在陪伴与离别之间辗转。能够拥有一份相伴许久的真挚情感,是何等幸事。

taytay 视音乐为毕生所爱,一直脚踏实地为音乐梦想努力,勇于挑战自我并在不同的音乐风格之间转换,且每张新专辑都取得了不断超越前者的斐然成绩。她为艺术家争取应有权益,为各种不平等现象勇敢发声,关注妇女、儿童、性少数群体,为慈善事业做出许多贡献。她对世界充满善意,却受尽诋毁。可她并未因此一蹶不振。她坚韧不拔,如生命力极强的爬山虎。她在名誉尽毁后浴火而归,用音乐作品回击那些如"黑云压城"般沉重的恶意。

无论陷入何种境况,她的音乐创作都未止歇……新冠疫情时期,她发行了由虚构故事构成的民谣姊妹专辑《民间故事》《永恒故事》、于无数失眠夜晚创作的电子流行专辑《午夜》。忙碌的时代巡演期间,她发行了基于"悲伤的5个阶段"而展开的最新专辑《苦难诗社》。一次又一次向世界宣告着她在音乐创作上的无限可能。她是举世无双、耀眼夺目的乐坛流行天后,是用一首首歌曲讲述动人故事的创作者,是用149场时代巡回演唱会创造20亿美元票房纪录的歌手,是千千万万霉粉心目中无可比拟的偶像。

而我,也有幸是千千万万霉粉中的一员,不仅拥有 taytay 歌声的陪伴,更因此结识了一群志同道合之人。我们在新专辑发行日不约而同地戴上耳机，准备好英语词典和纸巾；我们在演唱会大电影的霉粉派对一起欢度三个半小时而意犹未尽；我们在机场凭着"你怎么知道我要去看霉霉演唱会"的行李箱海报相认而交换友谊手链；我们在异国他乡的时代巡回演唱会现场观看taytay纵情演出，共度终于圆梦的美妙夜晚……我们会在人生每个阶段从她的音乐里不断感受到心弦共振的律动：怦然心动时听"I Think He Knows"满怀憧憬；分手悲伤时听"You're Losing Me"潸然泪下；愤怒不满时听"Call It What You Want"疏解情绪……庆祝22岁生日时要用歌曲《22》作吹灭蛋糕蜡烛的背景音乐；新年日要在朋友圈分享"New Year's Day"，约上三五好友去看落日与海鸥；去KTV必点一首"All Too Well"(10 Minute Version)，微电影看千万遍依然感叹"怎会有如此仙品"。

  taytay的音乐陪伴我已有9年，从考研、恋爱、毕业、工作、失业、骨折、分手、再就业，到如今这本打磨一年的书即将出版。我开始喜欢听taytay的歌曲是在她的低谷期，而在我的低谷期又用她的音乐治愈自己。我想，在我余下生命的每一天，也都会有她的陪伴——"Forever & Always"。

  如果说，2023年我的最大幸运是成功抢到了新加坡时代巡回演唱会的门票并如期观演，那么2024年的最大幸运便是成为《泰勒·斯威夫特：她说》的责任编辑。当我在3月底得知版权可获得的消息，当我把泰勒的名字写在出版计划里，当我在键盘上敲击着她的名字，一遍又一遍……那种感觉真是妙不可言！

  近两年来国内外出版的泰勒相关图书如雨后春笋般涌现，而我情有独钟于这本出版于2019年的书，原因在于它原原本本地呈现了泰勒的原话，未加任何他人注解。我想通过这本书，把最真实的泰勒，带给小草莓们！

不仅如此，我也期望能够让更多霉粉参与到本书的出版中来，把这本书做成"霉粉的小型团建"，希望这份参与感和成就感能为更多霉粉所拥有。

6月1日，我社官方小红书账号发布了译者招募的消息，收到133份试译稿。小编在此再次诚挚感谢每一位小草莓的热情支持！逐一读完大家的投稿，并经过对社内熟悉泰勒的编辑意见的采集，最终选定了试译作品极为贴合泰勒本人语言风格的译者。另外，这次招募还带来了意外收获，联系到了微博博主@TaylorSwiftCollection（简称TSC）！几个月后，在读到TSC写给泰勒的生日贺词的当天，便向执笔人称赞："写得真好，好到想收录进书里！"后来，应本书编排所需，收录一事也得以成真。

此外，机缘巧合之下，亦联系到霉粉译审王畅，对本书内容进一步把关。和其他读过译稿的编辑一样，她对译稿亦赞不绝口。11月，招募到一位霉粉插画师@一盘Dna（小红书）为本书设计书眉元素。一路以来，这支队伍日渐壮大。"今天我们相聚在这里，都是为了伟大的泰勒丝女士"。

当初，在跟国外版权方沟通的邮件里写道，"我希望能够用一杯星巴克的价格呈现一部好作品，让这本'霉粉圣经'实现霉粉人手一本"。前半句，我在过去一年中不懈努力着；后半句，对大家充满期望，希望能够收获读者朋友们的热情支持。

为了收获大家的喜爱与支持，本书策划的独特之处如下：话语部分采用中英文对照的格式，满足读者多样化的阅读需求；大事记部分，在2020年增加一条关于"侃爷录音门"事件的最终真相；在2019年初版的基础上，增加版权方2024年6月出版的Young Reader Edition版本中10条新增话语。此外，版权方计划于2025年4月推出的英文第二版近60条新增话语亦收录于本书。最终，囊括3个版本的本书共计457条话语。在此，向版权方的全力支持致以诚挚的感谢。

同时，感谢社领导与各位同事在本书出版过程中给予的支持与帮助，感谢编辑室伙伴在每个出版环节的悉心建议！在大家的共同努力下，使得本作品的呈现臻于完善。

对于一本书而言，最重要的是内容。对于一本引进版图书而言，除其内容，最重要的就是翻译。在此特别感谢本书译者孙澳。taytay的话语是本书的灵魂，而她的词句为中文版铸就了血肉。感谢她，在过去的6个月里乐此不疲地打磨一字一句。

最后，诚挚感谢taytay和所有小草莓们！是taytay和她的音乐与小草莓们产生的联结，让这份感情和陪伴变得弥足珍贵！

Love taytay till the end of time！

2025年1月5日

译名对照表

专辑译名对照表（截至 2024 年 12 月）

专辑名称	本书采用中文译名	发行日期
Taylor Swift	《泰勒·斯威夫特》	2006 年 10 月 24 日
Fearless	《放手去爱》	2008 年 11 月 11 日
Speak Now	《爱的告白》	2010 年 10 月 25 日
Red	《红》	2012 年 10 月 22 日
1989	《1989》	2014 年 10 月 27 日
reputation	《名誉》	2017 年 11 月 10 日
Lover	《恋人》	2019 年 8 月 23 日
folklore	《民间故事》	2020 年 7 月 24 日
evermore	《永恒故事》	2020 年 12 月 11 日
Fearless (Taylor's Version)	《放手去爱（重制版）》	2021 年 4 月 9 日
Red (Taylor's Version)	《红（重制版）》	2021 年 11 月 12 日
Midnights	《午夜》	2022 年 10 月 21 日
Speak Now (Taylor's Version)	《爱的告白（重制版）》	2023 年 7 月 7 日
1989 (Taylor's Version)	《1989（重制版）》	2023 年 10 月 27 日
THE TORTURED POETS DEPARTMENT	《苦难诗社》	2024 年 4 月 19 日

歌曲译名对照表（按本书出现顺序）

歌曲英文名称	本书采用中文译名	收录于专辑
The Outside	《局外人》	《泰勒·斯威夫特》
Our Song	《我们的歌》	《泰勒·斯威夫特》
Tim McGraw	《蒂姆·麦格劳》	《泰勒·斯威夫特》
You Belong With Me	《你应该和我在一起》	《放手去爱》
Love Story	《爱情故事》	《放手去爱》
Mean	《卑鄙》	《爱的告白》
Innocent	《无辜者》	《爱的告白》
Haunted	《摇摇欲坠》	《爱的告白》
Dear John	《分手信》	《爱的告白》
Enchanted	《着迷》	《爱的告白》
All Too Well	《回忆太清晰》	《红》
We Are Never Ever Getting Back Together	《我们再也回不去了》	《红》
I Knew You Were Trouble	《我知道你是大麻烦》	《红》
22	《22》	《红》
The Lucky One	《幸运儿》	《红》
Clean	《释怀》	《1989》
Shake It Off	《统统甩掉》	《1989》
Blank Space	《空白格》	《1989》
Welcome To New York	《欢迎来纽约》	《1989》
Look What You Made Me Do	《瞧你们让我做了什么》	《名誉》
Delicate	《易碎》	《名誉》
New Year's Day	《新年日》	《名誉》
ME!	《我！》	《恋人》
Never Grow Up	《不要长大》	《爱的告白》
Long Live	《不朽》	《爱的告白》
Everything Has Changed	《一切皆变》	《红》
Call It What You Want	《随你怎么说》	《名誉》
Speak Now	《爱的告白》	《爱的告白》

译名对照表

Lucky You	《幸运的你》	自制样带专辑
Fifteen	《15岁》	《放手去爱》
End Game	《游戏终结》	《名誉》
You Need To Calm Down	《你需要冷静》	《恋人》
Teardrops On My Guitar	《泪洒吉他》	《泰勒·斯威夫特》
Should've Said No	《本应拒绝》	《泰勒·斯威夫特》
White Horse	《白马》	《放手去爱》
Mine	《我的》	《爱的告白》
Wildest Dreams	《狂野的梦》	《1989》
Begin Again	《重新开始》	《红》
I Know Places	《藏身之地》	《1989》
Stay Stay Stay	《留下来》	《红》
... Ready For It?	《准备好了吗?》	《名誉》
Don't Blame Me	《别怪我》	《名誉》
King of My Heart	《心的主宰》	《名誉》
Bad Blood	《敌对》	《1989》
willow	《柳》	《永恒故事》
hoax	《骗局》	《民间故事》
Invisible	《隐形的爱》	《泰勒·斯威夫特》
Only The Young	《年轻一代》	单曲
Tied Together With A Smile	《面带微笑》	《泰勒·斯威夫特》
Picture To Burn	《烧掉的回忆》	《泰勒·斯威夫特》
Crazier	《更疯狂》	《乖乖女是大明星》电影原声
Back To December	《回到十二月》	《爱的告白》
This Is What You Came For	《你为此而来》	单曲
Better Man	《更好的人》	《红(重制版)》
Gorgeous	《如此动人》	《名誉》
The Archer	《弓箭手》	《恋人》
The Man	《人中翘楚》	《恋人》
cardigan	《羊毛衫》	《民间故事》

Anti-Hero	《反英雄》	《午夜》
Lavender Haze	《薰衣草迷雾》	《午夜》
Karma	《因果报应》	《午夜》
Bejeweled	《珠光宝气》	《午夜》
Question...?	《问题……》	《午夜》
Hits Different	《与众不同》	《午夜》（破晓版）
You're Losing Me	《你正失去我》	《午夜》（深夜版）
Carolina	《卡罗莱纳州》	《沼泽深处的女孩》电影原声
Cruel Summer	《残酷夏季》	《恋人》
Fortnight	《十四个日夜》	《苦难诗社》
I Can Do It With A Broken Heart	《纵然心碎，也能做到》	《苦难诗社》

致 谢

我们在此向威尔·卡尔（Will Carr）、约翰·克利玛（John Crema）、凯尔西·达姆（Kelsey Dame）、阿曼达·吉布森（Amanda Gibson）、艾琳·卡拉塞维奇（Erin Karasewski）、摩根·克雷比尔（Morgan Krehbiel）、爱玛·库珀（Emma Kupor）、伊丽莎白·帕帕斯（Elizabeth Pappas）及贾梅卡·威廉姆斯（Jameka Williams）致以感谢，感谢他们在本书手稿的筹备工作中做出的贡献。

图书在版编目（CIP）数据

泰勒·斯威夫特：她说 /（美）海伦娜·亨特编；孙澳译. -- 上海：上海社会科学院出版社，2025.
ISBN 978-7-5520-4710-3

Ⅰ.K837.125.76

中国国家版本馆CIP数据核字第2025896RS6号

上海市版权局著作权合同登记号：09-2024-0575

泰勒·斯威夫特：她说

编　　者：[美]海伦娜·亨特
译　　者：孙　澳
责任编辑：孙宇昕
封面设计：黄婧昉
版式设计：乔　安
书眉插画设计：@一盘Dna（小红书）
营销支持：@TaylorSwiftCollection（微博）
出版发行：上海社会科学院出版社
　　　　　上海顺昌路622号　邮编200025
　　　　　电话总机 021-63315947　销售热线 021-53063735
　　　　　https://cbs.sass.org.cn　E-mail: sassp@sassp.cn
排　　版：南京展望文化发展有限公司
印　　刷：上海雅昌艺术印刷有限公司
开　　本：890毫米×1240毫米　1/32
印　　张：9.5
字　　数：251千
版　　次：2025年8月第1版　2025年8月第1次印刷

ISBN 978-7-5520-4710-3/K·491　　　定价：68.00元

版权所有　翻印必究

TAYLOR SWIFT: In Her Own Words
Edited by Helena Hunt
Copyright © 2019, 2024, 2025 by Agate Publishing, Inc.
Published by arrangement with Agate B2, an imprint of Agate Publishing, Inc. c/o Nordlyset Literary Agency
through BARDON CHINESE CREATIVE AGENCY LIMITED
Simplified Chinese translation copyright © (2025)
by Shanghai Academy of Social Sciences Press Co., Ltd.
ALL RIGHTS RESERVED